Robert Hindmarsh

Letters to Doctor Priestley

Robert Hindmarsh

Letters to Doctor Priestley

ISBN/EAN: 9783337778545

Printed in Europe, USA, Canada, Australia, Japan

Cover: Foto ©Lupo / pixelio.de

More available books at **www.hansebooks.com**

LETTERS
TO
Dr. PRIESTLEY:

CONTAINING PROOFS OF THE

SOLE, SUPREME, AND EXCLUSIVE

DIVINITY OF JESUS CHRIST,

WHOM THE SCRIPTURES DECLARE TO BE

The Only God of Heaven and Earth;

And of the Divine Miffion of

EMANUEL SWEDENBORG.

BEING A

DEFENCE

OF THE

NEW CHURCH fignified by the NEW JERUSALEM

IN THE APOCALYPSE.

By ROBERT HINDMARSH.

'The Time cometh when I fhall fhew you plainly of the Father.
John xvi. 25.

LONDON:
PRINTED AND SOLD BY R. HINDMARSH,
PRINTER TO HIS ROYAL HIGHNESS THE PRINCE OF WALES,
No. 32, Clerkenwell-Clofe.
1792.

CONTENTS.

                                        Page

PREFACE   -   -   -   v

LETTER I.

Of Miracles, and the divine Mission of Baron Swedenborg   -   -   -   1

LETTER II.

On the sole, supreme, and exclusive Divinity of Jesus Christ   -   -   -   76

LETTER III.

Miscellaneous.

I. *Of the Connection between Religion and the Civil Power*   -   -   -   209

II. *Of the Human Form of God*   -   217

III. *Of the Union of Divinity and Humanity in the Person of Jesus Christ, and at the same Time of the Divine Omnipotence*   -   -   -   238

CONTENTS.

	Page
IV. Of the Holy Scripture, and the Science of Correspondences	266
V. Of the Second Coming of the Lord	303
VI. Of the Last Judgment	310
VII. Of the Resurrection	322
VIII. Of Marriages in Heaven	337
IX. That Love and Wisdom are Substances, and not mere Properties	351
X. Of the Divine Influx	362
XI. Of the Discovery of the Georgium Sidus	369
XII. Of Time and Space in the Spiritual World	373
XIII. Of Charity; and how it is to be understood, that neither Arians nor Socinians can be admitted into Heaven	388

PREFACE.

PREFACE.

ON the firſt appearance of Dr. Prieſtley's *Letters to the Members of the New Jeruſalem Church*, I was requeſted by ſeveral perſons to draw up an anſwer to him. This I declined for a conſiderable time, not doubting but ſome abler hand, with more leiſure than myſelf, would undertake the taſk. But a meeting of the Society in London being called to take into conſideration the expediency of a public reply, it was their unanimous requeſt, that I would immediately take up the pen, and defend the doctrines of the New Jeruſalem againſt the attack which had been ſo recently made upon them. Finding myſelf thus called upon, I no longer heſitated, but promiſed that I would devote the few leiſure hours I

had

had to spare from business, to the support of those great truths, which from many years close attention I have good reason to believe of heavenly extraction. How far I have succeeded in the attempt, must be left to the judgment of the candid and impartial reader, who, no doubt, is sufficiently aware, that on every possible occasion it is his duty to examine both sides of a question, before he ventures to decide in favour of either.

I may just observe here, that the following *Defence of the New Church* has been read in manuscript, from time to time, to the above-mentioned Society, who so far approved of it as to request, that I would publish it as an avowal of their sentiments, as well as of my own. Some others have also given it a perusal, of whose judgment I entertain a very high opinion; and the satisfaction, which these have expressed on the occasion, encourages me to hope, that my feeble endeavours in support of truth will not

prove

prove altogether useless. Yet as it is very possible there may be sentiments contained in this work, which do not in all respects accord with the views of every individual member of the New Church, on the same subjects, I do not wish to have it understood, that any errors discoverable in me are to be charged upon them; having simply stated my own opinions, with the reasons that have induced me to adopt them.

It is a common remark, that persons, who take up contrary sides of a question, too frequently treat each other with unbecoming asperity; imagining, no doubt, that their arguments will thereby gain a considerable accession of strength; or at least, that, as opponents, they have a right to indulge themselves in personal reflections, merely on account of their difference in opinion. But I hope nothing of this kind will appear in the following *Defence.* I have endeavoured, as much as possible, to avoid it. Yet should there be be any thing in it that will admit of such a construction, I beg it may be considered as unintentional; for I can assure the reader, I have no view to offend any person; having, to the best of my knowledge, been influenced by no other motive in writing, than the love of truth, that it may be first discovered, and then practised.

As human creatures born in ignorance, and designed by the great Creator of the universe to pass through various stages of intelligence, from the obscurity of *sensual apprehension*, to the brightness of pure *intellectual truth*, we are all, while in this first or present state of existence, continually exposed to error and deception. So many are the false appearances of things without, and so many are the prejudices and passions within, which combine to obstruct our progress in mental perfection, that unless we tread the ground of inquiry with the utmost circumspection and caution, paying every attention

tion that is due to the sentiments of others, as well as entertaining the most scrupulous distrust of our own hearts and understandings, instead of discovering what we all profess to be in search of, we shall only bewilder ourselves in the mazes of conjecture, and having the door of our mind shut against the light of truth, continue to grope in the dark.

The fallacies arising from the appearances of natural objects, when presented to the bodily senses, may easily be rectified, because of these the learned are sufficiently aware. But it is not so easy to detect the fallacies which arise from the appearance of intellectual objects, because few consider, that the human mind is furnished with senses peculiar to itself, just as the body is; and that for the most part, our first apprehensions of spiritual things are as imperfect and foreign to the real truth, as the first notions we entertain of natural things. The fact, however, is as here stated; and therefore it behoves

behoves us, if we are in earnest to obtain the prize of wisdom, to be perpetually on our guard against the delusion of appearances, ever holding our minds open for the reception of further light, and more just information.

As most of the objections, which Dr. Priestley has urged against the doctrines of the New Church, are the same as are usually made by many other persons on their first reading the writings of Baron Swedenborg, in consequence of not thoroughly understanding them; I have been the more particular, on that account, in obviating *all his objections;* so that the following *Defence of the New Church* may be considered not only as an answer to Dr. Priestley's *Letters*, but likewise to all other opponents who tread on similar ground. I have not shunned, in the smallest degree, an examination of any question, but have allowed to every argument of opposition it's full weight and importance. Those passages of scripture,
which

which the doctor has urged as the moſt decisive proofs in favour of his own ſyſtem, and againſt the doctrines of the New Jeruſalem, are conſidered with all the attention and candor I am maſter of; and ſuch anſwers and explanations are given, as I hope will prove ſatisfactory to every unprejudiced reader, who is in ſearch of truth purely for it's own ſake. Particularly I have taken pains to demonſtrate, as the fundamental article of the true chriſtian religion, the ſole, ſupreme, and excluſive divinity of our Lord and Saviour Jeſus Chriſt; proving by the moſt undeniable authority of the general tenor of the ſcriptures, that their grand deſign is, to reveal to mankind, not merely that there is a God, who created the univerſe and all it's furniture, but that this God is in a Human Form, that out of pure love and mercy he himſelf came down from heaven into the world to redeem and ſave mankind, and that he is no other than the Divine Man JESUS CHRIST. And here I muſt ſay,

if

if Jesus Christ be not the *true*, the *only* God, that the design of the scriptures is yet unfulfilled, and that christians to this day are as ignorant of, and unacquainted with, the supreme Governor of the universe, as the Athenians were, when Paul saw them pay their devotions *to the unknown God;* for to all who consider the Divine Being as superior to Jesus, or in any respect different from him, he is still a God unmanifested, invisible, unknown. But the great Jehovah hath manifested himself in the flesh, and thereby made himself visible and known to his creatures, not by any mere deputation, commission, or message, through the medium of another, but by his own personal and actual incarnation. Thus he, who in ancient times was the object of patriarchal worship, as Jehovah the Father in a human form, became in later times the object of apostolic worship, as the Messiah, Son, Redeemer of the world; and lastly, in his New Church is now worshipped as
Jehovah

Jehovah the Father, Son, and Holy Spirit, inseparably united in one divine person.

The scriptures throughout testify of Jesus, as he himself teaches in John v. 39; and this testimony is evidently the burden of all revelation. The historical, prophetical, and evangelical books are full of it, insomuch that it may with truth be said, they are *in labour* to bring forth their *only Son*, their *only Man*, JESUS CHRIST; the acknowledgment of whom, both in doctrine and life, as the alone Creator and Saviour of the world, is that new birth in every individual, which they so strenuously inculcate, and which is so worthy of their divine contents. But on the supposition that Jesus is a *mere man*, according to the view of Socinians, I must candidly confess, that the perpetual reference to the Messiah in the Old Testament, and to Jesus in the New, which is so striking as to escape the notice of perhaps none, would appear to me to be little better than a burlesque on the

fallen

fallen condition of the human race, if after all, the perfon, through whom they are to look for redemption and deliverance, is no greater, no abler, no wifer, no better than themfelves. For if Jefus be a mere man, nay if he be any thing fhort of the fupreme God himfelf, he muft have been unworthy of that high and exalted character which we find uniformly afcribed to him by prophets and apoftles; unworthy to be called by them the Saviour of the world, or to be confidered by us as the fingle Hero of divine revelation.

This fubject, however, with a variety of others clofely connected with it, will be found treated more at large in the following fheets. I have here only to add, that the fole, fupreme, and exclufive divinity of Jefus Chrift will admit of a thoufand times more abundant proof from the fcriptures, than could poffibly be comprized within the limits of the prefent work: and although this *Defence of the New Church* confiderably exceeds

the

the bounds I at firſt propoſed to myſelf, when I ſat down to write an anſwer to Dr. Prieſtley, yet, when compared with the magnitude of the ſubjects I have undertaken to defend and explain, perhaps it ſcarcely amounts to the value of a mite thrown into the increaſing treaſury of the New Church. However, ſuch as it is, I offer it to the world. What kind of reception it may meet with, or what effect it may produce in the mind of the reader, I do not pretend to anticipate: yet ſhould it become the means, under divine providence, of conveying truth to the breaſt of a ſingle individual, or of guarding one mind againſt the dangerous errors of Socinianiſm, I ſhall think myſelf happy in the reflection, that I have not ſpent my time in vain, but that as a member of ſociety I have been in ſome ſmall degree an inſtrument of uſe.

     ROBERT HINDMARSH.

London, Jan. 7, 1792=36.

NOTA BENE.

IN the following *Defence*, many of the quotations from scripture are rendered somewhat differently from the common English translation. But these variations are all made with a view to express more accurately the true sense of the original. The word *Jehovah*, for example, which in the Old Testament is for the most part translated *Lord*, is here retained: for although both terms evidently denote the same Divine Being, yet each conveys a peculiar idea distinct from the other. Thus, the term *Jehovah* means *the Lord not yet incarnate;* and the term *Lord* means *Jehovah incarnate*, or *in the flesh*, which is the same thing as *Jehovah in his Divine Humanity*. This is the reason why in those passages of the New Testament, which are parallel to others in the Old, the term *Lord* is used instead of *Jehovah*; as in Deut. vi. 4, 5; and Mark xii. 29, 30. Isaiah xl. 3; and Matt. iii. 3: for when the Old Testament was written, the Lord was *Jehovah;* but when the New Testament was written, Jehovah was the *Lord*.

☞ To those who may have occasion to quote the Works of Emanuel Swedenborg, it may be proper to observe, that all references ought to be to the *numbers* of the paragraphs, and not to the *pages*; for in different editions the pages vary, but the numbers remain the same.

A DEFENCE

OF THE

New Church, meant by the New Jerusalem

IN THE APOCALYPSE.

LETTER I.

Of Miracles, and the divine Mission of Baron Swedenborg.

IT is unnecessary, Sir, to make any apology for calling your attention to the following sheets, as I conceive myself in some measure entitled to that indulgence, in consequence of the *Letters* you have lately addressed *to the Members of the New Jerusalem*, among the number of whom I profess myself an humble individual. As it is my intention to obviate every objection you have brought against the credibility of Baron Swedenborg's testimony, as well as against the doctrines of the New Church, I shall take the liberty of making my observations in that order which appears to me most likely to clear the ground as we go. I therefore propose, in the present letter, to consider what is the most proper evidence of a man's inspiration and divine mission, and how far the pretensions of Baron Swedenborg are supported by such evidence as is at once both rational and satisfactory. In the course of this examination, I shall naturally be led to inquire into the true nature and tendency of miracles.

But here give me leave to make one observation, previous to my entering on the subject, which I wish both you and myself to bear in mind, and to consider as the condition of our correspondence. It is this, that during the present controversy (if such it must be called) no difference of sentiment, no opposition of argument, no strength of expression in favour of our respective opinions, shall by any means be deemed a breach of charity, or a personal reflection. With this condition in view, I now proceed with my subject.

In the first part of your Preface, you pay an handsome compliment to those members of the New Church, with whom you are acquainted; for which I am sure they have politeness enough to make you a suitable acknowledgment. I hope " the evident good sense, and good conduct," which you are pleased to say you discovered in them,

them, will not be confidered as any proof of their weaknefs and fuperftition, in having embraced a fyftem of divinity, which has been proved by Baron Swedenborg to be the only true chriftian religion, although in page xii you pronounce it to be a mere " vifionary " fcheme, and deftitute of all rational evidence."

To prevent the imputation of unfair conduct in mifreprefenting any of your affertions, and that every reader may judge of the propriety or impropriety of my anfwers; I think the moft candid, as well as moft juft mode of procedure will be, firft to ftate your own words, and then to make my remarks.

In page xii of your Preface you obferve as follows: " To many perfons it will appear " not a little extraordinary, that a fcheme of " religion fo vifionary, and fo deftitute of all " rational evidence, as that of Baron Sweden-" borg, fhould be fo firmly believed by fuch " numbers of perfons of unqueftionable good " fenfe, and the moft upright intentions; and " fome may be difpofed to fay, that *chriftianity* " *itfelf might have had no better an origin.*— " There is nothing, however, fo improbable in " itfelf, but what perfons of a certain turn of
" mind

" mind may *not* be pre-difpofed to believe. And
" they who already believe the infpiration of
" fome perfons, will eafily admit that of others,
" who, in their idea, carry on the fame fcheme,
" or one fimilar to it. *Thus the miracles of the*
" *popifh faints were received without much diffi-*
" *culty, after thofe of the apoftles and primitive*
" *chriftians.*—Any perfon of reputable charac-
" ter, and not apparently infane, gravely and
" repeatedly afferting his infpiration, and his
" intercourfe with God or angels, and advan-
" cing nothing contrary, or fuppofed to be con-
" trary, to what other acknowledged prophets
" had advanced before him, will be believed by
" fome; and the credit of thefe may in time be
" the means of procuring him credit with
" others. And thus it appears to me, that
" credit was acquired to the pretenfions of Ma-
" homet, and has been to thofe of Baron Swe-
" denborg."

In reply to the above, I fhall take the liberty to offer a few reflections as they occur. In the firft place then, if, as you acknowledge, " fuch
" numbers of perfons of unqueftionable good
" fenfe, and the moft upright intentions," do actually and firmly believe the teftimony of Baron Swedenborg; this is certainly a ftrong

prefumppresumption that they can see a *reasonableness* in his assertions, as well as a manifest *agreement with divine revelation* in all the doctrines of the New Church, which by your own confession you have neither eyes nor understanding to discern.

But, Sir, I do not know how to reconcile your mode of accounting for our embracing the doctrines of Baron Swedenborg, page xiii, with your polite assertions in page xii. You first say we are men of " *unquestionable good sense,*" and in the very next page pass us off as a set of the *weakest enthusiasts* in the world, who are prepared to give credit to any idle tale, provided it be but gravely and repeatedly asserted. One would imagine, that no person possessed of good sense, or in other words, of a sound understanding and solid judgment, (as you allow some of the members of the New Church to be,) would suffer himself to be deluded, either by the predisposition of his own mind, or the grave and repeated assertions of another, into such a visionary scheme as you suppose our's to be, unless he saw it had it's basis in truth, and was capable of being supported by rational evidence, as well as by the acknowledged oracles of divine revelation. Still less is it to be supposed, that

whole

whole societies and communities of men would embrace the doctrines of the New Jerusalem, (and that too even in opposition to former prejudices instilled into them from infancy by education and example,) unless they perceived in them an internal evidence of their own truth, and felt the firmness of the ground on which they stand.

There seems to be something very singular in the observation you make, when you say, that " some may be disposed to say, that *christianity itself might have had no better an origin*," than the system of religion which is now beginning to dawn upon the earth, under the name of the *New Church*, or *New Jerusalem*. You do not surely mean to insinuate your *doubts* concerning the truth of the christian religion, by saying so? Indeed, Sir, one would be almost ready to conclude as much, particularly as you add, " They " who already believe the inspiration of some " persons, will easily admit that of others, who, " in their idea, carry on the *same scheme*, or one " *similar to it*. Thus the miracles of the popish " saints were received *without much difficulty, " after those of the apostles and primitive christians.*" This certainly amounts (at least in my view) to the same thing, as if you had in plain terms said,

said, 'The miracles of the popish saints would 'never have received any credit, unless men 'had been *weak enough* first to believe those of 'the apostles and primitive christians.' It also, I think, fairly implies, that as you yourself have too much sense to believe the popish miracles, so you do not acknowledge those of the apostles; for the one, you seem to say, is a natural consequence of the other.—I do not wish to press you too hard on this point; I rather hope I may have misapprehended your meaning. But really, Sir, I could not help making these reflections in my own mind, while I was reading the above, and various other passages in your Letters.

As to the insinuation that the pretensions of Baron Swedenborg are no better than those of Mahomet, merely because he did not support them by miracles, if it proves any thing, it proves too much; for on this ground you will find yourself put to the necessity of denying the divine mission of many of the prophets, as well as of John the Baptist. What miracle, let me ask, did Joel, Amos, Obadiah, Micah, Nahum, Habakuk, Zephaniah, or Haggai, with several others whom I could name, perform, in order to convince the people, that they were the true
messengers

messengers of Jehovah? Not a single one that I know of. Will you therefore infer, that they were impostors, because they did not come with miracles in their hands? Had you lived in their day, you might with as good reason have objected to their *single* testimony of their own divine mission, as you now do to that of Baron Swedenborg. With equal propriety you might have said to Jonah, when he was proclaiming the destruction of Nineveh, 'Unless you will con-'vince me by a miracle, that you are sent of 'God, I will not believe a word you say.' Had the Ninevites reasoned in this manner, in all probability they would not have lived to lament their folly.

Again, what miracle did John the Baptist do, to convince the Jews that he was *more than a prophet*, as being the immediate forerunner of our Lord? If, as you say, p. 8, "the *only proper* " *evidence* of a divine commission is doing some-" thing that God alone could enable a man to " do," (meaning a miracle,) how happened it, that John, whose commission and character were more dignified, than those of any former prophets, did not display the necessary requisites for commanding the public attention? If to gain credit *simply as a prophet*, it is indispensably

bly neceffary to work a miracle; what may we not expect from him who comes to us as *more than a prophet?* John the Baptift, however, performed no miracle as a proof of his miffion, and yet he was pronounced by the Lord himfelf to be greater than Mofes, or any of the prophets, notwithftanding all the miracles which they performed. In proof of thefe affertions, I fhall juft beg leave to tranfcribe the following paffage from Matthew. Speaking of John the Baptift, Jefus fays, "What went ye out to fee? a prophet? "yea, I fay unto you, and *more than a prophet.* " Among them that are born of women, there " hath not rifen a greater than John the Bap- " tift," Matt. xi. 9, 11. And in John x. 41, 42, it is faid, " *John did no miracle;* but all things " that John fpake of this man, (Jefus,) were " true. And many believed on him there." The truth is, rational evidence is *ftronger* than any miracle, becaufe it reaches the *underftanding*, which no miracle ever did, or can do. I am therefore furprized, how any man, that calls himfelf a *lover* of truth, and a *fearcher* after truth, can yet *turn his back* on truth, together with found reafon, the *proper evidence* of truth, and call out for a miracle!

C

Having

Having seen that several of the prophets gave no proofs of their divine mission by working miracles, and that their testimony in many cases is admitted merely on their own bare assertions; let us now inquire whether it has been the general custom of mankind to give implicit credit to those who had the power of working miracles; and after viewing the effects naturally produced by them on the human mind, together with their real uses and design, we shall be the better prepared to take into consideration the divine mission of Baron Swedenborg.

In page 8, you say, " When Moses was ap-
" pointed by God to carry a message to his na-
" tion, and to the king of Egypt, he naturally
" said, Exod. iv. 1, *But behold they will not be-*
" *lieve me, nor hearken unto my voice; for they will*
" *say, the Lord hath not appeared unto thee.* In
" answer to this, God bade him throw down the
" rod that was in his hand, when it was instantly
" changed into a serpent, and he was ordered to
" shew the same sign to his countrymen, and to
" Pharaoh, iv. 5, *that they may believe that the*
" *Lord God of their fathers, the God of Abraham,*
" *Isaac, and Jacob, hath appeared unto thee.* Ac-
" cordingly he did exhibit this sign, and by this
" means satisfied them, that God had sent him."

It

It is true that the Lord enabled Moses to perform many miracles before his countrymen, in order to convince them that God had sent him. But that this conviction of their's was a mere *superficial impression* upon their outward senses, and carried with it nothing of *rational evidence* to their understandings, is plain from almost every part of their history. As soon as ever they had fairly escaped from the Egyptians, and were got into the wilderness, *the people absolutely murmured against Moses and Aaron* who had performed the miracles, and thereby brought them into a situation where they dreaded being destroyed by hunger and thirst. See Exod. xv. 24. Chap. xvi. 2, 3. They even accused Moses of a design and intention to kill them, and were on that account just on the point of stoning him to death, Exod. xvi. 4. If the miracles, which Moses and Aaron performed, had really operated upon their minds a full and rational conviction that they were sent by God, how is it possible they could so soon forget them, notwithstanding their greatness and frequency? The truth is, they only believed (or rather, were *compelled* against their wills to acknowledge) the miracles for the moment, while they were present before their *senses*. How else are we to account for their successively and almost continually rebelling against Jehovah, in whose name all the miracles were performed?

It was from a principle of selfishness and fear only, that they followed Moses out of Egypt and through the wilderness; *selfishness*, because they expected at last to arrive in a land of plenty; and *fear*, lest they should be destroyed by that power, which had so wonderfully manifested itself in the miracles. But no sooner did this fear subside in consequence of their temporary cessation, than they returned to the natural hardness of their hearts, and fell into the grossest species of idolatry, namely, that of worshipping a molten calf, the work of their own hands; and what is singular, even Aaron, who had himself performed the miracles, joined with the people who were witnesses of them, in ascribing all the power to the calf, and saying, "*These be thy gods, O Israel, which brought thee up out of the land of Egypt,*" Exod. xxxii. 4. Nothing then can be produced as a more plain and undeniable fact, than that the miracles which were performed before the children of Israel, were considered by them as downright acts of *compulsive authority;* and that the conviction arising from them was a mere *superficial impression* upon their

outward

outward senses, and carried with it nothing of *rational evidence* to their *understandings*.

But if I understand you right, you say, page 9, that Moses satisfied Pharaoh, as well as his countrymen, by the change of his rod into a serpent, that God had sent him. This, however, was not the case; for, Exod. vii. 8 to 13, " Jehovah said unto Moses and Aaron, When " Pharaoh shall speak unto you, saying, *Shew a* " *miracle for you;* then thou shalt say unto Aaron, " Take the rod, and cast it before Pharaoh, and " it shall become a serpent. And Moses and " Aaron went in unto Pharaoh, and they did so, " as Jehovah had commanded. And Aaron cast " down his rod before Pharaoh, and before his " servants; and it became a serpent. But Je-" hovah hardened Pharaoh's heart, that *he* " *hearkened not unto them.*" Your assertion, therefore, that the sign which Moses exhibited before Pharaoh, " satisfied him that God had " sent him," is in direct opposition to the plain matter of fact. Pharaoh saw with unconcern the miracle of the rod being turned into a serpent; for " the magicians of Egypt did in like " manner with their inchantments." So that he could not tell by that sign alone, whether he was sent by *God*, or by the *devil*. Neither was he convinced of the divine miffion of Mofes and Aaron, by their fmiting the waters, and turning them into blood; for " the magicians " of Egypt did fo with their inchantments." So, after the plague of the frogs, which the magicians likewife produced, Pharaoh "har-" dened his heart, and hearkened not unto " them." Nay, even on the duft of the earth being turned into lice, (which was a miracle that baffled the fkill of the magicians, for " with " all their inchantments they could not bring " forth lice,") ftill " Pharaoh's heart was har-" dened, and he hearkened not unto them." It was the fame with the plague of flies, the murrain, the boils, the hail and fire, the locufts, and the thick darknefs; for he would not let the Ifraelites go, till he was abfolutely compelled to do fo, by the flaying of the firft-born: and laft of all he purfued them, till he, with all his hoft, was drowned in the red fea. Now as you have, in page 2, exprefsly renounced any faith in the *calviniftic* plan, you cannot with any propriety avail yourfelf of that fyftem, by faying, that Pharaoh's unbelief was not chargeable on him, but on Jehovah, who had previoufly hardened his heart, on purpofe that *he fhould not let the people go*, Deut. iv. 21.

By

By way of digression, I will here put a question to you. If you can answer it, well; if not, then acknowledge fairly and openly, that there are mysteries in the holy word of the Lord, of which you are entirely ignorant, and which can only be understood by a knowledge of it's spiritual sense. The question I have to propound is this, How and why was it, that the magicians, as well as Moses and Aaron, could turn their rods into serpents, and all the waters of Egypt into blood, and bring up frogs upon the land, *and yet could not, with all their inchantments and mighty powers, produce lice?* See Exodus, chap. vii. and viii. You cannot surely say, that it is a greater miracle to produce lice, than to bring forth frogs, and to turn rods into serpents, and rivers of water into blood? Still less, I apprehend, will you venture to assert, as your most serious and deliberate judgment, that the production of lice is in itself a more rational and satisfactory proof of a *divine* mission, or more *worthy of the great Jehovah*, than the miraculous conversion of all the rivers, ponds, and pools of water in Egypt, into blood. According to the literal and obvious sense of the passage, however, by which you say you must in other cases be guided, it would appear that *such a miracle* is really greater, and more worthy

of

of God. But how and why it is, remains for you to explain.

To return. You say, p. 9, "Our Saviour did not expect to be believed upon his own word, when he declared that God had sent him; but said, John v. 36, " The works which the Father hath given me to finish, the same works that I do bear witness of me, that the Father hath sent me;" and we find that this was the circumstance that *convinced the Jews that he was a real prophet.*" Immediately after which you quote, as a proof of your assertion, the words of Nicodemus to Jesus, " Rabbi, we know that thou art a teacher come from God; for no man can do these miracles which thou doest, except God be with him," John iii. 2. These passages, you seem to think, establish your position, That miracles are more effectual in procuring credit to the divine mission of a prophet, than any other means. In this, however, you are again most egregiously mistaken. The Jews in general were *not convinced* by any or all the miracles which Jesus performed, that he was a real prophet, much less that he was the true Messiah, or Son of God. Of this they are standing proofs against your hypothesis to the present day. It is not even true, that Nicodemus
believed

believed the testimony of Jesus, although you have brought his own words in support of your doctrine; for in verse 11 of the same chapter our Lord in express terms tells him, " *Ye receive* " *not our witness.*"

But why do you take upon you to say, that " our Saviour *did not expect* to be believed *upon* " *his own word,*" but on account of his works only? The evangelist John says, chap. iv. 41, that " *many believed, because of his own word.*" And the Lord himself says, " He that heareth " *my word,* and *believeth* on him that sent me, " hath everlasting life," John v. 24. " He that " receiveth not *my words,* hath one that judgeth " him," John xii. 48. Again, it is said, " *As* " *he spake these words, many believed on him,*" John viii. 30. Was this *unexpected* by the Lord? No, truly; " for Jesus *knew from the beginning* " who they were that believed not," John vi. 64. And besides, " the *words* that he spake, are " *spirit,* and are *life,*" verse 63. It is very clear, then, that the Lord called the attention of the people more to *his words,* than to *his works;* the reason of which was, because his words were calculated to inform, instruct, and convince the understanding, in a more effectual manner than the most miraculous of his works. When he

D   found,

found, they would not hearken to his words, he then referred them to his works: "*Though ye* "*believe not me,* (says he,) *believe the works,*" John x. 38. "Believe me, that I am in the Fa- "ther, and the Father in me; *or else* believe me "*for the very works' sake,*" John xiv. 11.

That the Jews in general did not acknowledge Jesus to be a real prophet, and sent of God, notwithstanding all the miracles he performed, is easily proved by the following passages in the gospels.

1. After Jesus had cast out the devils, and permitted them to enter into the herd of swine, "the *whole city* came out to meet Jesus, and "when they saw him, they besought him that "he would *depart out of their coasts,*" Matt. viii. 34. Mark v. 17. Luke viii. 37. If they had believed him to be a true prophet, it is probable they would rather have besought him to dwell amongst them, than to depart from them.

2. When Jesus healed the man with the withered hand, "the pharisees went out, and "held a council *against him,* how they might "*destroy him,*" Matt. xii. 14. Mark iii. 6. Luke vi. 11. Would they have done so, if that miracle

racle had convinced them he was a prophet, and sent of God?

3. Again, when Jesus healed a blind and dumb man, who was possessed of a devil, "the pha-"risees said, This fellow doth not cast out devils, "*but by Beelzebub the prince of the devils,*" Matt. xii. 24. Mark iii. 22. Luke xi. 15. Here the pharisees were so far from acknowledging the *divine* mission of Jesus on account of this miraculous cure, that they even ascribed it to the power of the *devil!*

4. Again, when Jesus returned into his own country, and the people saw his "*mighty works,* "they were *offended in him.* And he did not "many mighty works there, *because of their un-*"*belief,*" Matt. xiii. 37, 38. Mark vi. 3, 5. But according to your doctrine, Sir, their *unbelief* ought to have been the *very reason* why he should have done mighty works, if he wished to convince them that he was a prophet; for it is certainly unnecessary, and even absurd, to work a miracle in order to convince a man that *already believes.*

5. When Jesus healed the woman who had an infirmity eighteen years, "the ruler of the sy-
"nagogue

"nagogue anfwered *with indignation*, becaufe he "had healed on the fabbath-day," Luke xiii. 14. Thus we fee, a fuperftitious prejudice in favour of the Jewifh fabbath, fo blinded the eyes of the chief ruler of the fynagogue, that he could difcern no traces of a divine hand in this extraordinary cure.

6. Although Jefus healed the high prieft's fervant's ear, in the prefence of thofe who came to apprehend him, yet fo far was this miracle from convincing them of his divine miffion, that they immediately "*took him*, and *led him*, and "*brought him into the high prieft's houfe*," &c. Luke xxii. 54.

7. Jefus performed a miracle on the fabbath day, by healing an impotent man; "and *there-* "*fore* did the Jews *perfecute him*, and fought to "*flay him*." And when Jefus thereupon took occafion to inform them, that his miracles were performed by the Father and himfelf conjointly, "the Jews fought *the more to kill him*, not only "becaufe he had broken the fabbath, but be- "caufe he faid alfo, that God was his Father, "making himfelf equal with God," John v. 16, 17, 18.

8. On

8. On Jesus raising Lazarus from the dead, many of the Jews who were present, and saw that extraordinary miracle, believed indeed on him; but some of them, it appears, did not; for they went their ways to the pharisees, and told them what things Jesus had done. And the chief priests and the pharisees convened a council, to consult how they might *put him to death, for working so many miracles.* See John xi. 45 to 57. Nay, the chief priests were so hardened, and incensed, that they even sought to *put Lazarus also to death,* although he had just been so miraculously raised from the grave. John xii. 10.

9. Notwithstanding all the miracles which Jesus performed before the Jews, it is said in Luke xxiii. 1, 2, that " the *whole multitude* of them arose, and led him unto Pilate, and began to *accuse him.*" Pilate, however, remonstrated with them; and declaring that he found no fault in him, proposed to set him free. But " *they all* say unto him, Let him be *crucified,*" Matt. xxvii. 22. Luke informs us, " they cried out *all at once,* saying, Away with this man, *crucify him, crucify him,*" Luke xxiii. 18, 21.

10. Lastly,

10. Laſtly, As a plain and poſitive proof, that the Jews in general did not believe on Jeſus, nor acknowledge him as a real prophet, and divinely commiſſioned, it is expreſsly ſaid, John xii. 37, " But though he had done ſo many mi-"racles before them, *yet they believed not on him*."

It is true, indeed, there are various paſſages to be found in the goſpels, which inform us, that great multitudes followed and careſſed him after they had ſeen his miracles: but it is very evident from our Lord's own declaration concerning ſuch perſons, that they followed him, not ſo much from any conviction of his divine miſſion, wrought in their minds by the miracles which he performed, as from a principle of low and groſs ſenſuality; for he ſays in plain terms, " Verily verily I ſay unto you, Ye ſeek me, *not becauſe ye ſaw the miracles*, but *becauſe ye did eat of the loaves, and were filled*," John vi. 26.

Agreeable hereto, it is obſerved in John ii. 23, 24, that although " many believed in his " name, when they ſaw the miracles which he " did," yet " Jeſus did not commit himſelf unto them, *becauſe he knew all men*;" plainly implying, that the faith which is founded merely on miracles, is not the true and genuine faith which

the

the Lord wishes to establish, because it resides only in the external man, and enters not into the internal, so as to form the *rational christian*.

Miracles then avail nothing towards a rational and permanent conviction of the truth. This is likewise particularly evident in the case of the poor cripple at Lystra, who was miraculously cured by Paul. "When the people "saw what Paul had done, they lifted up their "voices, saying, The gods are come down to "us in the likeness of men;" and they immediately prepared to pay him divine honours, Acts xiv. 8 to 18. But in the very next verse we are informed, that "there came thither certain "Jews from Antioch and Iconium, who per- "suaded the people, and *having stoned Paul,* "*drew him out of the city, supposing he had been* "*dead.*"

Where is it asserted in the Word of God, that no man ever was or will be divinely commissioned, without having the power of working miracles committed to him, as an undeniable proof of his mission? If such a condition is no where established, why do you take upon you to urge it as indispensably necessary? Our Lord says, "There shall arise *false Christs*, and *false* "*prophets,*

"*prophets,* who shall shew *great signs and won-*
"*ders,* insomuch that (if possible) they shall
"*deceive* the very elect," Matt. xxiv. 24. Mark
xiii. 22. If so, then signs and wonders, or
miracles, are no certain proofs of a divine mission; which is further evident from the following passage in the Apocalypse, "And I saw
"three unclean spirits like frogs come out of
"the mouth of the dragon, and out of the
"mouth of the beast, and out of the mouth of
"the false prophet; for they are the *spirits of*
"*devils, working miracles,* which go forth unto
"the kings of the earth, and of the whole world,
"to gather them to the battle of that great day
"of God almighty," Apoc. xv. 13, 14. Here
the power of working miracles is plainly and expressly attributed to devils. Again, when the
pharisees and sadducees desired that he would
shew them a sign from heaven, Jesus answered,
" A *wicked* and *adulterous generation* seeketh after
" a sign," Matt. xvi. 4. From which it appears,
that it is a mark of *wickedness* and *adultery* to require signs and miracles as the proper evidences
of divine inspiration. Therefore he told them,
they should have no sign, Mark viii. 12.

It would answer no valuable end, to adduce
more passages from the Word on this point; it
having

having been already clearly proved, that miracles in former ages were of themselves infufficient to work either faith or conviction in the human breaſt; that in many cafes they rather proved the occafion of men's hardening their hearts, by clofing the interiors of the rational mind; and that frequently they were not at all confidered as any genuine evidences of a divine miffion, becaufe they were equally within the power of wicked men and forcerers.

You may perhaps fay, 'Then for what end 'and purpofe were miracles performed?' I anfwer, Among others, for thefe great purpofes; firſt, that the Word of God might be written: fecondly, to compel the Ifraelites to do fo and fo, in order to *reprefent* the ſtate and progreſs of the fpiritual church; for they being merely external and fenfual men, having their interiors clofed, could, without danger of prophanation, be formed by miracles into the *reprefentative of a church*, but never into a *real church*. The third ufe of miracles was, to point out man's regeneration, which is the cure of his fpiritual maladies, and a miracle of miracles, being effected folely by the omnipotence of the Lord's divine human perfon. It was for this grand purpofe, that fo many miracles were wrought among

among the Israelites, by means of Moses and the prophets; and that the Lord himself, during his abode in the world, performed so many miraculous cures upon the blind, the deaf, the dumb, the lame, and the sick. For as all diseases originate in the vices of the spirit, and are no less than representative thereof; so the cure of men's bodily infirmities denoted the removal of those spiritual evils to which they correspond, and from which, as from their proper fountain, they have ever been derived.

* * *

Having thus demonstrated, that signs and miracles are not the only proper evidences of a divine commission, because they are equally capable of being performed by means of magical inchantments; having also proved, that the witnesses to such miracles in general gave little or no credit to the workers of them, but were merely struck with astonishment and awe during the moment of performance, though some even made it the occasion of hardening their hearts, attributing all the power to the devil; and having likewise seen the nature, end, and use of miracles; I shall now inform you on what authority the members of the New Church receive the testimony of Baron Swedenborg, and acknowledge him as divinely inspired, notwithstanding the

dispensation

dispensation he announces has nothing miraculous to accompany it. In doing this, I shall take the liberty of making such further remarks on the subject of miracles, as the nature of your objections may appear to require.

In p. xv. of your Preface, you tell us a story of "a Quaker going about the country, and "giving an account of a trance he was thrown "into, in which he had a sight of heaven and "hell:" and although you "do not remember "much of the vision at present," yet you say "it was entirely unlike any of the memorable "relations of Baron Swedenborg:" after which you add, "Now here is vision against vision, "or rather dream against dream, and which of "these are we to believe?"

Had you been kind enough to favour us with a specimen of what you do remember of the Quaker's vision, we might possibly have been enabled to form some judgment about it: but in the way you have stated it, it is out of any person's power to tell whether your inference be a just one or not, when you say, "Here is vision "against vision;" for you must admit it to be possible, that what appears *inconsistent* or *absurd* to *you*, may appear just the contrary to *another*.

And

And I apprehend you are at prefent fo little apprized of the infinite variety of appearances, which both the heavens and the hells are capable of prefenting, that were two different accounts of either the one or the other, as related by Baron Swedenborg, or by any other perfon whofe teftimony might be depended on, to be laid before you in a detached ftate, in all probability you would not hefitate to pronounce them abfolutely heterogeneous and contradictory: and yet for all this I fay it is *poffible*, that both accounts may in themfelves be true, and in the view of fome perfons clearly reconcileable to the laws of the fpiritual world, although to you and others they may appear oppofed to the nature and fitnefs of things. However, as in your comparifon of Baron Swedenborg with your old friend the Quaker, you have brought forward no fpecific point for confideration, except the credibility of his fingle teftimony, which you think not fufficient without *concurrent evidence*, of the want of which you complain, I fhall for the prefent confine myfelf more particularly to this objection.

Now, I fay, in fupport of the memorable relations which Baron Swedenborg has given relative to his intercourfe with the fpiritual world,

world, there is *a great deal of concurrent evidence,* and that too of the very beſt ſort; which, if you are deſirous of ſeeing it in preference to the evidence of truth reſulting from rational arguments, I will now lay before you, not only for your own meditation, but becauſe I believe it may prove uſeful to ſome others of my readers. The evidence I allude to is that of the holy ſcriptures, which you, in common with the members of the New Church, profeſs to believe. And I am the more inclined to adduce that evidence on the preſent occaſion, becauſe I obſerve you have omitted to take any notice of it, although in p. 68 of the Appendix to your *Letters,* you have tranſcribed a part of the very ſame ſection, n. 851, of Baron Swedenborg's *True Chriſtian Religion,* in which it is to be found, and of the weight and importance of which one would think you muſt have been ſenſible at the time.

" That ſuch things (ſays he) do really appear in the heavens, as are deſcribed in the above memorable relations, is clearly evident from ſimilar things being ſeen and deſcribed by John in the Apocalypſe, and alſo by the prophets in the Word of the Old Teſtament. In the Apocalypſe we read, that John ſaw the Son of Man in the midſt of ſeven candleſticks; that he ſaw
a taber-

a tabernacle, a temple, an ark, and an altar in heaven; a book sealed with seven seals, the book opened, and in consequence thereof horses going forth; four animals about the throne; twelve thousand chosen out of each tribe; locusts ascend from the bottomless pit; a woman bringing forth a man-child, and flying into a wilderness by reason of the dragon; two beasts, one ascending out of the sea, the other from the earth; an angel flying in the midst of heaven, having the everlasting gospel; a glassy sea mixed with fire; seven angels having the seven plagues; vials poured out by them on the earth, on the sea, on the rivers, on the sun, on the throne of the beast, on Euphrates, and on the air; a woman sitting on a scarlet beast; a dragon cast out into a lake of fire and sulphur; a white horse; a great supper; a new heaven and new earth; the holy Jerusalem coming down from heaven, described as to it's gates, it's wall, and foundations; also a river of the water of life, and trees of life bearing fruit every month; with many things besides, which were all seen by John, whilst as to his spirit he was in the spiritual world and in heaven. Not to mention what things were seen by the apostles after the Lord's resurrection, as by Peter, Acts xi. and by Paul; and also by the prophets in the Old

Testament;

Testament; as by Ezechiel, that he saw four animals, which were cherubs, chap. i. and x. and a new temple, and a new earth, and an angel measuring them, chap. xl. to xlviii; that he was carried to Jerusalem, and saw there abominations, and also to Chaldea, chap. viii. and xi; the case was the same with Zechariah, in that he saw a man riding amongst myrtle-trees, chap. i. 8; that he saw four horns, and afterwards a man with a measuring-line in his hand, chap. iii; that he saw a flying roll and an ephah, chap. v. 1, 6; that he saw four chariots and horses between two mountains, chap. vi. 1, &c. So again with Daniel, in that he saw four beasts ascending out of the sea, chap. vii. 1, &c.; that he saw the Son of Man coming in the clouds of heaven, whose dominion shall not pass away, and whose kingdom shall not be destroyed, chap. vii. 13, 14; that he saw the fighting of the ram and the he-goat, chap. viii. 1, &c.; that he saw the angel Gabriel, and conversed him, chap. ix; that the young man of Elisha saw chariots and horses of fire about Elisha, and that he saw them when his eyes were opened, 2 Kings vi. 17. From these, and several other instances in the Word, it is evident, that the things which exist in the spiritual world have appeared to many, both

before

before and since the coming of the Lord: what wonder then is it, that the same things should now also appear, at the commencement of the church, or when the New Jerusalem is coming down out of heaven?"

Such is the concurrent testimony of the holy scriptures, relative to the appearances in another life. Now, as the memorable relations of Baron Swedenborg are precisely of the same sort, having a similar tendency, and admitting of a similar (I do not say, *equal* degree of) illustration, it would appear, that a plain and downright opposition to the one, strongly implicates a secret denial of the other. But, do not think, Sir, that I mean to bring a charge of this kind against you, or any other person. It may be, that, in consequence of being educated from infancy in the belief of whatever is recorded in the scriptures, without any examination at all, many of us have never yet considered or ventured to call in question the evidence, which the prophets give of their own memorable relations. Much of what they said, you know, depended upon their own single testimony: yet their visions are universally admitted by the christian church to be true, whether they are comprehensible or not. What concurrent evidence is there, for example,

example, to prove the visions of John the Divine, as related in the Apocalypse? You will perhaps say, that they accord with those of Daniel, Ezekiel, and the rest of the prophets; and that from this harmony, together with the high character and eminent piety of the writer, results the proof of their divinity. Admitted: then, upon the same principle, why may not the harmony, which is plainly to be discerned in Baron Swedenborg's memorable relations, with those of the ancient prophets and apostles, be likewise admitted as satisfactory proof and evidence of their reality? especially as you allow the Baron to have been a man of acknowledged piety, and unimpeached character?

Supposing a great number of travellers, whose veracity we had no just reason to suspect, should in succession arrive in this country, and each of them assure us, that such and such were the laws, customs, and manners of a distant nation hitherto unknown; if there were an evident agreement in all their accounts, though related at different times, a reasonable man could not refuse his assent to their united assertions, however singular or strange the customs and manners of that distant nation might at first sight appear. And if, after an interval of seventeen hundred

hundred years since the other travellers had arrived, another should come from the same country, and by authority of the reigning prince, bring the same kind of testimony as his predecessors had done before him; together with an explanation of those former accounts, which to many were before unintelligible, but which the last traveller, in consequence of his acquaintance and familiar intercourse with the inhabitants of that distant nation for upwards of twenty-seven years, was enabled most completely and satisfactorily to do; what man is there, possessed of a sound understanding, and acquainted with the rules of evidence, that would object to this traveller's testimony, merely because he had no fellow-travellers, as witnesses, to attest the truth of his assertions? Yet, (excuse the liberty) you appear to me to be precisely in the situation of such an objector. The prophets and apostles are the travellers first mentioned; the distant country is the spiritual world;[*] the last traveller from that world is Baron Swedenborg, who, by commission from the Lord our Saviour, comes after a lapse of seventeen hundred years since the time of the apostles,

---

[*] The spiritual world is here compared to a distant country, not because it is such in reality, for it is close to us; but because it is so little known in the present day, and generally supposed to be at a distance.

apostles, with a testimony concerning that world, and it's inhabitants, similar to what they had before given; but in consequence of upwards of twenty-seven years' converse with angels and spirits, enriched with additional illustrations, and still further discoveries of the same.

If you reflect seriously on the above, I hope you will no longer have occasion to " wonder " at the strength of faith of Baron Swedenborg's " followers," but rather, with us, lament the infidelity of the times, when so many, who profess to believe the scriptures, refuse their assent to the first and fundamental principles of the christian religion.

Another proof of the divine mission of Baron Swedenborg arises from the manifest good tendency of all his writings, in almost every page of which he inculcates the necessity of leading a life of holiness and virtue. The two essentials, on which depends the whole of the law and the prophets, viz. an acknowledgment of the unity of God, and the loving him above all things, and our neighbour as ourselves, are in like manner insisted upon by Baron Swedenborg as the sum and substance of all religion, and the only means

means whereby our future happiness can be secured. Now as every man, as well as every tree, is known by his fruits, it follows, that that system of doctrines, which ascribes all glory and honour to the Creator and Saviour of the world, and which teaches love to him, and charity to all mankind, must proceed from God; and consequently, the message itself being proved divine, the bearer thereof must be estimated accordingly.

* * *

I now proceed to obviate some other objections you have stated against the testimony of Baron Swedenborg, and the want of miracles to support his pretensions: but as I observe there are many passages in your *Letters*, that require rectification, I shall be as brief as possible with each.

Page 10, you say, " Do we not object to the " divine mission of Mahomet, that he worked " no miracles?" Sir, if you have nothing more to object against the Mahometan religion than this, it appears to me, a Turkish magician might very easily convert you into a good Mussulman, by shewing you a few of his inchantments. Do you really suppose, that *no miracle can possibly be wrought*, except in favour

of

of the *true religion?* If you do, (which indeed you acknowledge in the fame page,) then your reafon and judgment are no guard either againſt the miracles of magicians, or the lying wonders of falſe Chriſts; but you are liable to become a prey to every deluſion. A member of the New Church, Sir, has other objections to Mahometanifm, than that of the want of miracles; and thoſe objections are of an intellectual, rational kind, and not ariſing from the groſſneſs of the bodily fenſes. But though the religion of Mahomet is far inferior to that of Jeſus Chriſt, yet it was permitted by the Lord's divine providence to be eſtabliſhed among the eaſtern nations, as being the only one they were capable of embracing. And it is remarkable, that they acknowledge one ſupreme God, and Jeſus Chriſt as his Son, whom they call the wifeſt of men, and the grand prophet, that came into the world in order to inſtruct mankind. A confiderable part of the Mahometans allow Jeſus Chriſt to be greater than Mahomet: and, if I am not miſtaken, there is a particular ſect among them, branded with the name of heretics, who acknowledge him as the only God of heaven and earth.

Again,

Again, you observe, p. 10, "In the Old Testament we read of numbers of prophets from Moses to Malachi, *most of whom* either worked what we usually call miracles, or foretold future events, which is exactly of the same nature, being equally within the province of *God alone.*" Here you virtually acknowledge, that at least *some* of the prophets neither worked miracles, nor foretold future events. But in p. 11 you say, that " to come from God with a message to man, is a very serious and important thing, for which *no man, however excellent,* hath any right to expect that his own word only should be taken." May it not then be hence fairly inferred, that, to be consistent with yourself, you must reject the testimony of all those prophets who gave no supernatural proofs of their divine mission? Whether you really do reject their prophecies on that account, or not, I cannot take upon myself to declare; but you have certainly given the world just reason to suspect your belief in the scriptures, together with the whole system of the christian religion.

You further remark in p. 61, " This great Being (God, of whose essence you say you know nothing at all,) " has at different times " com-

"commissioned various men, and especially Jesus
"Christ, to communicate his will to mankind;
"and he *always* sanctioned their missions by the
"power of working miracles, or doing such
"things, as no man could have done, if God
"had not been with him." Several of the prophets, we have seen, made no appeal to the test of miracles; and as for the circumstance of some of them foretelling future events, this could carry no weight or authority with it, until the accomplishment of their prediction. It is plain, therefore, that some prophets, at the moment of their announcing themselves to be the messengers of Jehovah, made no such miraculous display of supernatural powers, as you assert to have been invariably the case; and yet the same persons were accepted as prophets by the Jewish nation, and are still accounted such by christians.

In the preceding part of this letter it was proved, that miracles may be, and have been wrought by the power of the devil, or what amounts to the same thing, by magical inchantments. Your assertion, therefore, that the performance of miracles is within the province of *God alone*, falls to the ground, and cannot be be maintained, except in oppofition to the facts already ftated.

You quote Deut. xviii. to prove, that the true prophets were to be diftinguifhed from the pretended ones, by their foretelling things to come. They were fo; and in verfe 22 of that chapter it is faid, "When a prophet fpeaketh in "the name of Jehovah, if the thing follow not, "nor come to pafs, that is the thing which Je- "hovah hath not fpoken, but the prophet hath "fpoken it prefumptuoufly; thou fhalt not be "afraid of him." Now the prophet Jonah, by command of Jehovah, went through the ftreets of Nineveh, and without any conditions proclaimed it's overthrow within forty days. Yet fuch an event *did not come to pafs;* for God repented of the evil that he had faid he would do unto them, and he did it not; at which clemency of the Lord, Jonah his prophet was highly offended. How you, who confine your ideas to the *mere letter* of fcripture, reconcile thefe, and many other paffages, in all appearance more contradictory ftill, I know not. In my view, they are reconcileable only by means of the fpiritual fenfe, which is in every part of the Word, the real exiftence of which you neverthelefs deny.

Com-

Signified by the New Jerusalem. 41

* * *

Complaining of the want of miracles in support of the doctrines of the New Church, you make the following remark in p. 11. " To say, " that though the former difpenfations of re- " ligion required to be eftablifhed by miracles, " this new one, the moft magnificent of them " all, and which is to continue for ever, requires " none, is no better than faying, that though a " cottage may require to ftand upon a rock, a " palace, or a temple, like that of Solomon, " may be built upon the fand, or ftand without " any foundation at all." On this fubject I reafon in quite a different manner from you, and fay, As former difpenfations required the aid and affiftance of miracles in order to induce mankind to acknowledge them, this argues at leaft, that they did not carry with them that clear and rational evidence of their truth, which was of itfelf fufficient to gain credit among men: for wherever the truth of a thing cannot be eftablifhed by any other means than by miracles, it plainly implies, that it is involved in obfcurity, doubt, and uncertainty. Such was the cafe with all former difpenfations, which only *fhadowed forth* and *reprefented* the laft and moft magnificent of all, the *New Jerufalem.* This laft and greateft of difpenfations requires no
miracle,

miracle, becaufe the truths it difplays are of themfelves clear, rational, and fatisfactory. It is too dignified to ftoop down to the earth for any thing that refembles a miracle; for by fo doing, it's heaven-born glory would be tarnifhed, and a cloud would overfpread the fky, fo as to interrupt the beams of celeftial light proceeding from him who is the fun of righteoufnefs.

He that requires a miracle to convince him of truth, in preference to rational inveftigation, affifted by light from the holy Word, may be compared to a man, who takes a tinder-box out of his pocket, and in mid-day with flint and fteel ftrikes a light, to enable him to fee whether the fun is fhining or not. The flint and fteel are his natural fcience; the match with brimftone at the end of it is felf-love and felf-derived intelligence; the tinder-box is the natural mind, where all his fcientific knowledge is treafured up; and his dark pocket is himfelf.

In the darknefs of midnight a lighted torch, whofe virtues are derived from the earth, may be ufeful where there is no other luminous body to emit light; it may even *reprefent*, during

ring the darkness of the night, the sun itself. Yet when the moon arises, which is only another, though more perfect *representative* of the sun, the light of the torch is lost. But when the sun itself is risen, and shines with the full splendor of day, both the torch and moon, together with the stars, are no more thought of, their light being completely swallowed up by the superior brightness of the sun. Just so, in the midnight of the church universal, *miracles*, which do not go beyond the earthly or sensual principle, were granted to mankind, as a *torch* to lighten their footsteps, in the absence of heavenly truth. This was the time when the Israelitish and Jewish nation were led out of Egypt into the wilderness. Soon after, the *moon* arose, and some *stars*, as a still further light to their benighted posterity. I allude to the time when they were in possession of the land of Canaan, and were governed by *judges*, *kings*, and *prophets*. Last of all the *Sun himself*, the true light that enlightens every man coming into the world, rose upon the face of the earth; but before he arrived at the meridian, a thick cloud obscured him from the sight, and soon after he went down. This was the birth and crucifixion of our blessed Lord and Saviour *Jesus Christ*, by whom the primitive christian church was founded, and preserved in it's purity until the third century, when the dangerous errors of Arius and his adherents began to prevail. But now he comes a second time with all that fulness of meridian splendor, which is capable of dispersing the thick clouds of darkness from every mind that is in love with truth *for it's own sake*, and who is desirous of receiving illumination, *not from earthly torches*, but *from heavenly light*.

Our Lord says, " He that believeth on me, " the works that I do, shall he do also, and " *greater works* than these shall he do, because I " go unto my Father," John xiv. 12. It may be supposed, that the Lord here alluded to the miracles which he would enable his disciples to perform after his departure out of the world, in order to give effect to their ministerial labours. But as there can be no greater miracle, literally speaking, than the raising of the dead, which the Lord himself more than once performed; it is plain, that the works here spoken of, as *greater than miracles*, must be of a spiritual kind; in which case the above passage will bear the following interpretation. He that believeth on the Lord, that is, in heart and life acknowlegeth him as one with the Father, and the only God of heaven and earth, shall, by virtue of his

continual

continual affiftance, not only remove from himfelf, but alfo be the means of removing from others, all thofe evils and falfes which infeft the human mind, and which to fubdue requires more of a divine agency, than the performance of any vifible miracle whatever. To convert a finner from the evil of his ways, and inftead of the unclean delights of felf-love and the love of the world, to infufe the pure and chafte delights of heaven, fuch as the love of the Lord, and neighbourly love, is certainly a much greater work than healing the lame, the blind, and the deaf, or even raifing a thoufand dead bodies. But as this miraculous work of regeneration could not be effected, unlefs the Lord had glorified his Humanity, which is meant by his going to the Father; and as the Holy Spirit was promifed to the church after his glorification, by which is underftood the more effectual operation of Divinity when united to Humanity, therefore the Lord fays of the true believer, " Greater works than thefe " fhall he do, *becaufe I go unto my Father.*"

I will juft add here what a late ingenious writer, *a philofopher of the north,* fays, in anfwer to thofe who bring againft Baron Swedenborg fuch an objection as the following: " But he
" did

"did no miracles!"—"The miracle of all miracles (fays he) is *truth*. That is the effence of them all. When God did miracles in former ages, it was not to *prove* truth: for, *one and one is three*, cannot be true by a thoufand miracles; nor, *one and one is two*, lefs clear without any. God, then, did miracles—only to ftrike with awe the hard hearts of mortals, and *awake their attention*. This was not neceffary in an age of fcience and reafoning as now, when God has prepared all for the full perception of truth. From this obfervation you may fee, *that miracles are only for fools*, for men ftill brutes, ftill favage. For when all the miracles are paffed, there ftill remains the fame great duty—to fee and perceive the truth in your mind, without which neither faith nor worfhip exift."

Upon the whole, then, we may fafely conclude, that the ufhering in and eftablifhment of a new difpenfation of divine truth, like that of the New Jerufalem, which requires not the aid of miracles or other *extraneous* evidence to fupport it, but depends folely on it's own *intrinfic merit* for recommendation, from it's manifeft conformity to the true fenfe of holy fcripture, and the principles of found reafon, is an undeniable

deniable proof of it's superiority over every other system of religion in the known world.

* * *

In page 11 you hint, that Baron Swedenborg's communications with the spiritual world were no more than the effect of a warm imagination; and seem to insinuate, that "his intercourse with "God and the invisible world was by night. "In this case (you say) such a person *seeing an* "*angel in a dream*, is nothing more than his "*dreaming he saw an angel*." Now had you carefully examined Baron Swedenborg's writings, you would have found, that his intercourse with the spiritual world was when he was *broad awake*, and not during his sleep, which was like that of other men. In this particular, therefore, you have not done him justice. But if, as you say, a person's *seeing an angel in a dream*, is nothing more than his *dreaming he saw an angel*, what do you make of the dreams of the prophets? In what light do you consider those parts of the scripture, where it is said, that the angel of the Lord appeared to men *in dreams*, and foretold future events *in dreams* ? When the angel of the Lord appeared to Joseph in a dream, and warned him against Herod, Matt. ii. 12, 13, was this nothing more than *dreaming he saw an angel?* And when it is said, Jehovah himself

appeared

appeared to Solomon *in a dream by night*, 1 Kings iii. 5, does this imply nothing more, than that Solomon *dreamed he saw Jehovah?* Witticisms may do very well in some cases; but I hope you do not mean to apply them to subjects of a divine nature. I cannot help thinking, however, but many, on reading this part of your *Letters*, will be ready to conclude in their own minds, that you disbelieve and even despise the prophetical dreams, which are recorded in the scriptures.

* * *

You well observe, p. 12, that Swedenborg was aware of the objection which you and others might make to his testimony, namely, that he wrought no miracles in confirmation of it. But I am rather surprized, that you treat his answer so lightly, particularly that part where he says, that miracles carry compulsion with them, and take away a man's free-will in spiritual matters. " The same objection (you say) might
" have been made to the miracles of Moses and
" of Christ. It is the nature of all evidence to
" compel the assent. For no man can refuse
" his assent to what *appears to him* to be suf-
" ficient evidence. Whatever be the case of
" the *will* with respect to motives, the *judg-*
" *ment* is universally allowed to be *necessarily*
" *de-*

"*determined* by the force of arguments." If it is the nature of all evidence to compel the aſſent, why did not the evidence, which our Lord gave to the Jews, concerning himſelf, compel them to aſſent to his being the Son of God, and the true Meſſiah? Nay, why are *you* not compelled, by the miracles which Jeſus performed, to believe him to be *one with the Father*, that is, *very God?* And why do you not find yourſelf compelled to aſſent to the doctrines of the New Jeruſalem, by the rational and ſcriptural evidence which Baron Swedenborg has given? Sir, herein lies the excellence of rational evidence, that *it never compels the human mind;* but as it is itſelf free, ſo it cannot impart any thing contrary to liberty. It muſt be in a ſtate of freedom that it gains admiſſion to the underſtanding; and it will never make that man a ſlave, who has opened his houſe for it's reception. On the contrary, miracles, if they do not find men ſlaves, will ſoon make them ſuch.

To ſay, that " no man can refuſe his aſſent " to what *appears to him* to be ſufficient evi- " dence," is quite beſide the queſtion, and a mere play of words. You think there is a power in arguments capable of *neceſſarily determining*

mining the *judgment*, independent of the *will;* but herein you only discover what little attention you must have paid to the human mind, and how imperfect your knowledge is of the secret workings of man's heart. The Lord says, "If any man will *do his will,* he shall *know of the doctrine,* whether it be of God," John vii. 17. That is, if any man's *will* is inclined to good, then his *understanding* is fit for the reception of spiritual truth, and not before. Without this previous requisite, all the arguments in the world will have no weight with some minds. This is a truth so universally admitted, that it is even become a proverb to say, "There are none so "*blind* as them that *will not see.*" Also, "What "a man first *wishes* or *wills* to be true, he can "soon *make himself believe* true." On this very principle it is, that the civil laws of every country will allow no man to be a competent *judge* in any case, wherein he himself is interested by *passion* or *affection;* it being one of the first dictates of wisdom, founded on the uniform experience of ages, that the *will* of man is capable of exercising such a malignant influence over the *judgment* or *understanding,* as even to deprive it of the faculty of perceiving and acknowledging genuine truth.

But

But something further seems to be implied in your assertion, that " the judgment is necessarily " determined by the force of arguments;" namely, that all who have read your *Letters*, or other writings, are convinced of their truth, and consequently agree with you at least in judgment; for I dare say you think you have used weighty and powerful arguments to support your various hypotheses. But in this matter I believe you are much mistaken; and so shall I be too, if your *Letters* convince a *single member* of the New Church, either that Jesus Christ is not the supreme God, or that Baron Swedenborg was not inspired by him.

* * *

After quoting some excellent and highly rational remarks of the Baron on the subject of miracles, in which he particularly shews the reason why they were wrought previous to the Lord's coming into the world, and are not now, viz. because men were then mere natural men, incapable of seeing the spiritual or internal things of the church, whereas now they have a capacity of discerning them; you object as follows: " That any change was made in the " nature of men at the first coming of Christ, " or that any further change has been made in " man since what you call his second coming, is
" an

"an arbitrary suppofition of Mr. Swedenborg's, "for which he produces no evidence whatever." In anfwer to this I fhall obferve, that when any change takes place in fo large a community of men as that of the chriftian world in general, it is not eafily to be difcovered from any *particular acts* of particular individuals, or particular focieties; but may be feen by a comprehenfive mind, that is capable of collecting into one view the apparently detached operations of a thoufand contemporary and fucceffive focieties. This is the way to judge of that fpiritual light and liberty, which has lately made it's appearance in the world. The *precife moment* when it began, may be as difficult to determine, as it would be for you to point out the *firft day* in which Frenchmen began to think of civil liberty. That fome change or other has actually taken place among the nations of Europe, with refpect to what are called the *natural rights of man*, you yourfelf are one of the firft to publifh. This you can fee and acknowledge, becaufe it is made manifeft to the *outward fenfes*. But being unwilling to elevate your mind above the fphere of external objects, you do not perceive, that there is an equal degree of fpiritual liberty, operating *within* that which is natural, and even producing it as it's offspring; which latter,

however,

however, too often degenerates into licentiousness; and then, so far from deserving the name of liberty, it breaks the bonds of society, and while it pretends to support the sacred rights of man, actually tramples them under it's profane foot.

The great change that took place at the time of the Lord's first coming, consisted not so much in the adoption of any new external forms of worship, as in a new capacity men received for understanding the interior things of heaven and the church. Every thing before was typical or representative: but when he came, of whom all the scriptures testify, and to whom they all referred, then the whole cloud of shadows and representations that veiled the light of the sun, disappeared, and the minds of men received new illumination; as it is written, " The people that " walked in darkness, have seen a great light; " they that dwell in the land of the shadow of " death, upon them hath the light shined," Isaiah ix. 2.

A similar change has taken place in the minds of men since the year 1757, the period when (according to Baron Swedenborg) spiritual liberty was restored by the accomplishment of the laſt judgment in the ſpiritual world. And it may even be ſeen in the evident decline of eccleſiaſtical power, particularly in Roman Catholic countries. It may be ſeen in the general ſpirit of free inquiry that begins to pervade the world; in the expulſion of Jeſuits from different kingdoms; in the comparatively timid and cautious proceedings of the inquiſition, in thoſe countries where it is not yet aboliſhed; in the ſuppreſſion of monaſteries; in the pope's ſilent and humble reſignation of thoſe more than regal powers, which his predeceſſors had uſurped and impiouſly exerciſed over kings and princes; in the benevolent exertions of the friends of humanity for the abolition of ſlavery; in the new and ſucceſsful inſtitutions for the gradual inſtruction and reformation of the poor; in the improved regulations of priſons, and numerous other inſtances of national police; in the humane ſocieties formed for the recovery of perſons apparently dead; and, laſtly, it may be ſeen plainly and decidedly in the actual commencement of the New Church, called the New Jeruſalem, whoſe members require no miracles to convince them of truth, being in poſſeſſion of what is a thouſand times more excellent and ſatisfactory, namely, the true interpretation of the ſcriptures, ſupported by clear

and

and rational evidence. A community of this kind, rising up in the present day, and spreading itself over the face of the whole earth, is the most undeniable proof of Baron Swedenborg's assertions concerning the new light and liberty that has risen on mankind; for being a matter of fact, it bears down, by it's own weight, ten thousand arguments of opposition.

* * *

Speaking further of miracles, you say, p. 14. " If other methods fail to produce a general " conviction of the truth of your doctrine, " which you say is to fill the whole earth, " recourse must be had to the old, but effec- " tual method of miracles after all; and should " each of your temples be filled with the *glory* " *of the Lord* at the time of their consecration, " as was the tabernacle and temple of Solomon, " you would, I dare say, exult not a little. As " a similar glory invested our Saviour at his " transfiguration, all the three great dispensa- " tions of religion, you might then say, were " distinguished by a similar divine attestation." We do not say, that our doctrine is to fill the whole earth, so as to become the professed religion of all nations, to the exclusion of every other; for we consider the real visible church of Christ to be like the heart and lungs to the

Grand

Grand Man of the world, the church universal being viewed by the Lord as *One Man*, or rather as *One Woman*, Apoc. xxi. 2. It is not in any wise necessary, that the heart and lungs should actually or literally fill the whole body; it is sufficient if life is conveyed from them to every part of it. So likewise in respect to the New Church; there is no necessity for it's literally filling the whole earth, while life is communicated therefrom, like blood from the heart, to every nation and people of the world. But of this kind of reasoning I know you will require a miracle to be convinced, for I perceive nothing else will go down. As it is not, however, in my power to satisfy you in this particular, I must beg your indulgence while I deliver the sentiments of the New Church in her own language, even though the half of my remarks should be thrown away upon you.

Should our temples be filled with the glory of the Lord, like the tabernacle and temple of Solomon, we should, you think, exult not a little, and consider it as a divine attestation of the truth of our religion. Sir, our temples *are filled with the glory of the Lord;* for as at his transfiguration before Peter, James, and John, " *his face did shine as the sun, and his raiment was*
" *white*

"*white as the light,*" Matt. xvii. 2, so in his New Church he is worshipped and adored, in his Divine (transfigured) Humanity, as the glorious sun of righteousness, the source and fountain of life and light, and the one only and supreme God of heaven and earth. When we hear his holy Word read, we hear himself speak in his own divine language; and when, " begin-
" ning at Moses and all the prophets, he ex-
" pounds (by his ministers) *in all the scriptures*
" *the things concerning himself,*" we fall down in silent adoration at his feet, and having our
" understanding opened to understand the scrip-
" tures," we perceive, by the glory that visibly surrounds him, that in his glorified person " all
" things are fulfilled which were written in the
" law of Moses, and in the prophets, and in
" the psalms concerning him," Luke xxiv. 27, 44, 45. Thus all former dispensations of divine truth have their central point and full accomplishment in this last and most magnificent of all; their glory and honour is brought into the holy city, New Jerusalem; and the Lord God almighty, even the Lamb, Jesus Christ, is himself both the light and the temple of it. Apoc. xxi. 21, 22.

* * *

Your next observation, p. 15, is concerning Swedenborg's assertion, that in the center of Africa a revelation, similar to the doctrines of the New Jerusalem, is begun among the inhabitants of that country; and you seem to think, that we consider this circumstance "as "*a proof* that he was really inspired." But in this point you are again mistaken; for we cannot consider any thing as a *proof*, before the truth of it be fully ascertained. Neither does Baron Swedenborg himself relate the narrative with any view to establish his divine commission by such a kind of evidence. He simply declares the fact to be so, and leaves those who chuse to make inquiry into the truth of it. We embrace the doctrines he has published upon *quite another ground*, namely, because *we see with our own eyes or understandings*, that they are the doctrines of eternal truth, founded on the Word of God, and demonstrated by the acknowledged principles of right reason. We also, in cases where we have no other means of judging for ourselves, and in points that are not essential to salvation, receive his testimony on the credit of his own word; because we believe, both from his writings and his personal good character, that he was incapable of any fraud or deception. And in thus giving credit to Baron Swedenborg

denborg for what he folemnly declares he was an eye and ear witnefs of, we conceive we do no more than you yourfelf do, and every other perfon who admits the truth of *hiftorical facts* upon the fingle evidence of one writer or traveller.

But in p. 16 you obferve, " that neither Mr.
" Bruce's late travels into Abyffinia, nor the
" proceedings of the affociation for promoting
" the difcovery of the interior parts of Africa,
" give us as yet any reafon to think, that what
" Mr. Swedenborg defcribes as exifting in his
" time, is to be found at prefent. But we ex-
" pect foon to have further accounts from that
" hitherto unexplored part of the world ; and if
" it fhould appear, which I ftrongly fufpect,
" that there neither is, nor ever was any thing
" like a *New Jerufalem Church* in the center of
" Africa, your faith in Mr. Swedenborg's in-
" fpiration muft be very ftrong indeed, if it be
" not well fhaken."

Abyffinia, you will be pleafed to obferve, is not the country in which Swedenborg afferts that the new revelation has commenced. It ought not therefore to be expected, that Mr. Bruce, who penetrated no farther than Abyfsinia, should give the requisite information. Yet even the travels of that gentleman furnish us with strong presumptive evidence, that the inhabitants of Africa have a much better knowledge of the existence of the spiritual world, and a life after death, than many of those who fancy themselves to be in the full enjoyment of the light of christianity. But as neither the travels of Mr. Bruce, nor the proceedings of the African association, give the least proof of there being *no such a people* in the interior parts of Africa, as Baron Swedenborg describes, it is certainly too soon to conclude about the fact. From a *negative*, to infer a *positive*, is no sign of wisdom; it is beginning at the wrong end, and out of *nothing* attempting to produce *something*.

As to the particular name of *New Church*, or *New Jerusalem*, I do not know that we are to expect ever to find a set of people expresly so called in the center of Africa; but if it should at any time hereafter appear, that there is actually a race of men in the part alluded to by Baron Swedenborg, who worship one God in a Human Form, and who have any knowledge of his having been born a Man on this earth, and at the same time live in mutual love and peace,

peace, we may then safely conclude, that they are the people among whom the revelation has taken place, whether they be distinguished as the *New Jerusalem*, or by any other name. But until this matter is fully ascertained, it will not admit of an argument on either side; though even when fully established, I would not by any means wish the Baron's assertions to be considered of a miraculous nature, but simply as evidences that he had converse with angels and spirits. It is just in this point of view that he himself desired his friends to regard the many extraordinary particulars that transpired during his life-time, and which proved him to be possessed of supernatural knowledge. Some of these are already related in his theological works; but there are others, the truth of which has been attested by persons of undoubted character. I shall take the liberty of mentioning a few of them in this place.

1. Count Hopken, a Swedish nobleman, has confirmed the truth of the two following transactions. After the decease of the Count De Marteville, certain persons came to demand a debt of his widow, of a considerable sum of money, that they said was due to them by her deceased husband. This she knew was not a

just

just one, because it had been paid during his life-time; yet could not tell where the acquittance or receipt was put. In her trouble she applied to Mr. Swedenborg; and understanding that he had the privilege of conversing with the deceased, requested that (if possible) he would ask her late husband where the acquittance was. On the next day Mr. Swedenborg informed her, that he had seen and spoken to her deceased husband, who told him where he had put the acquittance, and that she would find it in the particular place he described. It was accordingly found in the same place; and this account was universally known to be true both at Court, and in Stockholm. The queen of Sweden herself, being afterwards on a visit at Berlin, confirmed the truth of this relation to several Academicians, whom she had invited to her table.

2. The second remarkable transaction is the following. The queen dowager of Adolphus Frederick, and sister to the late king of Prussia, soon after having heard of the foregoing account, and several others concerning Mr. Swedenborg, told the Senator Count Hopken, that she wished to speak to him. The Count, in going to carry the queen's orders, met Mr.

Mr. Swedenborg, who was on his way to the palace, with a defign to fpeak to that princefs. After having converfed on various fubjects, the queen informed him, that fhe had lately written a letter to her brother, a prince of Pruffia, who had fince died. The contents of her letter, fhe obferved, were of fo fecret a nature, that no perfon in the world had any knowledge of them, but that brother; and fhe wifhed Mr. Swedenborg to afk him, whether he had received her letter before his death; to which he replied, that he would give her an anfwer in a few days. At the time appointed Mr. Swedenborg waited on the queen, and related to her the whole contents of the faid letter, word for word, at which fhe was ftruck with the greateft aftonifhment. He further informed her majefty, that her brother had received her letter, and begun an anfwer to it, and that in the efcrutoire of the prince, was an unfinifhed letter, which he intended to have fent her before his deceafe. On this fhe fent to the king of Pruffia, and the letter was found as Mr. Swedenborg had directed, which the king fent to her. This circumftance was alfo publicly known at Stockholm, and much talked of out of the kingdom. The Baron, in a letter to the Landgrave of Heffe Damftadt, dated

July

July 13, 1771, confirms the truth of this relation, yet fays, "It is not to be accounted as any kind of miracle, but only as a memorable tranfaction, like thofe found in the work entitled, *True Chriftian Religion*, concerning Luther, Melancthon, Calvin, and others; which are only to be confidered as evidences, that as to the fpirit I have been introduced by the Lord into the fpiritual world, and that I converfe both with angels and fpirits."

3. A third memorable occurrence. On arriving at Gottenburg from London, Swedenborg was told that his houfe had been deftroyed by the flames, in the great fire that burnt almoft all the fouth fuburb of Stockholm, in 1759. "No," anfwered Mr. Swedenborg, "my houfe is not burnt, the fire only reached to fuch and fuch a part." What he faid was true; and the thing was then of fo recent a nature, that he could have had no particular account of it, either by letter or any perfon; for it was about three days before the arrival of the poft.

4. Mr. Springer, a Swedifh gentleman, whofe refidence for many years was in London, in a letter to the Abbé Pernetty, librarian to the late king of Pruffia, dated Jan. 18, 1782, relates

relates the following particulars. "Fifteen years ago, Mr. Swedenborg was about to depart for Sweden, and defired me to procure him a good captain, which I did. I made the agreement with a perfon named Dixon; and Mr. Swedenborg's effects were carried on board the veffel. When the captain came for Mr. Swedenborg, I took my leave of him, and wifhed him a happy voyage. Having then afked the captain, if he was provided with good and neceffary provifions, he anfwered me, that he had as much as was needful for the voyage. On this Mr. Swedenborg faid, " My friend, we have not need of a great quantity; for this day week we fhall, by the aid of God, enter into the port of Stockholm, at two o'clock." On captain Dixon's return, he related to me, that this happened exactly as Mr. Swedenborg had foretold."

Mr. Springer continues his letter in thefe words: " The whole of what he has related to me, concerning my deceafed friends and enemies, and of the fecrets which exifted only between them and me, is almoft paft belief. He even explained to me in what manner the peace was concluded between Sweden and the king of Pruffia, and praifed my conduct on that occafion.

K

occasion. He pointed out to me the three great personages, whose services I made use of in that circumstance, which was nevertheless a great secret betwixt us. I asked him how he could be instructed of these particulars, and who had discovered them to him? To which he replied, " Who informed me of your affair " with Count de C—— E——d? You cannot " deny the truth of what I have just related to " you. Continue," added he, " to merit his re- " proaches; depart not from the good way, " either for honours or money; but contrari- " wise, continue as constant therein, as you " have been hitherto, and you will prosper."

5. By the affidavit of Richard and Elizabeth Shearsmith, at whose house Baron Swedenborg lived and died, it appears, that a month before his death he predicted the very day on which he should depart this life, which happened accordingly. See a copy of the affidavit in the *Magazine of Knowledge*, &c. vol. ii. p. 300.

Besides the above extraordinary circumstances, which I have related only for the sake of those who will believe nothing without such kind of evidence, there are many others of a similar nature, the truth of which has been so

fully

fully attested, that none but an infidel can controvert them. These things, however, are not regarded by the members of the New Church, who look for and actually see *better* and *stronger* evidence of truth, than any miracle can afford. But as you, Sir, have called out for supernatural evidences, such as miracles, and the prediction of future events, here they are; make what use you can of them. We shall see whether they produce that conviction in your mind, which you say miracles unavoidably produce. If they do not, you will then be left without excuse. Without wishing to be considered as a prophet, I will nevertheless venture to prophesy, in the words of the evangelist, of all those who require signs and miracles, " If they hear not Moses " and the prophets, neither will they be " persuaded, though one rose from the dead," Luke xvi. 31.

Thus have I gone through all the objections you have urged against Baron Swedenborg, on the score of his not working miracles as a proof of his divine mission. You have seen, and are bound to acknowledge, that neither *signs*, nor *wonders*, nor *miracles*, avail any thing towards producing a rational conviction of truth in the understanding; consequently that such things are not the proper evidences of a man's infpiration. You may alfo be well fatisfied, if you will only be at the pains of examining, that the defcriptions which the Baron gives of the fpiritual world, exactly refemble thofe given by the prophets and apoftles in the Old and New Teftament; which, if the one be true, is a ftrong prefumptive proof that the other is alfo. This evidence, however, is only *external;* yet it is of great weight fo far as it goes. But we have better ftill, and that is of an *internal* nature; being an evidence that arifes from the fpiritual fenfe of the holy Word, by virtue of which we are enabled to fee what was never feen before, viz. that there is not only *no real contradiction* in that volume of infpiration, but that *every part*, even the moft minute, and apparently trivial and ludicrous circumftance therein recorded, is *divine* and *worthy of God*, containing within it's bofom fuch treafures of divine wifdom as cannot be exhaufted to eternity. It is the evidence arifing from this internal fenfe of the fcripture, proved and confirmed by it's literal fenfe, that principally authorizes us to acknowledge Baron Swedenborg not only as a divinely-commiffioned meffenger from the Lord, but as the *greateft* and *moft-enlightened* of any that has hitherto appeared

peared in the world. For as John the Baptist was declared to be greater than any that had preceded him, on account of his being the immediate fore-runner of the Lord at his *first advent*; so we consider Baron Swedenborg to be superior to John, or any other prophet or apostle, and that because he is the messenger appointed to announce the Lord's *second* and *most glorious advent*.

I know you will say, as you have already said, p. 17, that the " spiritual sense of the " scriptures cannot be attended to, till there be " some evidence of the reality of such a sense." And, " If you say that I am incapable of per- " ceiving this sense of the scriptures, you must " allow that you have no means of convincing " me, or any others who are in the same situa- " tion with me, how well soever you, who have " the illumination that I want, may be satisfied " with respect to all your doctrines." Were a blind man obstinately to deny the existence of the sun's light, until he had some evidence of it's reality, would you not pity him, and with a smile say, 'Why what evidence of the *light* can 'you have, while you are totally immersed in '*darkness?* Go to the oculist, let him cure you 'of your blindness, and then you will have suf-
'ficient

'ficient evidence of the reality of light.' It is in this way I would (without meaning any offence) addrefs myfelf to you, Sir, and to all others who are in a fimilar fituation. Get the eyes of your fpirit or underftanding opened, and then you will have ocular demonftration of the actual exiftence of fpiritual light; this being as obvious to the fight of a fpiritual or intellectual eye, as natural light is to a bodily eye. It is true, the members of the New Church have no power to communicate to you a perception of the internal fenfe of the Word; but for ourfelves, we as certainly know the reality of it, as you do the exiftence of the fun's natural light. We alfo know how you may obtain fuch a perception, if you are fo difpofed; and that is folely by applying in fincerity of heart to the one only true God Jefus Chrift, and by keeping his commandments. It is he alone that can open the eyes of the blind, and communicate that light which we all ftand in need of for our direction to heaven. He giveth liberally to them that *afk him*, and upbraideth none. And "if " any man will do his will, he fhall know of the " doctrine, whether it be of God," John vii. 17.

I cannot conclude this fubject better than by referring you to a memorable paffage in Baron Swedenborg's

Swedenborg's *Arcana Cœlestia*, n. 7290, where he treats of the nature of miracles. But as the original of that aftonifhing work is in few hands, being fo fcarce as not to be eafily procured, and the part alluded to not yet publifhed in Englifh, I fhall therefore take the liberty of tranflating and inferting it in this place. "With refpect to prodigies and figns, it is to be obferved, that they were performed amongft fuch perfons as were in external worfhip, and were not defirous of knowing any thing about internal worfhip; for they, who were in fuch worfhip, were to be compelled by external means: hence it was, that miracles were performed amongft the Ifraelitifh and Jewifh people, who were merely in external worfhip, and in none that was internal. It was alfo neceffary for them to be in external worfhip, when they would not be in that which is internal, in order that they might reprefent holy things in externals, and thus that communication might be given with heaven, as by fomething of a church; for correfpondences, reprefentatives, and fignificatives, conjoin the natural world to the fpiritual. Hence now it was, that fo many miracles were performed among that nation. But with thofe who are in internal worfhip, that is, in charity and faith, miracles are not performed,

being

being to such persons hurtful; for miracles force or compel to believe, and whatsoever is of compulsion doth not remain, but is dissipated. The internal things of worship, which are faith and charity, ought to be implanted in freedom, for then they are appropriated; and the things which are appropriated, remain: but the things which are implanted by compulsion, abide without the internal man in the external; for nothing enters into the internal man, except by intellectual ideas, which are reasons, the ground which receives them there being the rational principle enlightened: hence it is, that no miracles are performed at this day. That they are also of a hurtful nature, may appear from the following consideration; they compel to believe, and fix in the external man an idea that a thing is so or so; if the internal man afterwards denies what the miracles have confirmed, then there commences an opposition and collision between the internal and external man, and at length, when the ideas produced from miracles are dissipated, the conjunction of falshood and truth takes place, which is prophanation. Hence it is evident, how dangerous and hurtful miracles would be at this day in the church wherein the internals of worship are disclosed. These things are also signified by
the

the Lord's words to Thomas, " Becaufe thou
" haft feen me, Thomas, thou haft believed;
" bleffed are they who fee not, and believe,"
John xx. 29; confequently they alfo are bleffed, who believe, not by miracles. But miracles are not hurtful to thofe, who are in
external worfhip without internal, for with
fuch there cannot be any oppofition between
the internal and external man, thus no col-
lifion, and confequently no prophanation.

" That miracles do not contribute any thing
towards faith, may appear fufficiently plain
from the miracles performed with the Ifraelitifh
people in Egypt, and in the defert, in that
they were utterly inefficacious of any fuch thing
as faith amongft them: that people, although
a fhort time before they faw fo many miracles
in Egypt, afterwards the red fea divided, and
the Egyptians immerfed therein, the pillar of a
cloud going before them by day, and a pillar
of fire by night, manna daily rained down from
heaven, and although they faw the mount Sinai
fmoking, and heard Jehovah fpeaking thence, with
other things, yet notwithftanding all this, and in
the very midft of fuch things, they fell away from
all faith, and from the worfhip of Jehovah to the

worfhip

worship of a calf, Exod. xxxii. 1 to the end. Hence it is evident, what effect miracles have. Still less would they be effectual at this day, when men do not acknowledge that there is any thing from the spiritual world, and when every spiritual effect is denied, and attributed to nature; for a negative principle universally prevails, in respect to the divine influx and government in the earths: wherefore in the present day, if the man of the church were to see the most essentially divine miracles, he would first refer them to nature, and there defile them, afterwards he would reject them as phantasms or mere illusions, and lastly he would hold in derision all who should attribute them to a divine power, and not to nature. That miracles effect nothing, appears also from the Lord's words in Luke, " If they hear not " Moses and the prophets, neither will they be " persuaded, though one rose from the dead," chap. xvi. 31."

To the above I will just add the following remark. Although the miracles recorded in the Word were, at the time of performance, of a *compulsive* nature, because presented before the *immediate view* of the spectator, yet now they

they are not so, because they do not manifestly operate upon the senses of the external man, and there remain, as before, but may gain admission to the internal man, and there be rationally understood.

ROBERT HINDMARSH.

LETTER II.

On the sole, supreme, and exclusive Divinity of Jesus Christ.

I NOW come to consider the grand, the fundamental, and most important subject in the whole system of christian theology, namely, *the sole, supreme, and exclusive divinity of our blessed Lord and Saviour Jesus Christ.* That it should be my lot to stand up in this public manner as an asserter and defender of this great truth, is an honour that I did not expect to be called to, particularly as I know there are others much better qualified for such an undertaking than myself. However, as I have been earnestly invited, by many sincere lovers of genuine truth, to the task of defending the sole divinity of our Saviour against the objections which you have raised in your *Letters to the Members of the New Church;* and as I believe there is no employment, in which the faculties of the human mind can be more worthily engaged, than in magnifying the adorable Creator of the universe, and in publishing his

name

name among men as their Father, Redeemer, and Saviour; it is my intention to shew, according to the best of my ability, by a fair appeal to the Word of God, and a consistent interpretation of the same, 1. That all the arguments you have urged against the divinity of Jesus Christ, are no other than false reasonings from the mere *appearances* of things in the literal sense of the Word; and consequently that your whole system is built on the fallacy of the senses. 2. I will then prove, by scripture and reason united, that the Lord-Man Jesus Christ is the one supreme and only God of heaven and earth, who in his Divine Human Person is, and may be called, JEHOVAH-MAN.

But as I cannot do this by my own strength, being utterly incapable, of myself, either to do a single action, or to think a single thought, it behoves me to apply for wisdom and ability to him who is the fountain of life, and the giver of every good and perfect gift. May He therefore, who is the grand subject of this letter, assist in it's production, and afterwards accompany it with his divine blessing.

Before I enter upon the subject, I shall beg leave to make a few preliminary remarks on your

mode

mode of addressing the members of the New Jerusalem; in which I propose to shew, that a Socinian has no right to the name of a christian. As I cannot do this more effectually, than by addressing myself to one who avowedly professes himself to be such, you will excuse me, if, in opposing the *errors* of Socinianism, I also appear to oppose the *Socinian himself*. My design is not to wage war with the *person* of any man, but only with those *sentiments* which I think contrary to truth, and dangerous to christian societies. But as sentiments or opinions, abstracted from the persons who maintain them, are considered by many as mere nothings; and as the man and his opinions are so closely united, as, generally speaking, to be taken indiscriminately the one for the other; I hope I may be allowed without offence to make my observations to you as a *person*, while at the same time I would have them considered as directed against your *tenets* only.

Your first letter to the members of the New Church begins with these words: " My *fellow-* " *christians*, it is with peculiar pleasure that I " address any class of persons by this appel- " lation; and I am happy to observe, that you " value christianity *as much as I do*."

Were

Were an indifferent person to read this, he would naturally suppose, that it is from the great veneration in which you hold the person of Jesus Christ, that you thus congratulate any set of people who make profession of his name. Such a reader would doubtless say to himself, 'Surely Dr. Priestley is a zealous advocate for 'the divinity of Christ; and finding that the 'world in general begins to think too lightly of 'his sacred person, he seizes the present op- 'portunity of declaring his own faith in the 'Lord, and confirming others in the same 'duty.' This reflection would naturally occur to the mind of a person unacquainted with your peculiar tenets, on reading your first address to the members of the New Church: but were he to read your *Letters* throughout, it appears to me, he would have good reason to complain that you held out false colours at the beginning, by calling yourself a *christian*, when in reality you have no just claim to the title.

Without intending the smallest offence, give me leave to ask you a few questions. In the first place, Why do you call yourself a christian? Is it because you acknowledge the *divinity* of Christ? You answer, No. Is it because you believe the *history* of Christ, as related by the evangelists?

evangelists? You reply, Yes. Then by the same rule you are a Jew, if you believe the history of the Jews; and a Mahometan, if you believe the history of Mahomet. Christianity, if I apprehend it aright, is a system of religion that acknowledges the *divinity* of Christ, or in other words, that *Christ is God*. In what sense, then, can a person be called a christian, who does *not* acknowledge him as such? Does the bare belief of his being a *prophet*, like Moses or any other man, entitle you to be called after his name, any more than after the names of other prophets? Why, let me ask, do you call yourself a christian, or a follower of Christ, if you believe Christ to be a *mere man?* I really think, Sir, you expose yourself in this particular more than you are aware of. You think it *idolatry* to worship Christ, and yet you consider it an *honour* to be called after his name!

If I dwell longer on this part of your address to the members of the New Church, than you expected, it is because I conceive it to be of great importance, that we know each other on the first setting out on this business; for as you have thought proper to send us a friendly message, it is expedient that an explanation of characters take place as soon as may be; otherwise

we

we shall be talking to one another in the dark. Now, I can with safety and confidence take upon me to declare, in the name of all the members of the New Church, or New Jerusalem, that they are *christians* in the proper sense of the word, and that for the following reason, viz. because they acknowledge no other God in heaven, or on earth, but the Lord *Jesus Christ*. Thus they derive their name from the God they worship, and from no other *inferior* being, be he man, or be he angel.

Having given you this candid and explicit character of the members of the New Church, with the simple, plain, and obvious reason of their laying claim to the denomination of *christians;* I hope I may be allowed to make a little further inquiry into your religious profession, and again repeat my former question, Why do you style yourself a christian? It is not because you acknowledge Christ to be the *only* and *supreme God;* for this you reject with horror, and consider as no less than blasphemy. It is not because you allow Christ to be a *sharer in divinity;* for this you also deny with all your might, and openly declare him to be no more than a *mere man*, like Moses or any other prophet. What then can be be the reason? Perhaps it is because you happened to be born in a country, where the inhabitants call themselves christians; and so the name being popular, you may think it prudent to retain it? Or perhaps it is (as before observed) because you believe the facts recorded in the New Testament, while the Jews give credit only to those in the Old? But I hear you say, ' No, it is not for any of these ' reasons alone; it is also because Christ deli- ' vered such plain maxims and precepts of *mo-* ' *rality* as no other prophet had done before ' him.' I answer, It is true, the Lord manifested his divine will more plainly than had been revealed by the prophets; but still the *principle* of all his words and actions may easily be traced through every book of the Old Testament, and is particularly to be seen in the ten commandments. Therefore the circumstance of Christ's teaching moral duties, alone, is no just reason why a person should be called after his name; seeing that previous to his appearance on earth the world was already in possession of more perfect maxims of morality, than the generality of mankind were disposed to put in practice.

From the above observations, you will readily perceive, Sir, that I do not acknowledge you as a *christian* in the proper sense of that word; and yet, from principles of civility, I am willing to allow you every thing that I can, consistently with truth. You profess yourse f to be a *Socinian*, that is, one who completely and to all intents and purposes denies the divinity of Jesus Christ, making him a mere man, like any of us. You even virtually accuse the *Arian* for exalting him to a rank in creation above the highest angel, as if he was not sufficiently degraded by being considered as the highest *creature,* without pulling him down below the rank of angels, and placing him on a level with yourself. So inveterate and personal appears to be your prejudice against Him, by whose sole goodness and power you was first created, and are still sustained in existence; in whom you now live, move, and have your being; and from whom you derive that very faculty of reasoning, which you exercise (I trust ignorantly) to his dishonour!

The christian world in general acknowledges a trinity of divine persons; among whom it ranks as second in dignity, though sometimes as equal, our blessed Lord. It is for this reason alone, viz. because they with their lips annex *something of divinity* to the person of Jesus Christ, that they are distinguished by the name of christians. But as their division of the Deity into distinct persons, amounts to little less than a plain denial of the essential properties of the Godhead, they cannot be called christians in the true sense of that word. If then they, who nominally ascribe divinity to the person of Christ, cannot with truth and propriety be ranked under the denomination of christians, how much less can you, who openly, avowedly, and barefacedly degrade him below the character of an angel, and challenge him as a *mere man!* I do not by any means wish to offend you, Sir; but from the observations already made, I think even you yourself must see the impropriety of addressing the members of the New Church as *your fellow christians*, seeing that they disagree with you *in all respects* concerning the person of Christ.

You believe that Christ is not possessed of any real divinity inherent in himself as his own, but only what may have been communicated to him by inspiration: We, on the contrary, believe, that Jesus Christ is God-Man, and Man-God, having essential divinity residing in him as his proper own, for which he is beholden to no other being either in heaven or earth. You believe

believe he was no more than a prophet, like Mofes and the reft, fent of God to teach mankind his will: We, on the contrary, believe he is more than a prophet, becaufe, agreeable to his own words in Matt. xxiii. 34, *it is he that fends prophets*. You believe in the fimple humanity of Chrift, or in other words, that he was a mere man, like yourfelf: We, on the contrary, believe in his Divine Humanity; in which he is the fupreme and only God of heaven and earth, confequently the Only Man, and that all other men are men only by derivation from him. You believe he was the Saviour of the world in no other fenfe than Mofes was of the Ifraelites, that is, *under* another who is God: We, on the contrary, believe, that Jefus was the Saviour of the world, by virtue of his own perfonal power, and that falvation or redemption was effected by no other power or authority in heaven or earth, but his own divine arm. You confider him to be now the Son of Mary, if not of Jofeph: but we confider fuch an idea as impious and blafphemous. You believe that divine honours ought not to be paid to him: We, on the contrary, account all worfhip directed to any other than to Jefus Chrift, to be downright idolatry. In fhort, though you do not with your lips

exprefsly

expressly deny that he is Lord * and Master, you actually embrace every opportunity to degrade and dishonour him: while the members of the New and True Christian Church unite every faculty of their souls to exalt his name alone, to celebrate his praise alone, and to hail him alone as the one God over all, blessed for ever.

Such being the contrast between the christianity professed by Socinians, and that of the New Jerusalem, I leave you and all the world to judge with what propriety or truth you style us *your fellow-christians!*

Having thus animadverted on your way of addressing us, I now proceed to consider the arguments

---

* It is remarkable, that Dr. Priestley no where in his *Letters* calls Jesus *Lord*. Whenever that expression is mentioned by him, it is always by way of quotation either from the scriptures, or from Baron Swedenborg's writings, and never proceeds from him as an effect of his own sentiments. This circumstance brings to my recollection the words of Paul in 1 Cor. xii. 3: "No man can say that "Jesus is the Lord, but by the Holy Ghost." The Holy Ghost is the divine proceeding from Jesus; the sin against the Holy Ghost is the denial of his divinity; Arians and Socinians are guilty of this; therefore I judge that no Arian or Socinian can call Jesus *Lord*, without feeling a certain internal repugnance to the expression.

arguments you have brought againſt the divinity of Jeſus Chriſt, and to ſhew that they are all fallacious, being grounded in the mere *appearances* of truth in the literal ſenſe of the Word.

Page 18, you ſay, " I own that when I firſt " heard of this tenet of your's, that Jeſus Chriſt " was the ſame perſon with God the Father, " and that there is no other God than he, I " was exceedingly ſurprized." That you was exceedingly ſurprized on hearing it aſſerted, that Jeſus Chriſt is the ſame perſon with God the Father, and that there is no other God than he, I make no doubt; and I ſhould not have wondered much, had you gone backward and fallen to the ground, as the band of armed men did, when Jeſus declared the ſame thing by ſaying, *I Am*, John xviii. 6. But what will you ſay or do, when you find this grand truth proved and demonſtrated beyond the ſhadow of contradiction, as I hope, by the divine mercy of the Lord, I ſhall be enabled to do in the following pages!

" It is certainly no uncommon thing," (you ſay, p. 19,) " for the ſame thing, or the " ſame perſon, to be ſignified by two different " names, Jeſus, for example, and Chriſt, Simon " and

"and Peter; but then we always find, that the
"same character and description will apply to
"both, and except the literal significations of
"the term be referred to, we may, in any sen-
"tence, substitute the one in the place of the
"other; every thing that can be asserted of the
"one, being equally true of the other. Nothing
"is ever asserted concerning either of them,
"that is incompatible with the other; *nor will
"any speaker or writer,* knowing the use of lan-
"guage, *ever connect two names* which denote
"only the *same person* by the conjunctive par-
"ticle *and*. We say, for example, that Peter
"and John did this or that; but we never say,
"that Simon and Peter, Jesus and Christ, did
"this, using the plural number; because Peter
"and John are different persons. But Simon
"and Peter, Jesus and Christ, are the same
"persons; and therefore we naturally say Simon
"or Peter, Jesus or Christ, or else, joining the
"names, we say, Simon Peter, or Jesus Christ,
"did this or that, using the singular number
"only. Now look through the whole New
"Testament, where God and Christ are spoken
"of, and you will find by these plain rules
"concerning the use of words, which every
"body understands, and in speaking or writing
"strictly conforms to, that *God* and *Christ*, in

"the

" the ideas of the perfons who wrote thofe
" books, were as different perfons as Chrift
" and Peter, James and John."

The above argument, however plaufible it may appear to fome at firft fight, with refpect to the ftrictnefs of grammatical diction, is neverthelefs not a true one, becaufe it is founded on falfe premifes. To fay that " no fpeaker or writer, knowing the ufe of language, ever connects two names which denote only the fame perfon by the conjunctive particle *and*," is an affertion that militates againft, and is confuted by perhaps a thoufand paffages in the holy fcriptures, as well as in the apoftolic writings. I fhall produce only a few, which will be fufficient to fhew your inattention to the *language of infpiration*, and how vain a thing it is to build a fyftem of theology upon fuch a fandy foundation as the mere rules of grammar.

1. Abraham faid to his fervant, " I will " make thee fwear by the God of heaven *and* " the God of the earth," Gen. xxiv. 3. Here the God of heaven and the God of the earth are certainly the *fame perfon ;* and yet they are connected together by the conjunctive particle
and.

and. See also Gen. xxxi. 53. Chap. xxxii. 9. Exod. iv. 5.

2. It is said in the Apocalypse, that Jesus Christ " hath made us kings and priests unto " God *and* his Father," chap. i. 6. God and the Father are undoubtedly one and the same person; but if we are to form our doctrine from *conjunctive particles*, we must make two distinct persons of them.

3. John the Apocalyptist says to the seven churches in Asia, " Grace be unto you, and " peace, from him which is, and which was, " and which is to come; *and* from Jesus " Christ," Apoc. i. 4, 5. Now in verse 8 of the same chapter, the Lord Jesus saith, " I am Alpha *and* Omega, which is, and " which was, and which is to come, the Al- " mighty." Whence it follows, that he which is, and which was, and which is to come, and Jesus Christ, are one and the same person, notwithstanding the interposition of the conjunctive particle *and*.

4. So again, " The kingdoms of this world " are become the kingdoms of our Lord, *and* " of his Christ, and *he* shall reign for ever and
" ever,"

"ever," Apoc. xi. 15. Here, although it is said, *the Lord* AND *his Chrift*, as if they were two diftinct perfons, yet the paffage cannot be fo underftood, as is evident from the words immediately following, wherein both Lord and Chrift are united in one perfon, viz. *and* HE *fhall reign for ever and ever*. Befides, the term *Lord* is conftantly applied to Jefus Chrift in the New Teftament as his peculiar and diftinguifhing title, of which he was alfo pleafed to exprefs his approbation in thefe words: "Ye call me Mafter, and *Lord*; and ye fay "well, for fo I am," John xiii. 13.

5. "And they remembered, that God was "their Rock, *and* the high God their Redeemer," Pfalm lxxviii. 35. Here again God the Rock and the high God the Redeemer are one and the fame perfon.

6. The apoftle James, in his general epiftle, fays, "Pure religion, and undefiled before God "*and* the Father is this," &c. James i. 27. Paul faith, that "Jefus Chrift gave himfelf for "our fins, according to the will of God *and* "our Father," Gal. i. 4. "Giving thanks al- "ways for all things unto God *and* the Father," Ephef. v. 20. "Now unto God *and* our Father "be

" be glory for ever and ever, Amen," Philip. iv. 20. " We give thanks to God, *and* the " Father of our Lord Jesus Christ," Col. i. 3. " That their hearts might be comforted, being " knit together in love, and unto all riches of " the full assurance of understanding to the " acknowledgment of the mystery of God, " *and* of the Father, *and* of Christ," Col. ii. 2. " Whatsoever ye do in word or deed, do all in " the name of the Lord Jesus, giving thanks " to God *and* the Father by him," Col. iii. 17. " Remembering without ceasing your work of " faith, and labour of love, and patience of " hope in our Lord Jesus Christ, in the sight of " God, *and* our Father," 1 Thess. i. 3. " Now " God himself, *and* our Father, *and* our Lord " Jesus Christ direct * our way unto you,"
1 Thess.

---

* It is remarkable that the Greek word κατευθύναι, *may he direct*, is the 3 person singular of the 1 aor. opt. and not the 3 person plural. If God and Jesus Christ were two distinct persons, it would be more grammatical to use a plural verb: but as they are only one person, therefore it is with great propriety said in the singular number, " Now " God himself, and our Father, and our Lord Jesus Christ " (κατευθύναι) *direct* our way unto you." Something similar to this is found in the first chapter of Genesis, verse 1, " In the beginning God created the heavens and the earth." In the Hebrew the noun אלהים *Elohim*, is plural, *Dii, the*
Gods,

1 Theff. iii. 11.—In all these passages, and many others of a similar kind which might be adduced, God and the Father are spoken of *apparently* as distinct beings or persons; and in some of them Jesus Christ is no more distinguished from the Father, than the Father is from himself; for the conjunctive particle *and*, on which you lay so much stress, is equally interposed between all the three names. Thus the mystery of the incarnation is said to be the mystery of God, *and* of the Father, *and* of Christ. And Paul prays to be directed by God, *and* by the Father, *and* by the Lord Jesus Christ.

7. Again, " The great dragon was cast out, " that old serpent, called the devil *and* satan," Apoc. xii. 9. chap. xx. 2. Here the terms *devil* and *satan* are applied to one and the same dragon: and it is called the devil *and* satan, not the

---

Gods, and the verb ברא, *bara*, is singular, *creavit*, *he created:* literally in English, *The Gods* [he] *created the heavens and the earth.* The reason of this peculiarity in the Hebrew language, is to shew, that the regeneration of man as to his internal and external, (which is meant by the creation of heavens and the earth,) although conducted through the mediation of *angels and spirits*, (called Gods,) is yet after all effected by the *Lord alone.*

the devil *or* satan, as you seem to think it should be, in order to be conformable to the rules of grammar, which is a science, not of things, but of mere words.

Perhaps you will say, that the Greek word *και* ought, in the foregoing passages, to have been translated *even*, instead of *and;* in which case the phrase *God* AND *the Father* will read, *God* EVEN *the Father;* and the *devil* AND *satan* will be *the devil* EVEN *satan*. But this is granting more than I ask, and in fact giving up the point; for then instead of being, *God,* AND *the Father,* AND *Jesus Christ,* it would uniformly be, *God,* EVEN *the Father,* EVEN *Jesus Christ,* agreeable to the translation of 2 Cor. i. 3; and 1 Thess. iii. 13. So that, take the words which way you please, you are reduced to a perfect dilemma. If you make choice of the affirmative conjunction *even,* instead of *and,* you then acknowledge the supreme divinity of Jesus Christ, and that he is the high God, *even* the Father; but if, as I expect, you would rather retain the conjunctive particle *and,* you must at least be conscious, that your observations concerning the use of that word in the scriptures are not well founded.

S. In

8. In the following passage the preposition *from* is used: "Then Jehovah * rained upon Sodom, and upon Gomorrah, brimstone and fire *from* Jehovah out of heaven," Gen. xix. 24. Here it appears as if there were two Jehovahs, the one raining brimstone and fire from the other; which must necessarily embarrass the person, who confines his ideas to the mere literal expressions. Such a one, in a thousand instances, must either give up his understanding to be the tool of a blind faith, or else he must in his own mind conclude that the inspired writers *did not know the use of language*, or, what is worse than all, he must absolutely deny the sanctity and divinity of the Word.

The next thing I have to animadvert upon, is your assertion, that "through the whole New Testament, where God and Christ are spoken of, they are, in the ideas of the persons who wrote those books, as different persons as Christ and Peter, James and John." There is nothing like bringing you to the test. Let us see what the language of the New Testament is

---

* The English translation has the word *Lord*, instead of *Jehovah*, in this and other passages of the Old Testament. But I think it best to retain the word *Jehovah*, as in the original Hebrew.

is in this matter. If I have any understanding at all, the great God and our Lord Jesus Christ must, in the following passages, be *one and the same person*, according to the idea of the writers.

1. In the Apocalypse it is said, "We give " thee thanks, O *Lord God almighty, which art,* " *and was, and art to come,* because *thou hast* " *taken to thee* thy great power, and *hast reigned,*" chap. xi. 17. " I heard a loud voice saying in " heaven, Now is come salvation, and strength, "and the *kingdom of our God,*" chap. xii. 10. " Great and marvellous are thy works, Lord " *God almighty;* just and true are thy ways, " thou *King of saints,*" chap. xv. 3. " Allelujah, " for the *Lord God omnipotent reigneth,*" chap. xix. 6. In these passages salvation, and power, and the kingdom, are ascribed to the *Lord God omnipotent.* But in the following the *very same things* are ascribed to *Jesus Christ,* who is also called the *Lamb.* Jesus says, " I am Alpha and " Omega, *which is,* and *which was,* and *which* " *is to come, the Almighty,*" Apoc. i. 8. " The " kingdoms of this world are become the king- " doms of our Lord, and of his *Christ,* and *he* "*shall reign for ever and ever,*" chap. xi. 15. " The Lamb shall overcome them; for he is
" Lord

"*Lord of lords*, and *King of kings.*" chap. xvii. 14. "Salvation to our God which sitteth upon the throne, and *unto the Lamb*," chap. vii. 10. "The Lamb which is *in the midst of the throne*, shall feed them," verse 17.

Now let any unprejudiced person compare the above passages together, and he cannot but acknowledge, that in the idea of the writer God and the Lamb, or God and Jesus Christ, are *one and the same person*. It is said of God, that he *is, was, and is to come*: the same is said of Jesus Christ. God is called *almighty*: so is Jesus Christ. God is said to have taken his great power, and to *reign*, as *King of saints*: of Christ it is said, that the *kingdoms are his*, and *he shall reign for ever and ever;* and of the Lamb, that *he is in the midst of the throne, Lord of lords, and King of kings*. Under all these circumstances, is it possible that God and Christ can be two different persons? Can we for a moment suppose, that all the hosts of heaven should agree in dividing their worship between two Kings, two Lords, two Almighties, two First Causes, two Alphas and Omegas?—The very idea shocks me beyond description, and prevents my pursuing it any further.

2. The

2. "The *Lord God* of the holy prophets sent "*his angel* to shew unto his servants the things "which must shortly be done," Apoc. xxii. 6. In verse 16 of the same chapter it is said, "*I* "*Jesus* have sent *mine angel* to testify unto you "these things in the churches." As these two passages occur so near to each other, in one chapter, I cannot think with you, that in the idea of the writer "God and Christ are as dif- "ferent persons as James and John;" but have a clear perception given me to see, that the Lord God of the holy prophets and Jesus are one and the same divine person.

3. "And I saw no temple in the New Jeru- "salem, for the Lord God almighty and the "Lamb are the temple of it," Apoc. xxi. 22. A temple is *one single* building: how then can the Lord God almighty and the Lamb constitute that *one single* building, if they are divided into two different and distinct persons? But if we consider them as united in one person, then we shall plainly see, that the body of Jesus is that glorious temple. See John ii. 21.

4. In the New Jerusalem "there shall be no "night, and they need no candle, neither light "of the sun; for the *Lord God* giveth them "light," Apoc. xxii. 5. In the preceding chapter

ter it is said, "The *Lamb* is the light thereof," Apoc. xxi. 23. Whence I conclude, that the Lord God and the Lamb are the same person, and in the idea of the writer must have been considered as such.

5. " Blessed are they which are called to the " *marriage-supper of the Lamb,*" Apoc. xix. 9. In the 17th verse of the same chapter it is said, " Come and gather yourselves together unto " the *supper of the great God.*" The marriage-supper of the Lamb, and the supper of the great God, are the same thing; therefore the Lamb and the great God are one and the same person.

6. " We know that the Son of God is come, " and hath given us an understanding that we " may know him that is true; and we are in " him that is true, even in his Son Jesus Christ: " *This* is the *true God,* and eternal life," 1 John v. 20. Here it is evident, that John made no distinction between Jesus Christ and God; for he expressly says, that he is the true God and eternal life. And to caution us against worshipping any other than Jesus Christ, he immediately adds, " Little children, keep your- " selves from *idols,*" verse 21.

O 2 7. Jesus

7. Jesus says, "Whatsoever ye shall ask in my name, that will *I do*, that the Father may be glorified in the Son. If ye shall ask any thing in my name, *I will do it*," John xiv. 13, 14. In chapter xvi. 23, he says, "Whatsoever ye shall ask the Father in my name, *he* will give it you." If there be any consistency in the views or ideas of the speaker and writer, these passages, compared together, evidently prove that Jesus himself was the Father.

8. Lastly, Jesus said, " I and my Father are *one*," John x. 30. " Philip saith unto him, Lord, shew us the Father, and it sufficeth us. Jesus saith unto him, Have I been so long time with you, and yet hast thou not known *me*, Philip? He that hath seen *me*, hath seen the *Father*," John xiv. 8, 9. There needs no further proof in this matter; for Jesus himself expressly declares, that he and the Father are one and the same person. Philip, it seems, entertained an idea, as many others have done since him, that God the Father was a distinct person from Jesus; and observing that the Lord generally spake in parables, sometimes in pretty plain terms, and at other times obscurely, he was determined to put a direct question to him about the Father. He did so, and our

Lord's

Lord's answer was as explicit as it could be: "He that hath seen *me*, hath seen the *Father*." Still, however, the Lord saw, that the church at that time was incapable of receiving a full and clear revelation of this greatest and most sublime of all truths; therefore he continued to speak in parables and proverbs, reserving till a future day the glorious manifestation of himself, as being the *everlasting Father*, as well as the *Son* that was born *in time*. " These " things," says he, " have I spoken unto you " in proverbs: the time cometh when I shall " no more speak unto you in proverbs, but " *I shall shew you plainly of the Father*," John xvi. 25. The great day alluded to, in which he no longer speaks in proverbs, is the present; we now know for a certainty, who is the Father, having seen him more clearly and satisfactorily than ever Philip did; and for the first time the present day beholds the accomplishment of Isaiah's prophecy concerning the person of Jesus, " Unto us a *Child* is born, unto " us a *Son* is given, and the *government* shall be " upon *his shoulder*; and his name shall be " called Wonderful, Counsellor, *God*, Hero, " *Father of eternity*, Prince of peace," Isaiah ix. 6.

* * *

In

In page 20 you say, " Christ uniformly speaks
" of himself as having been sent from God,
" just as much as John the Baptist was; so that
" if the person *sending* can be the same with the
" person *sent*, John the Baptist may be God as
" well as Jesus Christ. I may say that I go
" from one place to another, but it is mani-
" festly improper to say that I *send* myself from
" one place to another. On your principles,
" Christ and his apostles might be the same
" persons. For Christ, addressing himself to
" his Father, says, John xvii. 18, *As thou hast*
" *sent me into the world, even so have I also sent*
" *them into the world*. It is evident, therefore,
" that Christ was a person as different from
" him whom he addressed as his *Father*, as his
" disciples were different from himself."

The whole of this objection arises from the want of knowing the difference between natural and spiritual language, and that spiritual ideas, in their descent from heaven, clothe themselves with such expressions as are accommodated to the state of men in the natural world. The garments of a man are not the real man; so neither is the literal sense of the Word, in many cases, real naked truth, but truth clothed with appearances, which may indeed prove a
stumbling-

stumbling-block to some, while to others they administer the delights of use. That Jesus Christ, although said to be *sent* by God the Father, was yet that very Father, may plainly appear from due attention to, and a right understanding of, the holy scriptures.

In all places where the Lord is said to be sent by the Father, we are to understand that God himself descended into the world as divine truth; which descent was effected by the assumption of the Humanity from the Virgin Mary. For the sake of distinction, the scriptures call divine good the Father, and divine truth the Son; because divine truth proceeds from divine good, comparatively as a son proceeds from a father. Hence it is said, that the *Son* of God descended, or was sent by the Father, meaning that God assumed the Humanity more particularly in respect to *divine truth*, than to divine good, although the latter was not separated from the former. By the word *sent* is also signified the same thing as *angel;* for the word *angel* in the original language signifies *sent;* as in Isaiah, "The *angel* of his presence saved them," chap. lxiii. 9; that is, divine truth *proceeding from* Jehovah saved them. The power of salvation is not
predicable

predicable of any one but a Divine Being, nor of any thing but a divine attribute.

Jesus said to his disciples, " It is expedient " for you that I go away; for if I go not away, " the Comforter will not come unto you; but " if I depart, *I will send him unto you,*" John xvi. 7. Here Jesus promises to *send* the Comforter, which is the Holy Spirit. Afterwards, " Jesus *breathed* on his disciples, and saith unto " them, Receive ye the Holy Spirit," John xx. 22. From which it is plain, that by the Holy Spirit is meant something proceeding from Jesus; and that *sending* signifies the same as *breathing* or *proceeding*. Again, the Lord having told his disciples, that he would *send* them *another Comforter*, which should abide with them for ever, immediately adds, " I will not leave you " comfortless, *I will come to you,*" John xiv. 18. He likewise says, " And lo, *I am with you* " *alway* even unto the end of the world," Matt. xxviii. 20. No terms can be more express than these; which therefore clearly and undeniably prove, that the person *sending* and the person *sent* are, in this instance at least, one and the same Being.

But

But you say, that, according to this way of speaking, John the Baptist may be God, as well as Jesus Christ, because it is equally said of him, that he was sent by God: also that Christ and his apostles may be the same persons, because they were sent by him: and it is very natural for you to ask, 'How shall we 'know whether they are, or not?' I will tell you: the method is easy and simple. Look through the gospels, look through the epistles, look through the Apocalypse, or any part of scripture, and see whether John the Baptist, or any of the apostles, is any where called Jehovah, Alpha and Omega, the First and the Last, the Beginning and the Ending, who is, who was, and who is to come, the Almighty, the I Am, the Mighty God, the Everlasting Father, the King of kings, and Lord of lords. If you can find none of these appellations given to any of them, you may rest assured they are neither God nor Christ, but that in dignity of person they all fall infinitely short of Him who alone is God-Man. John the Baptist says, " *I am not the Christ:* he must increase, but I " must decrease: he that cometh from above, " is above all," John iii. 28, 30, 31. He that is *above all*, must be *God alone*. " Behold the " Lamb of God that *taketh away the sin* of the " world,"

"world," John i. 29. Who can *take away sins*, but God? "The Son of Man hath power on "earth to *forgive sins*," Matt. ix. 6. "None "can *forgive* sins, but *God* alone," Luke v. 21. Therefore Jesus Christ alone is God.

There is no impropriety, you observe, in saying, "that I *go* from one place to another;" but a manifest one, you think, to say, "that I "*send* myself from one place to another." Strange as this may appear to you, and difficult of comprehension, it is nevertheless true, and what you yourself have actually done. By sending me your *Letters to the Members of the New Jerusalem*, you have in fact *sent yourself*, and I have you this moment before me. I do not so much consider your material *body* to be Dr. Priestley, as your *soul* which is within that body; and I know the soul or mind to consist of will and understanding, or affection and thought, and nothing else. Now I find your book contains your will and understanding, or your affection and thought, just as your person contains them; insomuch that it may with propriety be called *another self*, existing *without yourself*, or Dr. Priestley *proceeding from* Dr. Priestley. Thus whenever Dr. Priestley, or any other person, publishes a book of his own writing, he thereby actually *sends himself*

himself into the world; for the works of every man both contain and exhibit the real man, his *will* being therein by virtue of the design, motive, or end in view, and his *understanding* by virtue of the wisdom or thought whereby he expresses himself, as means to promote that end. There is this difference, however, between Dr. Priestley as a *man* or *person*, and Dr. Priestley as a *book* or *work*. As a *man*, he may change his state, and, rejecting his present errors, receive new life and new wisdom from the Lord. But as a *book*, or *work*, he cannot; that remains fixed and permanent, as an eternal monument of his present and past state of mind, to the production of which all the interior principles of his life conspired.

To render the subject now under discussion a little more familiar and plain, I will just relate a fact, which very lately happened; and you know facts are often more powerful than arguments. A gentleman came into my house, and seeing a *book* in my hand, said without any apparent reflection, " *Whom* have you got " there?" " Is *that* Dr. Priestley? or *who* else " is it?" I told him, *it was Dr. Priestley*, and that I was *hearing* what he had to *say* against *Baron Swedenborg*. " Well," added he, " and
" what

"what *does he say?*" When the gentleman left me, I began to reflect on his mode of accosting me, and soon found, that it is the *common language of every person*, to speak precisely in the same manner. Personification is congenial to the human mind; the ancients were fond of it, and the moderns are still in the habit of it, without being always conscious of the circumstance. "*Whom*," i. e. *what person*, (not *what book*,) "have you got there?—O, I see you "have Dr. Priestley in your hand," (not the *writings* or *book* of Dr. Priestley.) "What *does he say* against *Baron Swedenborg?*" (Not what *has he written* against the *writings* of Baron Swedenborg?) Such is the most familiar and common mode of speech. The reason of this personification is, because there is an influx general from the spiritual world into the minds of men, leading and directing them to reduce every thing to it's *first principles*, and thus in their very language to return effects back again to their causes, from whence they proceeded; so that in every effect they may contemplate the cause, and in every cause the end, which is man. This general influx is derived from one universal, which inculcates the unity of God, and teaches that, as all things came forth from him, so with respect to uses they must all

return

return back to him; "for all things were created by him and for him," Col. i. 16.

The common consent of mankind, in speaking of the *works* of any person, exactly as if they were the *person himself*, and this without any previous agreement among themselves to do so, is therefore to me a plain and clear demonstration, that such language is agreeable to the order impressed on creation, and that it is an effect produced in the natural world from causes originating in the spiritual world, where all ideas spontaneously fall into *corresponding* natural expressions.

It is for this reason, that the sacred scriptures, being written according to the laws of the spiritual world, do frequently speak of what proceeds from the Divine Being as though it were the Divine Being himself. Thus to the Holy Spirit, which is the divine proceeding of the Lord, John xx. 22, the same attributes and powers are ascribed, as to the Lord himself. Lying to the *Holy Ghost* is called lying unto *God*, Acts v. 3, 4. He that is born of the *Spirit*, John iii. 5, 8, is said to be born of *God*, John i. 13. Not to mention many other passages to the same effect. Again, the historical part

part of the Word is called Moses, Luke xvi. 31. chap. xxiv. 27. In like manner the Word of God itself, which proceeded from God, is also called God, John i. 1. It is further described as a Man, with eyes like a flame of fire, and having on his head many crowns, whose name is King of kings, and Lord of lords, Apoc. xix. 12 to 16.

As you seem to think there is such a great impropriety in saying, God *sent himself* into the world, though none in supposing that he *sent another person*, a prophet, for instance; I will reason a little with you on your own ground. To *send* a messenger on any errand, literally implies, that the person *sending* is at some distance from the persons to whom the message is *sent*. God is the *sender*, and men the persons to whom *sent*. Now you certainly acknowledge the *omnipresence* of God, that he is equally present here and every where. With what propriety then, let me ask, can it be said on your principles, that God *sends* a messenger to those, with whom he is to the full as present as with any messenger whom he can possibly send? He is already present with them, before the messenger arrives; nay, at every moment he sends him. To *send* further implies, in the

mere

mere literal sense of the word, that the messenger sent *quits* the presence of him who sends, and during his journey is in an intermediate state between the *sender* and the persons to whom he is *sent*. But this is absolutely impossible in respect to him who is *omnipresent*, for if God, as you say, p. 50, fills infinite space, being also in the *form of infinite space*, then the *sending* of any messenger to mankind can be nothing more than sending him from *one part of himself* to *another part of himself*; or, what is the same thing in your idea, from *one part of infinite space* to *another part of the same infinite space*. The doctrine, therefore, which you maintain from the mere literal and grammatical sense of scripture, is on the very face of it the most absurd, unphilosophical, and impossible, than can be supposed. For take it which way you will, look at it in every direction which your *hypothesis of mere words, and space, and matter*, will permit, and after all you must confess it amounts to nothing. If your ideas are derived from *words*, they will end in *words*; if from *space*, they will be dissipated like *space*; and if from *matter*, they will terminate in the *grave*.

All

All these things put together, and well considered, work, at least in my mind, a full and clear conviction, that God the *sender*, and Jesus Christ the *sent*, are always in the idea, and in many cases in the express language of scripture, one and the same Divine Being. But, for your satisfaction, if you still doubt it, I will bring further proof in what follows.

* * *

Because Jesus, previous to his glorification, or union with the Father, prayed to him *in all appearance* as to a person distinct from himself; therefore you conclude, that he could not *in reality* be that Father. " Christ," you say, p. 21, " constantly prayed to the person whom he " called his Father, and he directed his dis- " ciples to pray to the same person. *Father*, " says he, John xvii. 1, *glorify thy Son, that thy* " *Son also may glorify thee.* Was Jesus then only " speaking to himself? Sometimes, no doubt, " persons do so; but not in this manner." You acknowledge, then, that a person may and does speak to himself: but you say *not in that manner*. It is a pity but you had told us in *what manner* a man may speak to himself. David addresses his soul in the following manner. " Bless Jehovah, *O my soul;* and all that " is *within me*, bless his holy name. Bless
" Jehovah,

"Jehovah, *O my soul*, and forget not all his
"benefits; who forgiveth all *thine* iniquities;
"who healeth all *thy* diseases; who redeemeth
"*thy* life from destruction; who crowneth *thee*
"with loving-kindness and tender mercies;
"who satisfieth *thy* mouth with good things,
"so that *thy* youth is renewed like the eagles."
Psalm ciii. 1 to 5. "Why art *thou* cast down,
"*O my soul*? And why art *thou* disquieted
"*within me*? Psalm xlii. 5, 11. xliii. 5. David
here evidently speaks to his soul, and to all
that is within him. Will you therefore infer,
that David and his soul must necessarily be two
different persons? As well may you do this, as
conclude, that Jesus and the Father within him
were two, merely because he prayed to him
as if he were different from him.

As this seems to be one of your greatest objections to Christ being God, viz. his praying to him as to a different person, it may be proper to explain the reason of it; for until we understand something of that wonderful circumstance, we may reason to eternity, and never be a whit the wiser. And perhaps I cannot do it better, than by comparing it to the regeneration of an individual man. Every man, you know, consists of an internal and an external. The internal we will here call enlightened reason, and the external man's vicious propensities or inclinations. This comparison is also just, for the internal of the mind is the seat of rationality, and the external of the mind is the seat of vice or evil. Now this view of a single individual man at once presents the idea of an *apparent duality*, although we know for a certainty that both the internal and external constitute only *one man*.

Whenever a person is instigated by his lusts to commit a crime, the inclination commences in the external man, and would immediately rush into action, were it not for the check received from reason in the internal, which dictates to him, that the evil ought not to be done. If the man is disposed to be virtuous, he will constantly *have recourse* to this reason; and particularly in times of danger from his passions, he will *appeal* to reason, and as it were *cry out* with earnestness for all the powers which his rational faculty can afford him in the subjection of his evil propensities. Now what is all this, but the external of a man *praying* to the internal of the same man? And when by divine assistance he has successively resisted and overcome those evil inclinations,

he

he at length comes into the habit and practice of virtue, so that it may with truth be said, his internal and external are united, or in other words, the man is regenerated.

The above is a faint and very imperfect image of the Lord's glorification, or union with the Father. His internal was Jehovah, purity itself, life itself; his external was a Humanity or body derived from the Mother Mary, and consequently infirm, subject to temptations, hunger, thirst, death. By virtue of inclinations hereditarily received from the Mother, he was tempted to evils of various kinds, being in this respect like another man. But by virtue of the Divinity within him, in which he differed from every other man, he constantly resisted, opposed, overcame, and finally exterminated from his Humanity every thing derived from Mary. During this process, it was necessary for his external man, when assaulted by temptations, to pray to his internal man for that aid and assistance which no other power or principle could afford. It was in respect to his external man, previous to it's full union with his internal man, that he says, that *of himself he could do nothing*, and that *the Father is greater than he*: for his internal

internal being always perfectly divine, could not but be greater, while the external remained unglorified. But when the internal flowed fully into the external, which it could do when all hereditary evil or the maternal infirmities were exterminated therefrom, then the external was also made fully divine, or glorified, that is, perfectly united with the internal, so that the Lord is in all respects equal to the Father, being absolutely one and the same as the Father. This is what we are to understand by *all power being given unto him in heaven and in earth*, Matt. xxviii. 18.

But there is another reason why the Lord prayed to the Father as to a person different from himself; and that is, because he came into the world not only to effect our redemption by subduing the powers of hell which prevailed at that time, but also to teach us for ever after how *we* ought to pray. The whole process of man's regeneration is only a faint image of the Lord's glorification. If he had not been glorified, we could not be regenerated; if he had not prayed to the Father, we should not have known how to pray; for in all things he is our head and pattern. It may indeed appear, as if two distinct principles of intelligence

ligence were necessarily implied in all the prayers which the Lord uttered, the one principle being that which dictated the prayer, and the other that to which the prayer was directed. But this is a *mere appearance,* and not *really so,* as will be proved in another place, when I come to speak more particularly of the one and only divine source of all intelligence. So again it *appears* in all our prayers, as if there were a principle of intelligence *belonging to us* as our *proper own,* absolutely *distinct* and *underived* from that of the one intellectual Being to whom we pray. But this also is a *mere appearance,* and a fallacy arising from our *interior senses.** A man can *of himself* no more pray to the Lord, than he can hold the sun in his hand. It is the Lord alone in us that *prays to himself;* although it is done
apparently

---

* It is generally supposed, that man is endued with only the five bodily senses of *seeing, hearing, smelling, tasting, touching.* But he is also in the enjoyment of an equal number of spiritual senses, perfectly distinct from the former, though united together by correspondence. The sense of *seeing* corresponds to the affection of *understanding* and *becoming wise;* the sense of *hearing,* to the affection of *learning,* and also *obedience;* the sense of *smelling,* to the affection of *perceiving*; the sense of *tasting,* to the affection of *knowing,* or of *science*; and the sense of *touching,* in general to the affection of *what is good.*

apparently from the man; and no other prayer can have the least possible degree of efficacy or virtue in it. It is the same with *praise, thanksgiving,* and every other part of *divine worship,* which are only so far real acts of worship, and acceptable to the Lord, as the Lord himself is in them. So true are the Lord's words, "No man can *come* unto me, except it were "*given unto him of my Father,*" John vi. 65. "As the branch cannot bear fruit *of itself,* "except it abide in the vine; no more can ye, "except ye abide in me. For *without me* ye "can *do nothing.* If ye abide in me, and *my* "*words* abide in you, ye shall *ask* what ye will, "and it shall be done unto you," John xv. 4, 5, 7. Thus the Lord alone is the *Last,* as well as the *First,* the *Omega* as well as the *Alpha,* the All and in all. All comes *from* him; all is directed *to* him; and from *first to last* it is the Lord alone who operates in us and by us, from, to, and for himself. See Col. i. 16.

As I am now on the subject of prayer, I will here introduce a remark concerning our Lord's words in John xvi. 23, "Whatsoever ye "shall ask the Father in my name, he will "give it you." The construction generally put upon this passage is, that we ought to pray to

the

the Father *for the sake of the Son*, thus to the Father out of, and separate from the Son. Hence the prayers of almost all christian congregations are addressed to the Father alone, and conclude with words to this effect, *through Jesus Christ*, or *for the sake of Jesus Christ, his sufferings, death, and merits*, &c. &c. But that this is not praying *in his name*, nor according to *his directions*, is very plain from the *form of supplication*, usually called the *Lord's prayer*, which he dictated to his disciples, when they asked him to teach them how to pray. " After " this manner," says he, " pray ye, *Father of us* * " in the heavens," &c. This, compared with the above-mentioned passage in John, clearly points out, that the name of Jesus is *Father*; which is further confirmed by the prophet Isaiah, " Unto us a child is born, unto us a " Son is given, and his *name* shall be called the " *Everlasting Father*," chap. ix. 6. To pray therefore in his name, means to call upon him in the true spirit of prayer as our heavenly *Father*, who can alone supply all our necessities, alone redeem, regenerate, and save. And this
we

---

* My reason for beginning the Lord's prayer thus, *Father of us*, and not *Our Father*, may be seen in the *Magazine of Knowledge*, &c. vol. ii. p. 413.

we are to do, not for the fake of any perfon or thing *diſtinct from him*, but as the pfalmiſt David expreſſes it, *for his mercy's fake*, Pfalm vi. 4; or *for his name's fake*, Pfalm xxv. 11; or as the prophet fays, *for his own fake*, Ifa. xliii. 25. Jefus faid to his difciples, "Hitherto " have ye afked nothing in my name: afk, " and ye fhall receive. The time cometh, " when I fhall fhew you plainly of the Father. " At *that day* ye fhall afk *in my name:* and I " fay not unto you, that I will pray the Father " for you; *for the Father himſelf loveth you,* " *becauſe ye have loved me.*" John xvi. 24 to 27. From all which it is evident, that Jefus himſelf is the Father; and that when the time ſhould come for him to be plainly known as fuch, the members of his true chriſtian church would no longer confider him as a *Mediator* or *Interceſſor* diſtinct from the Father, but pray to him as the *Father himſelf* who loveth them.

I am aware that many of thefe fentiments will appear novel, becauſe hitherto the learned as well as the fimple-minded have been uſed to confider things in a very different point of view; not knowing the true nature either of the Divine Being, or of the exiſtence of man as a rational and free agent by continual derivation

tion from him, nor wherein human liberty effentially confifts, and how it is compatible with the fovereignty of him in whofe hands is the difpofal of all events from the day of creation to eternity. To Baron Swedenborg, as an inftrument in the Lord's hands, the prefent age is indebted for the difcovery of thefe more than metaphyfical truths; and I freely acknowledge, that all my prefent views have been opened in my mind through the medium of his writings, which appear to me to contain more true and folid wifdom, than the writings of all philofophers and all divines, in all ages, put together. I therefore from the fincerity of my heart, and as an act of the greateft friendfhip I am capable of fhewing, earneftly recommend the cool, deliberate, unprejudiced, attentive *ftudy* of them to Dr. Prieftley, and all others into whofe hands this *Defence of the New Church* may fall.

* * *

To return again to your objections. You go on, in p. 21, to obferve as follows. " When " Chrift directed his difciples to pray to their " *Father who feeth in fecret*, he furely did not " mean that they fhould pray to himfelf. If " he did, he certainly did not fpeak very in- " telligibly." If the *feeing in fecret* is a proof of divinity, and of being the Father, then Jefus is the divine Father; for he *knew all men*, John ii. 24. He *saw Nathanael before Philip called him, when he was under the fig-tree*, John i. 48. He *knew their thoughts*, Luke vi. 8; and many other places. I admit that such language as the Lord uses may not be intelligible to *some minds;* for " he hath *blinded their eyes*, and " *hardened their hearts*, that they *should not see* " with their eyes, *nor understand* with their " heart, and be converted, and I should heal " them," John xii. 40. That is, he *permits* some persons to remain in darkness, to prevent their being guilty of profanation, for no one can profane a thing, of which he is ignorant. But a time was to come, when he would speak more plainly of the Father, than ever he had done; when he would reveal to mankind, without any shadow of doubt, that he himself was the Father as well as the Son; and then men would see and understand more clearly than heretofore all that he had said when he was in the world. That day is at length come, and we have seen it.

You continue in the same page, " Besides, he " plainly distinguishes between praying to the " Father, and asking any thing of himself, " when he says, John xvi. 23, " *In that day ye* " *shall*

"shall ask me nothing. Verily, verily I say unto you,
"whatsoever ye shall ask the Father in my name,
"he will give it you." Was such language as
"this, which he constantly uses, calculated to
"lead the disciples to consider the Father and
"himself as the same person?" I answer, It
certainly was not calculated to give them an
immediate and *full* idea of his being the Father;
for this idea can only be brought about *gradually*.
Men must first believe Jesus to be the *Son of
God*, before they are capable of acknowledging
him as *God the Father himself*. If Jesus had
constantly and plainly told his disciples that
he was Jehovah the great God of heaven and
earth, they would not have believed him, because he had all the appearance of being a man
like themselves. He therefore usually called
himself the *Son* of God, and thus gradually
insinuated into their minds an idea of the divinity of his Humanity; which idea, however,
was not so clear as to be without all doubt;
for, as before observed, they were not prepared
for so full and open a revelation. Hence it was,
that the Lord, who best knows the times and
seasons, because he alone knows the states of
all hearts, almost immediately after the words
already quoted by you, adds, " These things
" have I spoken unto you *in proverbs*: the time
"cometh

"cometh when I shall *no more speak unto you in*
"*proverbs*, but I shall *shew you plainly of the*
"*Father*," John xvi. 25.

Now here I would beg leave to ask you what the Lord meant by speaking in this manner, if he had not some grand truth in reserve respecting the Father, which was improper to be fully communicated at that time, and which men would not have believed, had it been plainly avowed? Surely he could not allude to the doctrine maintained by you, that God the Father was a great *unknown Being* distinct from himself: for there were enough at that time of day who already believed in this manner. There could be no reason for speaking to the disciples on that subject *in parables*, if all the while he meant no more than what was generally believed by the scribes and pharisees his persecutors, as well as by the bulk of the Jewish nation. He must therefore have alluded to such a doctrine concerning the Father and the Son, as was not then understood, but which was to be made known at a future day, by a further and plainer revelation. Now we know not of any *plainer revelation* having taken place concerning the Father, than the words spoken by the Lord to his disciples, until the writings

of

Signified by the New Jerusalem.

of Baron Swedenborg appeared in the world; and these do contain a manifest and plain revelation from the Lord himself, that *He and the Father are One Divine Person*, just as the soul and body are one man. Thus his own words are now for the first time verified in his New Church, in that *he hath shewn us plainly of the Father;* which evident accomplishment of the scripture, is, among many others, one striking proof of the divine commission of Baron Swedenborg.

* * *

But you object, p. 22, against Jesus being the same with the Father, because, " speaking
" of the day of judgment, he says, Mark xiii.
" 32, that the time of it was not known
" either to the angels or to himself, but *to the*
" *Father only*. If the Son was the same with
" the Father, surely every thing that was known
" to the one, must have been known to the
" other also; especially as you suppose there
" was no principle of intelligence in Christ
" besides that of the Father, he having no
" human soul.

This is a very natural objection, and requires a particular answer. I shall therefore, according to my little measure of ability,

endeavour

endeavour to remove the veil that hangs over this grand myſtery, by a diſcloſure of the true ſource of intelligence, and the laws of it's deſcent from heaven to earth, from God to man. Afterwards I will apply the whole reaſoning to illuſtrate the circumſtance of the Lord's ſpeaking of the Father as if he were a perſon different from himſelf, and the appearance of his having within him two diſtinct principles of intelligence, although in reality he had but one, which was his own divine wiſdom. To do this effectually, would indeed require a volume of itſelf; but as I have not leiſure for ſuch an ample diſquiſition of the ſubject, I ſhall compreſs my ideas into as ſmall a compaſs as poſſible.

Firſt, then, it will be neceſſary to ſtate, that in reality there is *only one principle of intelligence in the univerſe*, which is God. Every other principle of intelligence is only *apparently* ſuch. Nevertheleſs ſuch appearances are agreeable to the laws of divine order inſtituted at the creation, which require that every man ſhould *ſeem to himſelf and others*, to think, will, and act, *of himſelf*. Without ſuch an appearance he could not exiſt one ſingle moment as a rational man, becauſe there would

be

be nothing in him that could *appropriate* the life flowing from God. Hence it is said in Gen. i. 26, 27, that God created man in *his own image*, after *his own likeness:* that is, he made him in all respects to have the *appearance* of being a God, to have the *appearance* of thinking, willing, and acting of himself, and consequently to have the *appearance* of a principle of intelligence within him distinct from God. Now as this was not a *real, genuine* truth, but only an *apparent* one, it is evident, that the *confirmation* of that appearance must have been highly criminal, because it amounted to a denial and rejection of the real truth, viz. that *God only* has life, love, and wisdom in himself. This was the origin of evil.

From these premises I infer, that all intelligence, whether in angels or men, comes from, and belongs to, God alone; that in order to be communicated to, and sensibly perceived by others, there must of necessity be in them forms or vessels receptive thereof; and that in it's descent from God it is varied according to the recipient forms into which it flows.

Man is born in utter ignorance, destitute of all thought and ideas, there being nothing
connate

connate in him, but the *faculty* of science, intelligence, and wisdom, together with an inclination to love not only such things, but also himself, his neighbour, and God. This being the constitution of man at his birth, he is utterly incapable of forming an idea, without the aid of his external senses, which are the inlets of all impressions from without, and the means whereby his internal connate *faculties* may come into actual exercise. These faculties in man may be called the *first principles* of his thought and affection, which cannot properly be said to *exist*, until they have a body wherein to exist, and this body is formed by scientifics from the senses, and by instruction. Hence no one can think a thought, or have any idea, without impressions from external objects which may serve as a body for his thought to dwell in; just as there can be no *sight*, which is something spiritual, without an *eye*, which is something natural.

But it ought to be well observed, that although impressions from external objects are made on us through the senses, yet they do not penetrate to the rational principle which resides in the internal, but stop in the natural principle, where they are met by the intellectual faculty,

faculty, and assumed merely as it's instruments of use. Thus the light of the sun flows into the eye, but not into the internal mind; yet the understanding meets that natural light, and being as it were cloathed with it, is thereby enabled to see the objects of the natural world, which it could not otherwise do. For what is natural or material cannot flow into what is spiritual, nor material ideas into immaterial or intellectual ideas; science cannot flow into reason, nor speech into thought; neither can the external flow into the internal; for this would be like the crasser flowing into the purer, the posterior in the prior, and the effect into the cause, which are all impossibilities. It appears indeed, in a thousand instances, as if that was the true order of influx; but it is a mere fallacy of the senses. All influx, on the contrary, is from the spiritual into the natural world, consequently all intelligence is so likewise; but the nearer it is to the external or sensual principle, and the fewer and more imperfect the vessels or sciences which any man has to contain it, so much the more obscure and faint is his intelligence. Hence the new-born infant, having no science or experience as a vessel for the actual reception of reason, has of course neither reason nor intelligence, but only the faculty or capacity of acquiring veffels for a future reception. As he grows up, he accumulates fcience by the ufe of his fenfes, and from the inftructions of his teachers, every day furnifhing him with an addītional ftock of knowledges, into which, as into their proper veffels, reafon, intelligence, and wifdom, continually flow from the fpiritual world. But all this while the principle of intelligence is the fame in it's origin; it only waits for the formation of a veffel to flow into; till that is effected, it cannot make it's appearance, nor even be perceived by man; but as fcientifics are provided by him from the external things of the natural world, light from heaven gradually flows into them, and the man becomes more and more intelligent and wife. Such then is the law of the defcent of intellectual light from God into the minds of men.

Having made thefe remarks on the nature of influx in general, and on the progrefs of man from mere ignorance to a ftate of wifdom and intelligence, I fhall now apply the fubftance of what has been faid to the cafe of the Lord, with a view to illuftrate, in fome fmall degree, the procefs of his glorification, and thereby fatisfactorily to account for his fpeaking of the

Father

Father as of a person that knew all things, but of the Son as of one who was ignorant of the day of the last judgment, while at the same time he himself was both that Father and that Son.

God from eternity was a man in *first principles*, but not actually such *in the ultimates* * till the incarnation. He often declared by the prophets, that he himself would descend into the world, assume human nature, be born as a child, and during his abode in the world be called the Messiah, the Son of God, Immanuel, Redeemer, &c. At the appointed time he came; a virgin conceived without the aid of man; Divine Truth itself, such as is contained in the Word, impregnated her; and a God-Man was born; at which all the hosts of heaven rejoiced. This divine child was called Jesus Christ. In assuming this form, the pure Divinity descended from his high abode, first into the angelic heaven, from thence into

the

---

* Paul, in his epistle to the Hebrews, chap. vii. 9, 10, says of Levi, that " he paid tithes in Abraham; for he " was yet in the loins of his father when Melchisedec met " him." This is as much as saying, that Levi was a man in *first principles*, long before he was actually a man *in the ultimates*.

the womb of Mary in the natural world, where he cloathed himself with material substances from her body; and at last was born as any other child. Thus the divine principle of intelligence became as it were *obscure*, in consequence of being surrounded with such gross substances from Mary, as were not capable of receiving the full influx of divine life from within. Therefore, agreeable to the established laws of influx, as before mentioned in page 129, the divinity could not fully manifest itself in the infant form, until by instructions, and scientifics derived from the natural world, proper vessels were formed to receive it. Hence it is written, that " Jesus *increased in* " *wisdom* and stature, and in favour with God and " man," Luke ii. 52. As the same false appearances of things presented themselves to him, as do to every other man, these furnished him with occasions for meditating upon them, and detecting their fallacy; which he was always enabled to do, by appealing to that divine principle he was conscious resided within him. While he was in the act of appealing or praying to the Father within him, it would indeed appear as if the principle of intelligence in the Son was distinct from that of the Father; but they were in reality no more distinct in

Jesus,

Jesus, than in David when he called upon his soul, and all that was within him, to praise the Lord.

For further illustration, we will consider the Lord, as having three degrees of perception of truth; a first or internal, called *intellectual;* a second or middle, called *rational;* and a third or lowest, called *scientific.* When he thought from the latter, he was ignorant of many things, and therefore needed *instruction:* when from the rational, he was in the clear perception of truth, as the Son of God, yet by assistance from a superior principle called his Father: but when he thought from the intellectual, (if that can be called *thought*, which is essential and perfect wisdom and love united) he spake as Jehovah the Father himself, who knew all things, even the hour of the last judgment. From the shade of the *scientific* man, he advanced to the light of the *rational* man, and from this to the full perception of the divine *intellectual* man. During the whole process of his glorification, he continually removed the imperfections and infirmities necessarily attendant on the gross human nature, till at last he completely united in himself the infinite perfections of Divinity with the ultimate

mate form of Humanity. Thus he that was God, became perfect Man; and he that was Man, became perfect God.

Now let us fee what ufe can be made of the foregoing obfervations, in illuftrating the paffage of fcripture alluded to in Mark xiii. 32, " But of that day and hour knoweth no man, no " not the angels which are in heaven, neither " the Son, but the Father." Here, you fay, Jefus evidently diftinguifhes between himfelf and the omnifcient God, attributing to the Father what he denies to himfelf. Not fo; Jefus, in this paffage, no more diftinguifhes between himfelf and the Father, than he does between himfelf and the Son; and for all that is expreffed to the contrary, he might as well have alluded to himfelf as being the Father to whom the time *was* known, as to himfelf as being the Son to whom it was *not* known. If merely his fpeaking *of the Father* be a fufficient proof that he was *not* that Father, then his fpeaking *of the Son* is to the full as good a proof that he was *not* that Son. To fay that he meant *himfelf* by the term *Son*, and *another* diftinct from himfelf by the term *Father*, is a mere *petitio principii*, a begging of the queftion. He fpeaks of the Father, I will admit,

apparently

apparently as of a third perfon; but he alfo fpeaks *in like manner* of the Son. Therefore, according to this view of the fubject, the whole of the objection has loft it's weight, and falls to the ground; for although it is true, that the Lord in other places frequently calls himfelf the *Son* of God, yet it is equally true that he is fometimes declared to be the *Father*, and the *very God*.

But not to take this advantage of the weaknefs of the objection, I will, for argument's fake, (or rather for the fake of manifefting the truth,) allow it all the importance, which you feem to think it carries with it. How eafy is it to fee, from the preceding remarks on the various difcrete degrees of intelligence in one mind, that the Lord meant to inftruct us, that *truth* not yet fully united to divine *good* (fignified by the *Son* as diftinguifhed from the *Father*) was not poffeffed of that infinitely-complete perception of all things, which it would have when the perfect union was accomplifhed; or, in other words, that himfelf, in the capacity of *Son*, could not manifeftly exhibit thofe full perfections of divinity, which the laws of order required him to exercife as *Father*. That Jefus is the Father, as well as the

Son,

Son, is also plain from this circumstance, that he is the *sole judge* of the living and the dead, for into his hands all judgment is committed. Now as no one can be a *competent* judge of every creature in the universe, who is so defective in capacity as *not to know* even the time *when to commence it;* and as the sitting in judgment over the thoughts, intentions, and motives of all hearts, as well as over their every word and action, implies to the full as much an infinite capacity, if not more so than the mere knowledge of the day when such an event is to take place; I infer, that he who knows the greater, cannot be ignorant of the less; that he, who is equal to the one, is sufficient for the other also; consequently that Jesus being qualified to *execute* judgment, must know the proper time *when* to do it; and that therefore he himself was that very Father to whom he alluded, as alone knowing the day and hour of that great event.

There is one circumstance highly necessary to be observed in reading the holy scriptures, if we would attain to a right understanding of their contents; without a due attention to which, many passages will unavoidably appear dark, perplexed, and contradictory to others.

What I allude to, is, the frequent use of *apparent* truths in the literal sense, instead of those that are *genuine*, together with the necessity of an inversion of the terms, in order to obtain the spiritual sense. My meaning will be best explained by an example. It is frequently said in the Word, that God is angry, that he punishes, casts into hell, and destroys the wicked. These are only *apparent* truths, not *real* or *genuine*; for the Lord is love itself, and mercy itself, and it is not within the power of love and mercy to punish, or bring evil upon any one. To come at the genuine truth, then, there must be an inversion or change of terms, at least in our idea. Thus, instead of supposing that the Lord is *angry* and *casts into hell*, we must understand that he is *merciful* and *does good*, and that it is man who is angry with the Lord, and casts himself into hell; for such is the genuine truth, as is particularly evident in Psalm cxxxvi. 10, 15 to 20, where the destruction of the Egyptians, &c. is attributed to his everlasting mercy. The Lord, in his own person, when on earth, represented not only the Word itself, but also the state of the church on earth; so that what is spoken of the Lord, will in many cases admit of being applied to man. Take an example: " Jesus
"charged

"charged his disciples, that they should tell no man that he was Jesus the Christ," Matt. xvi. 20. Here it is said of Jesus, that he charged his disciples not to publish him abroad, although he came into the world and chose his disciples for that very purpose. This passage, therefore, appears to be one that is more immediately applicable to the state of the church, and descriptive of it's non-reception of truth, than to the Lord, who certainly willed that all men should receive and acknowledge him. In another place it is said, that *he could do no mighty work there, because of their unbelief,* Mark vi. 5, 6; where *non-ability* is ascribed to the Lord, on account of *unbelief* in the people. From these and other passages of a similar nature, it is very evident, that many things spoken of Jesus have a *relative* application to the state of the church at that time, and ought to be interpreted accordingly.

Agreeable to these observations, the circumstance of the day and hour of the last judgment being hid from the Son, and known only to the Father, will admit of the following explanation. The *Father* signifies the Lord as to divine good, and in respect to the church the reception thereof under the description of charity,

charity. The *Son* signifies the Lord as to divine truth, and in respect to the church the reception thereof under the form of faith. Now the end of the church, signified by the last judgment, being principally in consequence of the destruction of charity, which has immediate reference to divine good or to the Lord as Father, it is therefore said, that the Father only knoweth the time, and not the Son; by which is signified, that the last state of the church is determined by the defection of charity, and not so much by the want of faith; for immediately on the expiration of charity, the church ceases to be any longer a church, notwithstanding all it's faith. As long as charity remained, the church remained; but as soon as ever that was lost, the judgment took place. This is a short sketch of the spiritual sense of the above passage. But for a further and more particular explanation, I refer you to the *Magazine of Knowledge concerning Heaven and Hell*, vol. ii. p. 187, where you will find the subject treated, I hope, in a satisfactory manner, by a writer under the signature of *M. B. G.*

* * *

In Matt. xxviii. 18, Jesus says to his disciples, "*All power is given unto me in heaven and* "*in earth.*" And in Luke x. 22, "*All things are delivered to me of my Father.*" You quote these two passages, in p. 22, as a proof of the distinction between the Father who *gave* the power, and Jesus who *received* it; and then immediately you put the following question, "Can the *giver* and *receiver* be the same person, any more than the person *sending*, and the person *sent?*" I have already shewn, that the person *sending* and the person *sent* may be one and the same; I will now prove, from the authority of scripture, that the *giver* and *receiver*, in the following instances, not only *may be* one and the same person, but clearly and absolutely *can be no other.*

Jehovah says by the prophet Isaiah, "I am Jehovah, that is my name, and *my glory will I not give to another*," Isa. xlii. 8. The glory of Jehovah consists in his being possessed of all divine and infinite perfections, of which *omnipotence* is one. Jehovah the Father gave to Jesus *all power*, as is expressly declared; therefore unless Jesus was the same person as the Father, Jehovah gave his glory of omnipotence to *another*. But as this cannot possibly be true, I conclude that Jesus and Jehovah are one and the same person, consequently

that

that the *giver* and *receiver* are one and the same also.

Peter says, that Jesus Christ " received from " God the Father, honour and glory," 2 Pet. i. 17. As God cannot give his glory to *another*, and it is here said that Jesus received it from God, it is plain that Jesus himself must be God, and thus that the *giver* and *receiver* are one and the same person.

When Jesus would instruct his disciples of the union subsisting between himself and the Father, that it was like the union subsisting between the soul and body of one man, he did it in such terms as these: " As the Father " hath *life in himself*, so hath he *given* to the " Son to have *life in himself*," John v. 26. Now he that hath *life in himself*, must be essentially God: and as it is impossible for God to communicate to *another* being the essentially divine property of having *life in himself*, for this would be *one God creating another God*, which is a manifest absurdity; and as it is said that the Father *gave* to the Son (meaning to Jesus Christ) that divine property of having life in himself in all respects as God the Father had; it is evident, that the Father and the Son

can

can be no other than one and the same God, consequently that the *giver* and *receiver* are one and the same person.

It is said of the Lord God almighty, that *he has taken to himself* his great power, Apoc. xi, 17. Now although it may seem, according to the literal sense of these words, that there was a time when the Lord God almighty had not that great power which he now has, but that it was lodged in some *other hands*; just as, when it is said of Jesus, that *all power is given unto him*, it may appear as if he received it from *another*, there being no greater impropriety in the one case, than in the other; yet no one will pretend to build an argument on such ground against the real divinity of the Lord God almighty. Why then, Dr. Priestley, do you make that an argument against the sole and supreme divinity of Jesus Christ, which equally and as strongly operates against the great Jehovah himself?

Jesus not only hath *all power* in heaven and in earth, but *every other* attribute of divinity that can possibly be conceived. Infinity, immensity, and eternity are his. He is self-essent and self-existent; the I Am, Independent,

dent, Sole, Supreme, from eternity the First, and to eternity the Last; for, says he, " *All* " *things* that the *Father* hath, are *mine,*" John xvi. 15. No divine attribute then can be wanting in him. The *fulness* of the Godhead must necessarily dwell in him, not as a power or principle distinct from him, but as *one with him,* like the *soul and body* in man. Were we to suppose it *possible* for the Father to be a God distinct from Jesus Christ, then, agreeable to the above passage in Matthew, he must have resigned his kingdom and power to Jesus Christ, and consequently is no longer the God of heaven and earth. But Jehovah will not, cannot give either his glory or omnipotence to *another.* He may and hath given it to *himself;* that is, the Divinity of Jehovah hath given it to the Humanity of the same Jehovah; for Jesus, who is God in the Humanity, and who received all power from the Father, says, " *I and my Father are one,*" John x. 30; one, not by unanimity, but absolutely and inseparably, being as incapable of division without a complete and total denial of the whole Godhead, as the soul and body of man are, without death.

* * *

The

The next thing I have to remark upon, is the conclusion you draw from the following passage in John, " This is life eternal, that " they might know *thee the only true God*, and " Jesus Christ whom thou hast sent," chap. xvii. 3. What has already been advanced concerning the *apparent* distinction between the person of the Father and that of the Son, may equally be applied to this and many other passages in the Word. Permit me, however, to bring to your recollection the testimony of John in respect to Jesus Christ the Son of God. He says, 1 Epist. v. 20, " *This* * *is the true God*, " and eternal life." Now you know there cannot be *two* true Gods. Jesus calls his *Father* the true God, and John calls *Jesus* the true God. If both propositions be admitted, then no conclusion can be more regular or certain, than that *the Father and Jesus are one and the same God*. The apostle Jude likewise agrees with us of the New Church in ascribing " glory and majesty, dominion and power both
" now

---

* It will avail nothing to say, that the definitive pronoun *this* refers not to Jesus Christ, but to the Father; the plain sense of the words being evidently such as they are here taken, viz. that Jesus Christ is the true God and eternal life.

" now and ever, to the *only wife God our Sa-*
" *viour,*" verfe 25.

Our Lord fays, that *life eternal* confifts in knowing the *Father and Jefus Chrift*. This appears to me exceedingly unfavourable to the Socinian fcheme; for if Jefus Chrift be no more than a *mere man*, I cannot fee how the knowledge of him, any more than of any other prophet, can be one of the effential conditions and conftituents of life eternal. To know the *true God*, one might naturally expect to be neceffary to falvation; but that the knowledge of a *mere man*, be he who he may, fhould be to the full *as neceffary* and *as effential* to our future happinefs, as the knowledge of the *only true God*, is a fuppofition which, I think, even a Mahometan or a Pagan would blufh to maintain. And is this the *fcheme of chriftianity* which Dr. Prieftley invites the members of the New Jerufalem to embrace!—My good friend, let me intreat you to re-confider this matter, and ferioufly weigh in your mind the confequences of fuch a delufion. If Jefus be no more than a prophet, like Mofes, or Jonah, or Amos, or any others, what virtue can there be in the knowledge of him, any more than of them? But if he be the *Divine Human Form* of God, then the acknowledgment of him muſt be *as eſſential* to ſalvation, as the acknowledgment of the *Father*, ſeeing that both the *Father* and the *Son*, the *eſſence* and the *form*, together conſtitute only one God.

In John iii. 16, and other places, Jeſus calls himſelf the *only-begotten* Son of God: but in what ſenſe this is to be underſtood, deſerves ſome conſideration. If Jeſus was a mere man, it would not be ſaying the truth to call him the *only-begotten* Son of God, ſeeing that all men, who are born again, are equally ſaid to be begotten of God, and even called the ſons of God. The expreſſion, however, of *only-begotten* is repeatedly applied to Jeſus Chriſt, which is therefore evidently repugnant to the ſuppoſition of his being a mere man. But if we conſider Jeſus Chriſt as the Humanity of Jehovah, then it is with great propriety ſaid of him, that he is the *only-begotten of the Father;* for the divine *eſſence*, which is meant by the Father, being individual, has begotten to itſelf a divine *form*, which is alſo individual; and thus Divinity and Humanity are united in one God, as ſoul and body are united in one man,

which

which union is signified by the only-begotten Son dwelling in the bosom of the Father.

It is on account of this strict union between the Father and the Son, that it is said, "He that honoureth not *the Son*, honoureth not the Father," John v. 23. "He that believeth on *the Son*, hath everlasting life," John iii. 36. "This is the will of the Father, that every one who seeth *the Son*, and believeth on *him*, may have everlasting life," John vi. 40. "Whoso denieth *the Son*, the same hath not the Father," 1 John ii. 23. "God hath given to us eternal life; and this life is *in his Son*. He that hath *the Son*, hath life; but he that hath not *the Son*, hath not life," 1 John v. 11, 12. From all these passages the following plain conclusion naturally results, viz. That the Son is the *continent* of the Father, just as light is the *continent* of heat, as the form is the *continent* of the essence, or as the body is the *continent* of the soul; and he that sees the one, sees all that can be seen of the other. If I wish to converse with a man's *soul*, I must approach his *body;* for there the soul is, and no where else. And while I address the body, I at the same time address the whole man, both soul and body together. But were I to attempt to

address

addrefs the foul feparately or diftinct from the body, it would not only be abfurd in itfelf, but could not poffibly be attended with any effect; for if the *fulnefs of the foul*, or the *whole foul*, refides *in* the body, and not *out of it*, to the body alone muft the *direct* and *immediate* approach be made. On this very principle it is, that the members of the New Jerufalem approach Jefus Chrift alone, as knowing that the *fulnefs of the Godhead*, or the *whole Divinity*, centers in his Humanity, and is no where elfe to be found. Thus by approaching him, they at the fame time approach the Father, becaufe the Father is in him, as the foul is in the body. Were we to attempt to "climb up any other " way," by addreffing the Divinity feparate from the Humanity, we believe we fhould be "*thieves and robbers*," inafmuch as fuch a conduct would be no lefs than robbing the Lord's Humanity of all it's Divinity. See John x. 1.

* * *

Another ftumbling-block, which feems to lie in your way, is the paffage in John xx. 17, " I afcend to my Father and your Father, " to my God and your God." " Here furely," you fay, p. 22, " are two different perfons in-
" dicated. Can any perfon be faid to afcend
" to

"to himself?"—I answer in the affirmative. If you will not believe me, hear what Paul says: "Without controversy great is the mystery of "godliness; *God* was manifest in the flesh, "*God* was justified in the spirit, *God* was seen "of angels, *God* was preached unto the gen- "tiles, *God* was believed on in the world, "*God* was *received up* into glory," 1 Tim. iii. 16. God was received up into glory! Who received him there? Doubtless God *received himself* there. *Jesus*, I know, was manifest in the flesh, *Jesus* was justified in the spirit, *Jesus* was seen of angels, *Jesus* was preached unto the gentiles, *Jesus* was believed on in the world, and *Jesus* was received up into glory. Therefore *Jesus* was God, and ascended up to himself.

Again, David says, "God is gone up with a "*shout*," Psalm xlvii. 5. Where, I pray you, could *He go to*, who is *omnipresent*, if not up to himself? Parallel with this is the passage in John xx. 17, where Jesus says, "*I ascend* "unto my Father and your Father, and to my "God and your God." In the first passage, *God goes up*, in the second, *Jesus ascends*. Now as God cannot go any where, but where he was before by virtue of his *omnipresence*, it must

be

be understood that *God went up to God,* that is, *to himself.* And as in verse 28 of the same chapter of John, Jesus is called *God* in express terms, I therefore conclude, and I trust without any violence to truth, that the meaning of the second passage is, that *Jesus ascended to himself,* or which is the same thing, though in other words, that *God went up to God.*

As I have already explained, according to my view of the subject, the internal sense of John xx. 17, respecting the Lord's ascension into heaven, and published it in the *Magazine of Knowledge concerning Heaven and Hell,* vol. i. p. 273 to 277, there is no necessity for inserting it here; neither do I conceive it would be of much use to those who deny the reality of such a sense, as I am sorry to observe is the case with the gentleman, to whom these *Letters* are more immediately addressed. I shall therefore proceed to the examination of other objections.

* * *

At the foot of p. 22, you say, "Lastly, our "Saviour says, John xiv. 28, that *his Father* "*was greater than he.* Can any person be greater "than himself?" There are some in cases in
which

which a man may be greater than himself; and of this you yourself seem to be apprized, for you continue, " The same person may, " no doubt, be greater at one time than he " was at another; but here he speaks of the " same time. Also, a man in one capacity " may be greater than he is in another; as a " general at the head of his army may be said " to be greater than he is at his fire-side. But " here our Saviour speaks *absolutely*." Rather say, he speaks *relatively*; for so the truth is. He was telling his disciples, that he was *about to ascend to the Father;* which was as much as to say, that his Humanity was *not yet perfectly united* to his Divinity; and *until* this was the case, and *by how much* it was *not* united, just *so far* he was inferior to the Father: but *by how much* it *was* united, *so far* he was equal to, and one with the Father. Hence we find him speaking in two ways; at one time having respect to the Humanity *as not yet glorified*, in which state he speaks of the Father as *greater than himself*; and at another time having respect to the Humanity *as glorified*, in which state he says, " *I and my Father are one.*"

Before a man's passions are properly subdued, and when he is tempted to commit a rash action,

action, if he is a wife man, or in purfuit of wifdom, he will *look up* to his reafon and underftanding for affiftance, hereby virtually acknowledging that his reafon is greater than himfelf. In this fituation of mind he may with great propriety fay, ' *Of myfelf* I cannot
' refift thefe temptations, being as it were im-
' merfed in all kinds of vicious inclinations,
' which have their abode in the loweft regions
' of the mind: I will therefore afcend into it's
' fuperior regions, and elevate myfelf into the
' light of reafon, for *my reafon is greater than my*
' *paffion*.' Now here, notwithftanding the man's reafon is greater than his paffion, and thus the man himfelf greater in one refpect than he is in another refpect, ftill both his reafon and paffion conftitute but one perfon. It was juft fo, comparatively fpeaking, with the Lord: his Father was the Divinity within him; himfelf was the Humanity. While the Humanity was fubject to temptations, the Father was greater than him, becaufe the Divinity could not be tempted. But when the Humanity was fully united to the Divinity, then neither could the Humanity be tempted, any more than the Divinity, becaufe all the properties of the latter centered bodily in the former. Hence the Lord fays, " I and my Father are *one*."

There

There is therefore no difficulty at all in comprehending how and in what respect the Father was greater than Jesus; and yet after all, that both he and the Father were one and the same divine person.

* * *

The explanation you give, p. 23, of our Lord's words in John x. 29, is to me very extraordinary and unnatural, implying consequences not only irrational and absurd, but even blasphemous, utterly destructive of the universe, and together with it the Creator of the universe himself. I cannot indeed think you was aware of any such inferences being deducible from your doctrine; but I see they necessarily result from the Socinian method of interpreting scripture. Our Lord's words are as follow: " My sheep hear my voice, and I know them, " and they follow me. And *I give* unto them " eternal life, and they shall never perish, " neither shall any pluck them out of *my hand*. " My Father who gave them me, is greater " than all; and none is able to pluck them out " of *my Father's hand*. I and my Father *are one*," John x. 27 to 30. *I and my Father are one*, " that is," you say, " no person can overpower " *me*, but he must overpower *the Father also*." Here let us pause a moment to consider the consequences of such an interpretation as this, according to the Socinian faith. You, Sir, as a Socinian, maintain that Jesus Christ was a *mere man*, both as to his soul and his body; that in consequence of this mere humanity, he was, like any other man, liable to sufferings and death; and that the Jews, whose prejudices he opposed, at last actually crucified him, or, agreeable to your own expression, *overpowered him*. Now if, as you say, the meaning of the Lord's words above recited is, that " no one can overpower him, but he must over-" power the Father also," it will then follow, that the Jews, by crucifying the *mere man Jesus*, at the same time actually *overpowered the supreme God!* Such is the unavoidable consequence of interpreting the Lord's words in the way you have done.

But if we pursue your notions a little further, we shall see something, if possible, still more absurd. You believe, that when a man dies as to the body, all consciousness of life or existence perishes with him; thus that both soul and body together lie dead in the grave. Now, if the Father was overpowered at the same time that Jesus was overpowered, when he was crucified and buried, then the
Father

Father must have been in a state of torpor and death, as well as Jesus: I would therefore beg leave to ask, By what power was it that Jesus was raised from the grave? He could not raise himself, because you say he was a mere man; and besides, he had been so *overpowered* by the Jews, that all his own powers were become extinct. Neither could the Father raise him, because *his* powers were also extinct, in consequence of the Jews overpowering Jesus; for " *no person,*" you say, " *can overpower Jesus, but he must overpower the Father also.*" Again, if, as you say, p. 50, God has no other form or shape, than that of *infinite space*, it will follow, that when Jesus was overpowered, *infinite space* also was overpowered; since whatever misfortune befals the *essence* of any being, must likewise necessarily happen to his *form*. Hence it is plain to see, that the method of interpreting the scriptures, which Socinians are obliged to have recourse to, is the most irrational, absurd, and self-contradictory, that can possibly be imagined; nay, that it even militates against the very being of a God, against the existence of a heaven and a hell, or a life after death, and against every thing spiritual or divine; instead of God, setting up nature, or, what amounts to the same thing, *infinite space*, as the object of worship, of which neverthelefs no proper idea can be formed in the human mind.

After having made thefe remarks on your mode of interpreting our Lord's words, I will now point out what appears to me to be a much more rational and confiftent explanation. Jefus fays, " *My sheep* hear *my voice*, and follow " *me*. And *I give* unto them eternal life, " neither fhall any pluck them out of *my hand*. " My Father who *gave them me*, is greater " than all, and none is able to pluck them out " of my *Father's hand*. I and my Father *are* " *one*." Here it is plain, the sheep *belong to Jefus*, and *he gives* them eternal life. He indeed fays, that no one can pluck them out of his *Father's hand;* but he alfo fays, None fhall pluck them out of *my hand*. Wherefore the Father's hand, and the hand of Jefus, muft be one and the fame; for the fheep cannot be in *two different perfons'* hands at the fame time. If the Father be a different perfon from Jefus, then the fheep are not in the Father's hand at all; for he gave them away *out of his own hand* into the hand of Jefus. But as the paffage plainly implies, that, notwithftanding the Father's giving them away *into the hand of Jefus*, they ftill
remained

remained *in his own hand* likewife; no other conclufion can be fairly drawn, than that Jefus and the Father are one and the fame perfon. And this is the very conclufion that our Lord himfelf has drawn; for immediately after making the *apparent* diftinction between himfelf and the Father, he teaches us how to underftand him, and in exprefs terms fays, " I and my Father *are One*."

It is therefore impoffible to reconcile our Lord's words concerning the Father and himfelf, in any other way, than by confidering the Father to be the Divinity, and Jefus the Humanity, of one and the fame God. For as in the cafe of an individual man, the foul *gives* or *transfers* all it's power to the body, and yet at the fame time *retains* it to itfelf; fo the Divinity *gives* or *transfers* all it's power to the Humanity, and yet at the fame time *retains* it to itfelf; or in other words, the Father *gives* all his power to the Son Jefus, and yet *retains* it to himfelf; for after all they are only one and the fame divine perfon.

* * *

You fay, p. 23, that the *conftant* language which the apoftles ufed, when they fpake of our Saviour and God, " demonftrates, that they
" confidered

"considered *him* as being a person different from God." I allow, that the greatest part of their writings wears this aspect; and I have already hinted the reason why it could not be otherwise, viz. because it is agreeable to order, that divine truth, like every thing else, should be gradual in it's manifestation. The light of the natural day does not come on instantaneously; first of all the twilight, then the day-dawn, and last of all the direct beams of the sun. It is the same with every art and science hitherto discovered; the same with the growth of man, both as to his intellectual and animal powers; the same with the production of plants and trees from small seeds till they arrive at their full maturity, and are capable of bearing fruit; in short, it is the same with every thing in nature that surrounds us. Why then should the light of revelation alone be deemed sudden or instantaneous? Is not the understanding (which is the eye of the mind) as susceptible of injury from the *too precipitate* influx of divine truth into it, as the eye of the body is from that of natural light? Most certainly it is. For this reason our Lord said to his disciples, "I have yet many things to say unto you, *but ye cannot bear them now,*" John xvi. 12. Hence also he spake to them

mostly

moftly in parables, at the fame time informing them, that a day was coming when the parables, which he then uttered, would be clearly unfolded, and when by his Holy Spirit (a new fpiritual revelation) he would fpeak more plainly to his Church, than it was as yet capable of bearing.

But although the apoftles were not fo clear concerning the union of the Father and Son in one perfon, yet it is remarkable, that many paffages are to be found in their writings to confirm this grand truth. Such are the following among many others. "Hereby per-"ceive we the love of *God*, becaufe *he laid down* "*his life for us*," 1 John iii. 16. Jefus Chrift alone laid down his life for us: therefore Jefus Chrift alone is God, and this according to the plain declaration of John.—" Jefus Chrift is " the *true God*, and eternal life," 1 John v. 20. Jude fays, that certain men " deny the *only* " Lord God, and our Lord Jefus Chrift," verfe 4. Paul fays, there is " *one* Lord, *one* " God and Father," Eph. iv. 5, 6. Now Jefus Chrift is conftantly called the *Lord* by all the apoftles: therefore the Lord Jefus and the only Lord God muft be one and the fame perfon; otherwife Paul was miftaken when he faid there

was

was only *one Lord*.—Again, "Jesus Christ the "same *yesterday, to-day, and for ever*," Heb. xiii. 8. This is a character applicable only to Jehovah that *changeth not*, Mal. iii. 6. "*In Jesus* "*Christ dwelleth all the fulness of the Godhead* "*bodily*," Col. ii. 9. All the fulness of the Godhead cannot dwell in Jesus Christ, in any other way, than as all the fulness of the soul dwells in the body: therefore God and Jesus Christ must be one and the same person, as the soul and body are one man. The same apostle further says of our Lord Jesus Christ, that "he is the blessed and *only Potentate*, the *King* "*of kings*, and *Lord of lords; who only* hath "immortality, dwelling in the light which no "man can approach unto, whom (as the "Father) no man hath seen, nor can see; to "whom be honour and power everlasting, "Amen," 1 Tim. vi. 15, 16. I might fill many pages with passages of a similar tendency, all selected from the apostolic epistles; but the above are sufficient to establish the sole, exclusive divinity of Jesus, and to disprove your assertions in p. 23 and 24, that "the apostles "*constantly* spake of him as a person different "from God;" for they *very often* speak of him in such terms, as can have no other meaning than that he is God.

"I have

* * *

"I have considered (you say, p. 24,) all that "you alledge," in favour of Jesus Christ being the same person as God the Father, "and find "them only to be a *few passages*, which, "literally interpreted, *might indeed imply as much*, "but which very easily admit of a very dif- "ferent interpretation; and in all cases we in- "terpret what is *figurative* and *obscure*, by what "is *clear* and *express*." By your saying we have only a *few passages* by which to support the exclusive divinity of Jesus Christ, I am convinced you have not informed yourself sufficiently of the evidence which Baron Swedenborg adduces from the scriptures, in proof of this matter. And if you have not paid a proper attention to the evidence, it is impossible you could have digested the subject, or formed a right judgment about it. The passages of scripture, on which the exclusive divinity of our Saviour is founded, are exceedingly numerous; and, when viewed in their true light, afford the most satisfactory proof, that God the Father and Jesus Christ are one and the same person. Many of these passages are adduced in the present *Defence*; but many more might be pointed out in aid of the same doctrine, were it necessary. Let
what

what has been said, and what still remains to be said on the same subject, answer in this behalf.

You admit that what is figurative and obscure ought to be interpreted by what is clear and express: but it is remarkable you will allow nothing to be clear and express, except such passages as *appear* in the literal sense to favour your own sentiments. Those which *you* say are *obscure*, are to *others clear* and *explicit;* while those which you take to be *genuine truths,* are evidently no more than the *appearances of truth*, the confirmation of which is like grasping at the shadow, and losing the substance. So long therefore as you continue to view the scriptures from a *negative* principle, I fear it will be impossible for you to see your mistake. By a *negative* principle I mean a *pre-conceived* denial and rejection of the divinity of Jesus Christ. My reasons for thinking that you are really influenced by such a principle, are grounded on the whole tenor of your theological writings, and particularly on the following passages in your *Letters to the Members of the New Jerusalem*. " Whatever particular passage may " seem to intimate" that Christ and God are one person, " must have some other meaning;
" and

"and even if we could not explain it other-
"wife, we ought to *content ourfelves* with *ac-*
"*knowledging the difficulty,* or fuppofe *fome error*
"to have *crept into the text,*" p. 25. "Should
"any being, in the complete form of an angel,
"tell me, that God had the form of a Man,
"and that this God was Jefus Chrift, I fhould
"tell him that he was a *lying fpirit,*" p. 60.
Such is the language you hold out concerning
our bleffed Saviour, which, for your fake, I
was extremely forry to read, becaufe it carried
fo much the appearance of a *fixed, determined
refolution not to be convinced,* by any argument
whatever, of the divinity of Jefus Chrift.
And I well know, that where the *will* tyrannizes,
the *underftanding* muft be a flave.

* * *

You feem, p. 25, to be aware of the great
ftrength of our Lord's words to Philip, and
how completely they overthrow your whole
fyftem. "Philip faith unto him, Lord, fhew
"us the Father, and it fufficeth us. Jefus faith
"unto him, Have *I* been fo long time with you,
"and yet haft thou not known *Me,* Philip?
"He that hath feen *Me,* hath feen *the Father,*"
John xiv. 8, 9. Of which paffage you give the
following explanation. "Jefus, you cannot
"deny, was ufed to fpeak in figurative lan-
"guage,

"guage; and where is there a more common figure of speech than to say, *we see a person in his works*, and especially *in those persons* who are commissioned to say or do any thing in his name? We even say, that God, who is invisible, is to be seen in his *works*. Now the power and wisdom of God were manifest in Christ, who spake and acted by immediate commission from him; and seeing the manifestations of divine wisdom and power either in the works of nature, or in the sayings and miracles of the prophets, is all that we can see of God, who is himself invisible."

This explanation of our Lord's words appears to me to be a mere evasion, and in the end destroys itself. For, in the first place, you arbitrarily substitute the *works* of Jesus, instead of his *person*. When Philip said, *Shew us the Father*, our Lord directed him to *himself*, in his own *proper person*, and not to his *works*, as you endeavour to make your readers believe. Had it been the Lord's design to answer Philip by a reference merely to the *works* of the Father, he would certainly have pointed him to the visible creation, or else to the sayings and miracles of the prophets, which, you say, *is all that*

that we can see of God. But instead of this, he told Philip, that the sight of *him* was the same thing as seeing the *Father*, and that because the Father dwelt in him, as the soul does in the body. Afterwards, indeed, he desired Philip to believe him *for the very works' sake,* verse 11; but then what was he to believe? Why, he was to believe the truth of what the Lord had just before told him, viz. " He that hath seen " *Me*, hath seen *the Father.*" And if, by reason of his having the *appearance* of a mere man, Philip could not discern the divinity of his *person*, he was nevertheless enjoined to believe it *for the very works' sake.*

But again: You believe, that Jesus was no more than a common man, like any of the prophets or apostles: and you say, that all we can see of God, is either in his works, or *in those persons* who are commissioned to say or to do any thing in his name. Upon this supposition, then, it will follow, that when Philip desired to see the Father, the Lord might with as much propriety have referred him to John the Baptist, or any other of the prophets, as to himself. Nay, to come closer still, and more evidently expose the fallacy of your principles, he might have said, ' He that hath seen *Philip*,
' hath

'hath seen *the Father;*' for Philip also (being an apostle) had the power of working miracles committed to him, and in this respect equally manifested the works of God, from whom, you say, as from a Being different from either of them, they derived all their power. But the absurdity of such an hypothesis as this, needs only to be brought to light, to be rejected by every rational christian. And I doubt not but the judicious reader already agrees with me, that the explanation you have given of the foregoing passage, is forced, unnatural, and destructive of itself.

* * *

Another passage which you observe we quote in proof that Jesus and the Father are one and the same person, is that of Paul, Coloss. ii. 9. "*In him dwelleth all the fulness of the Godhead bodily.*" "But this," you say, p. 26, "might be the case without Jesus himself being God, when the divine power was manifested by him. Nay, the very phraseology of this passage is unfavourable to your hypothesis, for that which dwells in a person cannot be the same thing with himself, but must be different from him."

I wonder, Sir, how you could run the risk of exposing yourself, by letting such unguarded expressions escape your pen. Have you forgotten, that the *soul* of every man *dwells* in his *body?* Or do you mean to say, that a man's soul is not the man himself, but something *different from him?* Are all your ideas of humanity confined to the mere corporeal frame? If so, you must be a *materialist* with a witness, admitting nothing to enter into the constitution of man, but what you can see with your eyes, hear with your ears, smell with your nose, taste with your tongue, or touch with your hands. The apostle James says, " The *spirit* that *dwel-* " *leth in us,* lusteth to envy;" and he makes no distinction between the spirit of a man, that dwells in him, and the man himself. See chap. iv. 2, 5. Here the phraseology of James, respecting a man and his soul, agrees with that of Paul, concerning Jesus, that in him dwells all the fulness of the Godhead; and in both cases, by that which dwells in the person, is signified the same thing as the person himself.

I have already observed in a former part of this *Defence,* p. 142, that Jesus was possessed of *all power* in heaven and earth, with *every other attribute of divinity,* agreeable to his own words in John xvi. 15, "*All things* that the *Father* "hath, are *mine.*" With this passage the saying of Paul perfectly coincides: therefore what has been advanced concerning the one, will equally apply to the other also. But as a proof that the *fulness of the Godhead* is the same thing as the *fulness of Jesus,* I shall here adduce the following passage from John i. 16, "And of *his* "*fulness* have all we received, and grace for "grace." These words were spoken of Jesus Christ, and, compared with those of Paul, plainly, testify, that he and God the Father are one and the same person.

* * *

You acknowledge, p. 27, that the same titles are given to Christ, as to God. But you add, "Beings the *most different* in their natures may, "in several respects, resemble one another, and "act a *similar part,* so as to be entitled to the *same* "*appellations,* without being the same persons." And in answer to the arguments we urge from those passages in the prophets, in which Jehovah is so frequently and so solemnly declared to be the *only Saviour,* and the *only Redeemer,* you say, that "both he who saves by another, and that other "who saves by his orders and directions, may "be equally called a *Saviour;*" thus that Jesus Christ was no more a Saviour by his own
power,

power, than Moses was, who under God delivered the Israelites from Egypt, or than the judges who delivered them from their various enemies. But you forget what the prophet Isaiah says concerning Jesus who was to come into the world, that he is a Redeemer and Saviour *by his own proper power.* " Who is this that
" cometh from Edom, with dyed garments from
" Bozrah? this that is glorious in his apparel,
" travelling in the *greatness of his strength?*"
Who? It is no less than Jehovah himself, " *I*
" *that speak in righteousness, mighty to save.* I
" have trodden the wine-press *alone,* and of the
" people there was *none with me.* The day of
" vengeance is in my heart, and the year of
" *my redeemed* is come. And I looked, and
" there was *none to help;* and I wondered that
" there was *none to uphold:* therefore *mine own*
" *arm* brought salvation unto me, and my fury
" it upheld me. *I will tread down* the people in
" mine anger, and *I will bring down* their
" strength to the earth. He said, Surely they
" are *my people,* children that will not lye. *So*
" *he was their Saviour.*" Isa. lxiii. 1 to 8.

Now it is no where said of Moses, that he saved or delivered *by his own proper power,* but always by a power which he derived from
another

another different from himself, namely, Jehovah, in whose name, and by whose express command he brought the Israelites out of Egypt. But of Jesus it is said, that he saved and redeemed *by his own mighty arm;* and when any of the apostles performed miracles, it was always *in the name of Jesus,* which is a plain and full acknowledgment, that their power so to do was derived from *him alone.* To do any thing *in the name of the king,* implies by the *authority of the king:* hence to heal the sick, the lame, the deaf, and the blind, *in the name of Jesus,* means to perform those cures by the *sole power* and *authority of Jesus,* which nevertheless cannot belong to any mere man, but exclusively to him who is both God and Man in one person.

Of Jesus it is remarkable, that whenever he performed a miracle, or delivered a precept, it was always in *his own name,* and by *his own authority;* in this respect differing from both prophets and apostles, who constantly spake and acted in the name of *another,* attributing all their wisdom, power, and authority, to God from whom they derived them. When the chief priests and elders of the people demanded of Jesus, by what authority he did such and such things, and who gave him that authority,

he

he refused to tell them; plainly intimating, that it was by *his own* authority, and by *none other;* for had it been derived from any other being, or had he himself been a person different from God, as a faithful prophet and messenger, he would doubtless have taken that opportunity of acknowledging his master, and ascribing honour to whom honour was due. But no such language as this was held forth by him: on the contrary, he spake as *one having* [*self-derived*] *authority*, and not as the scribes.

Moreover, it is said of Jesus, that " *he shall* " *save his people from their sins,*" Matt. i. 21. A mere man cannot surely do this. Noah, Daniel, and Job, could deliver only *their own souls* by their righteousness, Ezek. xiv. 14, 20; and even this could not be effected without the Lord's righteousness imparted to them. But Jesus is the Lamb of God that taketh away the *sins of the world.* He hath power to *forgive sins,* and actually *did forgive them.* Yet none can forgive sins, but God only. See Mark ii. 5, 7, 9. Luke v. 21. Herein then is Jesus distinguished from all other prophets, and, by his divine prerogative of forgiving sins, known to be God alone.

* * *

You juftly obferve, p. 27, that we lay great ftrefs on Chrift being called *the Alpha and the Omega*. We do fo, and confider the title as a ftriking characteriftic of the great Jehovah. "But," fay you, "this is no more a proper "name of God, than *Saviour*, or *Father*. It "may fignify the chief, or founder of any "thing; as Chrift is, *under God*, of the chriftian "difpenfation." This interpretation, however, is by no means applicable to the term *Alpha*, which being *abfolutely* the firft letter of the Greek alphabet, muft imply that Jefus is *abfolutely* the *primary* and *fole founder* of the chriftian religion, not as a fubordinate minifter *under* another, but as the real felf-exiftent fountain and fource of all life, from whom, by whom, and for whom all things are. To put any other fenfe upon the appellation *Alpha*, would be to deny the import of the word, and to fubftitute another (*Beta*, for inftance,) in it's ftead. Mofes was the founder, *under God*, of the Jewifh difpenfation. Was he therefore the *Alpha?* You muft know, that fuch a title cannot belong to any one who acts *under the directions of another*, but exclufively to *that other* who *gives* the directions, from whom the difpenfation originates, and who makes ufe of fuch inftruments, as in his divine wifdom he fees

moſt

most fit to promote his grand end, the salvation of mankind.

The true signification of Alpha and Omega, as applied to Jesus Christ, is, that he is the essential and only Being from first to last, from whom all things derive their existence; consequently that he is the essential and only love, the essential and only wisdom, the essential and only life in himself; and thus the essential and only Creator, Saviour, and Illustrator from himself; hence that he is the all in all both of heaven and the church, who alone is Infinite and Eternal, and Jehovah the Lord. All this and infinitely more is implied in the name *Alpha and Omega*, which is given to Jesus Christ exclusive of every other being whether in heaven or on earth, as in Apoc. i. 8, 11. chap. xxi. 6. chap. xxii. 13.

* * *

You say, p. 28, that a person being occasionally denominated by the name of God, is no proof that he is God; and that Christ is no more *Jehovah our righteousness*, because he is so called in Jer. xxiii. 6, than the city Jerusalem is, she being also called by the same name in Jer. xxxiii. 16. But you, who confine your ideas to the literal sense of the Word only,

give

give no information what we are to understand by Jerusalem being called *Jehovah our righteousness;* having, I apprehend, no method of reconciling the passage to your reason, but that which you mention in p. 25, of supposing *some error to have crept into the text.* This may be the shortest way of getting rid of the difficulty, but by no means a satisfactory one to those who believe the Word of God to be perfect, as we have it in the originals. It is, however, a curious circumstance, that you, whose whole system is founded on the *mere appearances* in certain parts of the *literal sense,* should yet urge the apparent inconsistency of one passage against us, who maintain that *every part* of the Word is to be understood *spiritually:* just as if *we* were the persons who rested in *the letter,* and *you* the advocate for *the spirit!* But, Sir, the argument is our's, not your's; and the above (if taken according to the common translation*) is one of the many passages which we have to bring forward, as proofs that the scriptures, in a thousand instances, are not to be understood literally, but spiritually. For that Jerusalem

the

---

* Commentators are not all agreed about the true translation of Jer. xxxiii. 16: but in which ever way it is taken literally, the internal sense must be, that the Lord alone is entitled to the name of *Jehovah our righteousness.*

Signified by the New Jerusalem.

the city cannot be Jehovah the Creator, is self-evident; and therefore, if there be any meaning at all in calling a city by the name of Jehovah, we must have recourse to the spiritual sense, which being abstracted from persons and places, can alone afford a rational and true interpretation of the words. In this sense, Jehovah our righteousness is the Lord as to divine good; the city Jerusalem is the New Church in respect to it's doctrine of charity and faith united; her name denotes her quality. Thus combining the different significations into one sentence, the spiritual meaning is simply this, That the New Church will receive it's quality of love and wisdom, good and truth, charity and faith, from the Lord alone, who is himself the all of love and wisdom, the all of good and truth, and the all of charity and faith, both in the church universal, and in every individual member thereof. See what was advanced and proved concerning the Lord praying in man, p. 117; and concerning the one only source of intelligence in the universe, p. 126.

Still you cannot believe that Jesus was God himself; for you say, " Though it should be " Christ, and not the *prophet's son*, that was
" called

"called *Emmanuel*, which signifies *God with us*, it will not follow that he was God;" because "princes are sometimes called gods, to denote their power, and men are called devils to express their bad dispositions." That you write under the influence of a *strong prejudice* against Jesus Christ, is very manifest from the above words; although I admit you may not be sensible of it, on account of it's having become *habitual* to your mind; and whatever is *habitual* or *natural* to a man, is not sensibly perceived by him. It seems you would rather allow the *prophet's son* to be called *Emmanuel*, or *God with us*, than Jesus; notwithstanding it is expressly declared at the birth of Jesus, that then "was fulfilled that which was spoken of the Lord by the prophet, saying, Behold, a *virgin* shall be with child, and shall bring forth a Son, and they shall call his name *Emmanuel*, which being interpreted, is *God with us*," Matt. i. 22, 23. How can it be, that a mere man (as you together with the Jews suppose Jesus to be) could be born of a *virgin mother?* Since the creation of the world, such a thing was never heard of, except in the *single instance* of our blessed Lord, who for that very reason could not be a mere man; for having no human father, the interior essence of his life or foul muſt be different from that of all other men; and it is well known, that every man's foul is derived from his father, and the body from his mother.

But to bring the matter to an iſſue. Either you believe that Jeſus had a *mere man* for his *father*, or you do not. If you believe the former, you are, in this reſpect, a downright Jew: I know no difference between you. If the latter, then you allow Jeſus to be *more than a mere man*, in which caſe all you have written againſt him falls to the ground, and has no more weight in it than a ſtraw. But you expreſsly maintain, that Jeſus was no more than a mere man; therefore the whole world has a right to infer, that your *private* creed is, that Joſeph, his *ſuppoſed* father, was his *actual* father.* Your ſyſtem of materialiſm alſo

---

* Since writing the above, I have found to my great ſurprize, that you have publicly declared in your firſt Letters to the Jews, that you "do not believe in the mira-
" culous conception of Jeſus; but that you are of opinion
" he was the legitimate ſon of Joſeph." From your principles, I always ſuppoſed, that this muſt be your private creed; but I did not apprehend, you would venture to go the length of publiſhing it to the world; for I underſtand, the time was, when you thought it dangerous to your

alfo implies as much; for whoever afcribes to matter the fource of intelligence, by fuppofing that fpirit is incapable of thinking, unlefs while acted upon by an influx from material fubftances, virtually afcribes the production of a foul, which in itfelf is fpiritual, to caufes in themfelves merely natural: and by the fame rule, the creation of the univerfe is by fuch a perfon attributed to nature, inftead of God. Nay, the very idea which he has of the being of a God, when explained by himfelf, is no other than that of nature, or which amounts to the fame thing, infinite fpace, as expreffed in

character, to be fufpected of fuch an antichriftian fentiment. You deny the authenticity of the firft chapter of Matthew's gofpel, poffibly becaufe Jefus is there faid to be born of a virgin, and called Emmanuel, God with us. But if you admit the fecond of Luke to be genuine, that fufficiently proves that Jefus was not the fon of Jofeph. When Jofeph and Mary his mother returned from Jerufalem, the child Jefus tarried behind. So they turned back, to feek him. "And when they faw him, his mother
" faid unto him, Son, why haft thou thus dealt with us? Be-
" hold, *thy father* (meaning Jofeph) and I have fought thee
" forrowing. And he faid unto them, How is it that ye
" fought me? Wift ye not that I muft be about *my Father's*
" bufinefs?" Luke ii. 48, 49. Here Jefus plainly denied that Jofeph was his Father; for when he was in the temple, teaching the doctors, he was not about Jofeph's bufinefs, but his Father Jehovah's.

in your *Letters to the Members of the New Church*, p. 50. But while the Word of God endures, it muſt remain an eternal truth, that Jeſus was conceived without the mediation of a man, deriving his ſoul from Jehovah the Father, and a body only from the Virgin Mary; which ſoul, being of itſelf *indiviſible*, and therefore unlike the ſoul of a finite man, muſt be Jehovah himſelf. Conſequently the whole Divinity was included in the Lord's Humanity from his firſt conception; but on the glorification of his human eſſence, that alſo was made completely divine, by the putting off or diveſting himſelf of every thing that was derived from Mary; and by virtue of it's perfect union with the Father, who was it's ſoul, it became the Divine Humanity, or in other words, the Viſible Jehovah in a Human Form.

As to the circumſtance of princes being ſometimes called *gods*, on account of their great power, which you think is the reaſon why the name *God* is occaſionally given to Jeſus, without however any intention in the writer of ſetting him forth as the true God; I have to obſerve, that an evident diſtinction is made in the uſe of the term, when applied to men or angels, and when applied to the living God.

In the former cafe, it is ufually faid, that fuch an one is *a god*, or fuch and fuch perfons are *gods*. But in the latter cafe, Jehovah is emphatically ftyled *God*, or *the God*, viz. of heaven and earth. And although in the originals the ufe of the particles, *a, the*, &c. may not be fo certain and precife as in Englifh, yet the context will invariably point out when they are to be underftood, and when omitted, according to the nature of the fubject treated of. Now it is worthy of notice, that whenever the term *God* is applied to Jefus, it is done in the fame manner, and with the fame degree of emphafis, as when applied to the great Jehovah. So in the following paffages: " They fhall call his " name *Emmanuel*, which being interpreted, is, " *God with us*," Matt. i. 2, 3. " In the be-" ginning was the Word, (Jefus,) and the Word " was with God, and *God was the Word*. And " the Word was made flefh," viz. in the perfon of Jefus, John i. 1, 14. " *God* (i. e. Jefus) was " manifeft in the flefh," 1 Tim. iii. 16. " This " (Jefus Chrift) is *the true God* and eternal life," 1 John v. 20. " Thy throne, O *God*, is for " ever and ever," Pfalm xlv. 6. Thefe words were fpoken of Jefus Chrift, and quoted by Paul, Heb. i. 8, who applies them to him as the Son of God. Whence it follows, that Jefus

being

being diftinguifhed by the title *God* in a manner widely different from that in which either angels or men are fpoken of; and having alfo names and qualities attributed to him, which can belong to none other than to the great Jehovah, he muft of confequence be the fole, the fupreme, the everlafting God of heaven and earth.

* * *

You think it fomething extraordinary, p. 28, that we, who ftrenuoufly affert the unity of God, and reject the idea of *three divine perfons*, as manifeftly implying *three Gods*, fhould yet contend for a *trinity*, although the expreffion is not to be found in the fcriptures. And you conclude, rather haftily, that we have adopted the term merely as a facrifice to popular prejudice. In this, however, you are much miftaken, as I hope to fhew you prefently. You even bring a charge againft the writer of the Preface to the *Summary View of the Heavenly Doctrines of the New Jerufalem*, for urging as a plea in favour of Baron Swedenborg's writings, that he afferts and defends the divinity of our Lord and Saviour Jefus Chrift; which plea you treat as a mere apology addreffed to the weaknefs and prejudices of the multitude. But you forget, or perhaps never confidered, that that fmall pamphlet

pamphlet was principally intended for those who profess to believe in the divinity of Jesus Christ, and not so much for Arians or Socinians, who deny it. It was therefore with great propriety that the writer addressed his readers in the language he did. -Had he intended it as an appeal to Socinians, he would, without doubt, have introduced the subject in a different manner, and reasoned with them on principles more suited to their state of mind. But be this as it might, you may rest assured, that neither that writer, nor any other member of the New Church, seeks a shelter for truth in the prejudices of mankind; of which your present opposition to the doctrines we maintain, is at least one striking proof; for had we in view secretly or insensibly to insinuate our tenets into the public mind, by flattering either the weakness or errors we discovered, we should hardly have declared ourselves in so plain and open a manner as we have done. And I believe nothing but the love of truth for it's own sake, together with a desire to contribute to the general happiness of mankind, has induced the members of the New Church to exert themselves in publishing and spreading through the kingdom at large those new but grand discoveries of divine truth, of which they

they have received the most deliberate and powerful conviction in their own minds.

I before observed, that you object to the doctrine of a *trinity*, because that expression is not found in the scriptures. On the same principle you may object to a thousand other words equally in use, when the subject of conversation is theology. But I apprehend it is sufficient, if the *thing* signified by *trinity* is clearly discoverable in the sacred writings; and that it is so, I think will appear from the following passages: " The angel said unto Mary, " The *Holy Spirit* shall come upon thee, and " the power of the *Highest* shall overshadow " thee: therefore also that holy thing that shall " be born of thee shall be called the *Son of God*," Luke i. 35. Here mention is made of *three*, viz. the *Holy Spirit*, the *Highest*, and the *Son of God*, which is evidently the same thing as a *trinity*. Again, " When Jesus was baptized, " lo, the heavens were opened unto him, and " he saw the *Spirit of God* descending like a " dove, and lighting upon him. And lo, a " *voice from heaven* saying, This is *my beloved* " *Son*, in whom I am well pleased," Matt. iii. 16, 17. Mark i. 10, 11. " John the Baptist " bare record, saying, *He* that sent me to bap-
" tize

"tize with water, *the same* said unto me, Upon whom thou shalt see the *Spirit* descending and remaining on him, the same is he which baptizeth with the *Holy Spirit*. And I saw, and bare record, that this is the *Son of God*," John i. 32, 33, 34. In both these passages a trinity, though not expressed by the very term, is yet discernible by every reader. But it is more plainly declared in the following words of our Lord to his disciples, " Go ye, and teach all nations, baptizing them in the name of the *Father*, and of the *Son*, and of the *Holy Spirit*," Matt. xxviii. 19. Also in these words of John, " There are *three* that bear record in heaven, the *Father*, the *Word*, and the *Holy Spirit ;* and these *three* are *one*," 1 John v. 7. To this may be added the further evidence arising from the circumstance of the *Lord*'s praying to his *Father*, and speaking of him, and with him, and declaring that he would send the *Holy Spirit*. The apostles also, in their epistles, make frequent mention of the *Father*, the *Son*, and the *Holy Spirit*. Hence then it is evident, that there is such a thing as a *divine trinity*, consisting of Father, Son, and Holy Spirit.* The

---

* See this subject more fully treated of in Emanuel Swedenborg's *True Christian Religion, containing the Universal Theology of the New Church*, n. 163 to 188.

The actual exiſtence of a trinity being thus eſtabliſhed, it only remains to be conſidered in what ſenſe we are to underſtand it, whether as a trinity of diſtinct perſons in the Godhead, or as a trinity of eſſentials in one divine perſon. And as this cannot be better illuſtrated, than by a reference to the three general eſſentials of man, who is ſaid to have been created *in the image, and after the likeneſs of God,* let us firſt ſee how far a human trinity can be diſcerned in him as a ſingle individual, and then we ſhall be able in ſome meaſure to comprehend how the divine trinity exiſts in the ſingle perſon of our Lord and Saviour Jeſus Chriſt.

"There are (ſays Baron Swedenborg) general, and alſo particular eſſentials of every one thing, which all together conſtitute one eſſence. The general eſſentials of every one man, are his ſoul, body, and operation; and that theſe conſtitute one eſſence, is evident from this circumſtance, that one exiſteth by derivation from the other, and for the ſake of the other, in a continued ſeries; for man hath his beginning from the ſoul, which is the very eſſence of the ſeed, and which is not only the initiating, but alſo the producing cauſe of all the parts of the body in their reſpective order, and afterwards of all acts proceeding from the foul and body united, which are called operations; wherefore, from this circumstance of the production of one from another, and their confequent infertion and conjunction one with another, it is evident, that thefe three are of one effence, and therefore they are called three effentials.

"That thefe three effentials, viz. foul, body, and operation, did, and do exift in the Lord God the Saviour, is univerfally acknowledged. That his foul was from Jehovah the Father, can only be denied by Antichrift, for in the Word of both the Old and New Teftament he is called the Son of Jehovah, the Son of the Moft High God, the Only-begotten; wherefore the divinity of the Father, anfwering to the foul in man, is his *firft effential*. That the Son, who was born of the mother Mary, is the body of that divine foul, is a confequence of that birth, inafmuch as nothing is provided in the womb of the mother except a body, conceived by, and derived from the foul : this, therefore, is a *fecond effential*. That operations conftitute a *third effential*, is a confequence of their proceeding from foul and body together; for the things that proceed are of the fame effence with the things from which they proceed.

ceed. That the three essentials, which are Father, Son, and Holy Spirit, are one in the Lord, like soul, body, and operation in man, is evident from the words of the Lord, declaring that he and the Father are one, and that the Father is in him, and he in the Father; and that in like manner he and the Holy Spirit are one, inasmuch as the Holy Spirit is the divine proceeding out of the Lord from the Father." See *True Christian Religion*, &c. n. 166, 167.

From the above observations it is plain, that a trinity, consisting of three essentials, is necessary to the full constitution of every single man; for were we to suppose any one of the essentials to be wanting, in that case man would not be man, in the proper sense of the word. As for example, let us picture to our imagination a man destitute of his first essential, which is the soul; what is he but a lifeless corpse, a mere lump of earth? So in respect to the second essential, what idea should we form of a soul without an organized body, wherein it may reside and be manifested, as in it's proper form? Or how could it exist in such a state of abstraction from all substance, as to have neither eyes to see, ears to hear, nor any other organs by which it might perceive the delights of life? Would it even amount to so much as a vapour, or breath of wind? We know that such a *mere soul* as this never did nor can exist; for without a substance there can be no property; and that, of which nothing can be predicated, must be a non-entity. Again, supposing both a soul and body to exist, without a third essential called operation, what would a man, in such case be, but a mere statue? Nay, would not the two first essentials, viz. soul and body, fall into decay, and perish, without the third, which is their proceeding operation; just as love and wisdom would perish, without their third essential, which is use?

A trinity, then, is absolutely necessary to the existence of man, as well as of every created subject in the universe; and notwithstanding your assertion, p. 30, that " the three terms," or three essentials, " are not correlative, having " no proper correspondence," it is manifest that they bear the most intimate and strict relation to each other, and form the most perfect correspondence, that unity of essence can produce. As you do not admit, any more than myself, the doctrine of a *trinity of divine persons*, such an idea evidently amounting to a *trinity* *of Gods*, it is unneceffary, in writing to you, Sir, to point out the abfurdity of fuch a notion, which even many of the Athanafian trinitarians themfelves now begin to be afhamed of.* Suffice it to obferve, that as man was created in the image and likenefs of God, and as in him is clearly difcernible a human trinity of foul, body, and operation, and yet he is but one man both in effence and perfon; fo we have both reafon and fcripture to conclude, that in the Lord God and Saviour Jefus Chrift there is a divine trinity, confifting of Father, Son, and Holy

---

* Some of the moft eminent among the Athanafian trinitarians, feeing the abfurdity of fuppofing, that the one God can exift in *three perfons*, inftead of this phrafe fubftitute that of *three offices* or *characters*. Hereby indeed they evade one abfurdity; but they entangle themfelves in another, namely, in praying to *one office* for the fake of *another office*, that it would be pleafed to fend a *third office* to fanctify and regenerate them. Thus inftead of addreffing God as an *object*, a *fubftance*, and a *form*, they call upon *three offices* one after another, when yet an office, as fuch, has neither eyes to fee, nor ears to hear their wants. God, then, does not confift in three offices, any more than in three perfons; but he confifts in *divinity* and *humanity* united in one perfon, from which proceeds *holy operation*; and thefe three, when diftinctly conceived by the human intellect, may moft properly be termed *three effentials* of one God, anfwering to a fimilar diftinction in man, of *foul, body,* and *fpirit*, or *proceeding operation*.

Holy Spirit, and yet he is but one God both in eſſence and in perſon.

* * *

Having now refuted, either directly or indirectly, every objection you have urged againſt the divinity of Jeſus Chriſt; and having proved, that he alone is the ſupreme Lord of heaven and earth, in whom the complete trinity reſides, or, as Paul expreſſes it, in whom dwelleth all the fulneſs of the Godhead bodily; I will add a few remarks on the cloſing part of your third Letter.

You addreſs the members of the New Church in the following terms, p. 30. "With " a change in your phraſeology, and very little " in your ideas, you are as proper unitarians, " as we who are uſually called *Socinians*. For " we ſay, that the *Word*, by which all things " were created, and which dwelt in Chriſt, was " the *one true God*, beſides whom there is no " other, and that without this divine principle " Chriſt was a mere man, as other men are." That we are unitarians, and that in the true and proper ſenſe of the word, (though not as generally underſtood,) I admit; for we inſiſt upon the abſolute, unequivocal unity of God, as the fundamental principle of all religion,

par-

particularly of the new and true chriftian religion, which we profefs. But while we affert the unity of God, we alfo maintain a divine trinity, not of perfons, like the Athanafian trinitarians, but of three effentials in one perfon, as already explained. Why then do you endeavour to make the world believe, that the principles of the New Church are but a ftep removed from thofe of Socinianifm? I hope you do not mean to rank every one among the number of Socinians, who believes that there is only one God. Jews, Mahometans, and Pagans, agree in this point; and what is more, they, *in common with Socinians*, and too many others who *call themfelves chriftians*, all unite in worfhipping *the fame unknown God;* with this difference, however, that chriftians might know, if they would, in preference to all others in the world, who the one living and true God is, namely, the Saviour and Redeemer of the world, Jefus Chrift. Imagining that it was fcarcely poffible for any defcription of chriftians to ftand forward in defence of the abfolute unity of God, except thofe of fimilar principles with yourfelf, it feems you have thought yourfelf juftifiable in declaring that the members of the New Jerufalem muft be fomething akin to Socinians, becaufe because the divine unity is their first and fundamental article. But you have certainly been too hasty in drawing such a conclusion; for I assure you, that no two descriptions of men in the universe are more opposed to each other, with respect to theological principles, than the *Socinian* and the *member of the New Jerusalem*. I will not even except the *Jew;* for he, not having received a christian education, does not form so full and perfect a contrast to the true christian, as a Socinian does, and is therefore on that account less guilty than him, for denying the divinity of Jesus Christ, and ranking him as a mere man. Nay, it appears very plainly from Mr. David Levi's Letters to you, Sir, that did he but believe the authenticity of the New Testament, he would not hesitate a moment to acknowledge the divinity of Jesus Christ, because he says it is therein asserted from beginning to end; and he wonders, with great reason and justness, how any person can call himself a christian, who, like you, Sir, rejects the chief corner-stone of christianity. The immense difference between your system and our's, I have already noticed in a former part of this *Defence;* to which I shall here add the following observation, That so far from there being any agreement,

ment, either in words or in reality, between Socinianism and the religion of the New Church, the relation which the former bears to the latter is like that of darkness to light, cold to heat, the nadir to the zenith, shadow to substance, matter to spirit, falshood to truth, the worship of a God in the shape of infinitely-extended space, (which is the same thing as no God at all,) to the worship of the true and living God in a Human Form, who is the adorable and ever-blessed Lord of the universe, Jesus Christ.

You acknowledge, that the Word, by which all things were created, and which dwelt in Christ, was the one true God, besides whom there is no other; but you do not allow that Jesus Christ was himself that Word, he being, as you say, no more than a mere man that had no existence till his birth in this world. Now if it can be made to appear from scripture, that Jesus Christ himself was that Word, by whom all things were created, I hope you will be candid enough to renounce your errors, embrace truth for the sake of truth, and like a man and a christian, submit to acknowledge him as your creator and sovereign, who condescended so far as to clothe himself with flesh and bones for the redemption and salvation of you, in common with all his other fallen creatures.

The evangelist John says, " In the beginning was the Word, and the Word was with God, and God was the Word.* All things were made by him; and without him was not any thing made that was made. And *the Word was made flesh*, and dwelt among us," John i. 1, 3, 14. Here it is expressly declared, first, that God was the Word, by whom all things were created; and secondly, that *the same God was made flesh*, and dwelt among us. To be made flesh can have no other meaning, than to become a *Man*. *God* therefore, having become *flesh*, when the *Word* became *flesh*, must at the same time have actually become a *Man*. This, Sir, is a conclusion drawn even from *your own premises*, to which I wish you to pay particular attention. How you will reconcile it to your declaration, p. 50, where you deny that God has any thing of a human form, I must leave to your ingenuity. I own I am incapable of doing it for you; and I fear the dilemma, in which I see you involved, is so absolute, that

you

---

* This translation is according to the original Greek.

you have no way left to extricate yourself, but by an honest and candid confession of your mistake.

Again, Jesus Christ, you acknowledge, was the only man in whom the Word dwelt. But there was in him no flesh belonging to the Word, different from his own flesh. Therefore, both by scripture and your own concessions, the flesh of Jesus Christ must be that very flesh which John meant, when he said, "*The Word was made flesh.*" Hence I infer, that Jesus Christ, who was the Word made flesh, was also the true God that created heaven and earth.

In Apoc. iv. 11, the four and twenty elders fell down, and said, " Thou art worthy, O " *Lord*, to receive glory, and honour, and " power: for thou hast created all things, and " for thy pleasure they are, and were created." In chap. v. 12, ten thousand times ten thousand cried out, " saying with a loud voice, Worthy is " the *Lamb* that was *slain*, to receive power, and " riches, and wisdom, and strength, and honour, " and glory, and blessing." Here the same glory, honour, and power, are ascribed to the Lamb that was slain, (i. e. to Jesus who was crucified,) as to the Lord the Creator of all things. Therefore I conclude in the words of Paul, that " by him (Jesus Christ) were all things " created that are in heaven, and that are in " earth, visible and invisible, whether they be " thrones, or dominions, or principalities, or " powers: all things were created by him, and " for him," Col. i. 16.

Further: " *In the Word was life*, and the " life was the *light* of men," John i. 4. Jesus says, " *I* am the way, the truth, and the *life*," John xiv. 6. " *I* am the *light* of the world," chap. viii. 12. You say the Word only dwelt in Jesus, as something distinct from him, but was not in reality Jesus. But by the above passages it is evident, that Jesus, who was the life and light of men, was *in the Word*, as well as the Word *in him*: so that whatever is said of the one, may be equally applied to the other also. Hence again results my first and last position, viz. That Jesus Christ alone is God.

It is said of the Word of God, that *he sat* upon a white horse; that he is called Faithful and True; that he doth *judge* and *make war*; that he had *eyes* like a flame of fire; that

that on *his head* were many crowns; that he had a name written which no man knew but *himself;* that he was *clothed* in a vesture dipt in *blood;* that out of *his mouth* went a sharp sword; that *he treadeth the wine-press* of the fierceness and wrath of almighty God; and that he hath on *his vesture* and on *his thigh* a name written, *King of kings, and Lord of lords,* Apoc. xix. 11 to 16. The whole of the above is evidently the description of one in a *Human Form;* and yet it is expressly said to be that of the *Word of God.* The Word of God is therefore *a Man—a King —a Lord.* But that it is no other than the Divine Man Jesus Christ, is plain from the particulars of the description, which are elsewhere applied to him in nearly the very same terms. As for instance, it is said of Jesus, that he is the *faithful* and *true* witness, Apoc. i. 5. chap. iii. 14; that all *judgment* is committed unto the *Son,* John v. 22; that the *Lamb* shall overcome, in *war,* the ten kings, for he is *Lord of lords, and King of kings,* Apoc. xvii. 14; that the eyes of the Son of Man were as a *flame of fire,* Apoc. i. 14; that out of his mouth went a *sharp two-edged sword,* verse 16; that he had a *new name written,* which no man knoweth, but he who receiveth it, Apoc. ii. 17; and of our Saviour Jesus Christ it is said, in
allusion

allusion to the work of redemption accomplished by him, that he *trod the wine-press alone*, and that his *garments were stained with blood*, Isaiah lxiii. 3. Seeing then the very same things are alike spoken of the Word, which you have acknowledged to be God, and of Jesus Christ whom you consider as a mere man, it follows, that the *Son of God* and the *Word of God* are one and the same divine principle, both having been made flesh in the single *person* of our Lord Jesus Christ.

To make it, if possible, still more manifest and undeniable, that the Word of God and Jesus Christ are the same, I shall add the following considerations. In the first chapter of John's gospel, it is said of John the Baptist, that he came to bear witness of the *Word*, as it's immediate fore-runner, " and he cried, " saying, This was he of whom I spake, He " that cometh after me, is preferred before me; " for he was before me," verse 15. In the same chapter the same words are applied to Jesus Christ, in the most decided and unequivocal manner: " The next day John seeth " *Jesus* coming unto him, and saith, Behold " the Lamb of God which taketh away the " sin of the world. *This is he* of whom I said,

" After

"After me cometh a *Man*, which is preferred "before me; for *he was before me*," verse 29, 30. In the first passage John evidently speaks of the *Word;* and in the latter he says expresly that *Jesus is he* of whom he spake. It is also said, verse 14, that the *Word* was full of *grace and truth;* and in verse 16, that *grace and truth* came by *Jesus Christ*. The *Word* is called the true *light* which lighteth every man that cometh into the world, verse 9: and Jesus says, "*I am the light of the world*," chap. viii. 12. And further, Paul declares, 1 Cor. i. 24, that Christ is the *wisdom of God*. Now the wisdom of God can be no other than the *Word of God*. Therefore the truth of my proposition again appears, That the Word of God, and Jesus Christ the Son of God, are one and the same divine principle manifested in the flesh; consequently, that as the Word of God is the true God, who was made flesh, so Jesus Christ is the same God who manifested himself in a Human Form.

* * *

You ask, p. 30, " What is the difference, " excepting in words, between saying that " Jesus was a man *united* to God, and a man " *inspired by God*, when in this case you can- " not pretend to have any proper idea to the
" word

"word *united*, or can say wherein it differs "from *inspired?*" If there be no difference in the meaning of the two expressions *united* and *inspired*, why do you object so much to the use of the former, when speaking of Jesus, and insist that the latter only is applicable to him? You know that the term *union* implies such an incorporation of two principles into one, as to preclude every idea of separability: whereas the term *inspiration* bears no such signification. A man may be *inspired* by God, as the prophets were, to write or utter whatever may be dictated to him: but he is not therefore *united* to God; for it is possible he may still be an ungodly or disobedient man, as was the case with several of the prophets mentioned in the Old Testament, viz. Balaam, Jonah, Hosea, &c. To be *united* is to become *one* like soul and body in man, or like heat and light in the sun's rays, or like essence and form, affection and thought, cause and effect. These comparisons, though they may sufficiently explain my meaning, yet fall infinitely short of conveying a perfect idea of the intimate union subsisting between the Lord's Divinity and Humanity; for the subject being in itself divine, and of course infinite, the full knowledge thereof must ever

transcend

transcend all finite capacities, whether human or angelical. Nevertheless, as we are so constituted, that an idea of the Divine Being can in some small degree be formed in a finite understanding, it is lawful for us to illustrate the mode of his existence by such things in the created world as may be supposed most to resemble it.

Such then being our idea of the *union* subsisting between Jesus and the Father, or the Humanity and the Divinity, and such the difference between it and mere *inspiration*, say not that we confound the one with the other, or that we are incapable of distinguishing between them. We know how to ascertain the difference between *union*, *conjunction*, and *inspiration*; *union* having respect to Jesus and the Father, *conjunction* to man and the Lord, and *inspiration* to the descent of divine truth from heaven to earth, particularly as manifested in the holy Word. No *mere man* can ever be so united to Jehovah, as to be *one with him*. In the person of Jesus alone such *union* was effected; for he says, " *All things* that the " *Father* hath are *mine*," John xvi. 15. " I " and my Father are *one*," chap. x. 30. Wherefore he alone must be a Divine Man. The union subsisting between the Lord and his church, considered as mere men, is more poperly termed *conjunction*, because it is between two parties who are still separate and distinct from each other, and must for ever remain so; for the ardour of the divine essence is so intense, that were any mere creature to approximate too near it, he would instantly be consumed like a stick thrown into the body of the sun. *Inspiration*, again, differs both from union and conjunction in this, that the person inspired may have no perception in himself of the truth of what he asserts, being no more than a kind of passive organ for spirits to speak by and through. Several of the prophets were, during the time of their inspiration, *possessed of spirits*, who occupied their bodies according to their own pleasure; in which situation some appeared to be insane, as Saul, when he stripped himself, and lay down naked all day and all night; see 1 Sam. xix. 24. Others received their inspiration by dreams and visions, consequently when they were not in the use of their external faculties. But those prophets, by whom the Word was written, for the most part merely wrote down what was dictated to them by spirits from the Lord, the very words which they wrote

having

having been first audibly pronounced in their ears.

After saying, that Man and God are more different in their natures, than the iron and clay in Nebuchadnezzar's image, and as incapable of forming any proper union, as those substances; from your great desire for our conversion, you add, p. 31, " Say then, in in-
" telligible language, that Jesus was a man,
" but that God was with him, and acted by
" him; and we shall be agreed in words, as
" well as in reality, and every desirable con-
" sequence will flow from it. You will then,
" as now, disclaim all plurality of Gods, to-
" gether with different persons in the trinity,
" and you will effectually secure the truth of
" all the declarations of Christ, as proceeding
" from God, *just as much as if he himself had*
" *been God.*" We already declare, in language sufficiently intelligible, that Jesus is a Man; but we go further, and acknowledge him to be the *Only Man* in the universe, from whom all other men derive those very faculties which constitute them men. Every rational and considerate person knows, that man is not man merely by virtue of his external form or body, but principally by virtue of his spirit or soul, which is a form recipient of love and wisdom

from God. This form we call the will and underſtanding, his will being a receptacle of love with all it's derivative affections, and his underſtanding being a receptacle of wiſdom with all it's derivative thoughts. Theſe are the fundamental conſtituent principles of humanity, without which man would be no better than a brute beaſt, but in proportion to his reception of which he becomes more and more a man. If then love and wiſdom, or, which is the fame thing, good and truth, are the only proper ſtandard of humanity, from which even the human form itſelf is derived; how plain is it to ſee, that God, who is the ſole fountain of love and wiſdom, muſt be the *Only Man*, from whom all others are by derivation called men! And how rational to ſuppoſe, that as the human ſoul, which is a mere receptacle of life, aſſumes to itſelf a body which it forms into it's own likeneſs, ſo Jehovah, who is eſſential life, has aſſumed to himſelf an actual Humanity, by virtue of which he is now the only ſelf-exiſtent Man in ultimate or laſt principles, as he was from all eternity the only Man in firſt principles.

From the above ſpecimen of our ſentiments concerning the Humanity of Jeſus Chriſt, you will

will readily perceive, Sir, that the members of the New Church agree with you neither in words, nor in reality. And although with you we disclaim a trinity of divine persons, as amounting to the same thing as a trinity of Gods, yet we do it upon quite different principles from those of a Socinian. The principles on which we build, are the following: 1. That there is one God only, whose essence is love and wisdom. 2. That love and wisdom must belong to a substance, whose form is verily Human; consequently that the one God, the Creator of the universe, is a Divine Man. 3. That the Lord and Saviour Jesus Christ is that one God. 4. That the Word of God contains a spiritual as well as a literal sense; that it is holy and divine in every part; that there is nothing in it redundant by human interpolations, or defective by omissions of negligence; the Divine Providence of the Lord having preserved it entire, in the original languages, till the present day. These are all *affirmative* principles, leading the mind to the true knowledge of things as they are, and thus to the positive perception of the delights of wisdom, as manifested in the two kingdoms of spirit and nature. But the principles from which you reason, are all of a *negative* quality, and in

direct

direct opposition to our's, being as follow: 1. That there is one God, of whose essence we know nothing at all, p. 61. 2. That the substance of this God is equally unknown to us; that he has no form at all, much less a human form; but if he has any form, it can be no other than that of infinite space, p. 44, 49, 50. 3. That Jesus Christ has nothing of divinity residing in him as his own, being no more than any common man, p. 21, 24, 30, 60. 4. That the Word of God does not contain a spiritual sense; that in various parts it is neither holy nor divine, but absolutely false, in consequence of the interpolations and dangerous glosses of designing men, which the Divine Providence has never interfered to prevent, p. 17, 57.*

Such is the difference between your principles and those of the New Church, which I have thus contrasted, for the purpose of preventing any person mistaking the one for the other. You seem indeed to think it is of no consequence whether Jesus be God or not; for you say, that if we will but set him down as a mere

* See also Dr. Priestley's first Letter to the Jews, p. 41; and his second Letter, part 2, p. 10, where he asserts, that the first chapter of Matthew is not authentic, and that the gospel of Luke "abounds with the most manifest improbabilities."

mere man, by whom God acted, we shall "effectually secure the truth of all the declara-"tions of Christ, as proceeding from God, "*just as much as if he himself had been God;*" which declaration of your's, if it has any meaning at all, must argue, that you consider it the same thing whether we worship the true God, or a false God; for in either case, you intimate, the consequences will be the same. Thus you make no distinction between truth and error, and that in a point which is of the highest moment, and on which our everlasting welfare depends.

The confession of a God, and the declaration that he is one, without knowing or caring *who he is*, may do very well for a Socinian, but never for a member of the New Jerusalem. With us it is by no means an indifferent matter whether Jesus Christ, or any other, be the true God; for according to the idea we entertain of God, such must the whole system of our theology be, which is founded thereon. If Jesus be not God, then the scriptures fall to the ground, and perish; revelation must be a dream, and all religion a farce. But if Jesus be God, then the scriptures remain in their purity, and we can understand them, as testi-
fying,

fying, from beginning to end, of Him alone. Therefore Him only are we bound to acknowledge; Him only to worſhip, as Creator from eternity, Redeemer in time, and Regenerator for evermore. He alone is Father, He alone is Son, and He alone is Holy Spirit. Jehovah of hoſts is his name, the Holy One of Iſrael, the mighty God of Jacob. He is Alpha and Omega, the Firſt and the Laſt, the Beginning and the End, the I Am, who is, who was, and who is to come, the Almighty. Thus there is one Lord, one God in the church, who out of his great love and mercy hath, by the aſſumption of Humanity, made himſelf viſible, approachable, and in ſome meaſure comprehenſible as a Divine Man. To Him be glory and dominion for ages of ages. Amen.

ROBERT HINDMARSH.

LETTER III.

Miscellaneous.

HAVING in the preceding Letters, I trust, sufficiently obviated the objections which you raise against the divinity of Jesus Christ, as well as against the extraordinary commission of Baron Swedenborg, I propose, Sir, in the present Letter, to make such further remarks as the remainder of your objections shall appear to require. The subjects, on which I may be led to speak, being various, my observations will naturally be of a miscellaneous kind.

* * * * *

I. *Of the Connection between Religion and the Civil Power.*

In p. 2, you say, that the members of the New Church "assign the same source to the "corruptions of christianity," as you do, viz. "false philosophy, and the interference of the "civil powers in matters of religion." From what authority you take upon you to assert this,

I know not. This, however, is moſt certain, that we by no means agree with you in theſe points. Falſe philoſophy, indeed, or ſuch as is founded on the mere fallacies of nature, as your ſyſtem of materialiſm moſt evidently is, has been one great cauſe of excluding from the human mind all perception of ſpiritual and divine truth; for while the underſtanding is ſhackled by, and confirmed in, the *appearances* of truth, every thing will be ſeen in an inverted point of view. So far therefore as men have reaſoned from fallacious principles, ſo far have they contributed to the corruption of chriſtianity as exiſting in the preſent day, whether it has been done in favour of a trinity of divine perſons, or in oppoſition to the one and only true God Jeſus Chriſt.

But I cannot paſs over in ſilence your aſſertion, that we aſſign, with you, as the cauſe of the corruptions of chriſtianity, " the in-
" terference of the civil powers in matters of
" religion;" which interference of the civil powers you call, in the ſame page, a " moſt
" unnatural alliance with the church of Chriſt."
Now, Sir, if you had given the writings of Baron Swedenborg a deliberate and attentive peruſal, and thereby informed yourſelf of the

true

true drift of the New Jerusalem doctrines, (which, previous to any attempt to confute them, you certainly ought to have done,) you might easily have discovered, that even in this particular we differ very essentially from you. We consider religion, or what in the present case amounts to the same thing, christianity, to be an *active* principle in man, influencing his life and conduct *in all the civil concerns of society;* and not as an *abstract theory* floating in the brain, without any application to uses of life. Hence it is, that we consider an alliance between the church and state, in any country, to be similar to the alliance between the soul and body; and that as in the latter case both ought to correspond and act in conjunction for the good of an individual, so likewise in the former case both ought to be united in giving energy and effect to the welfare of a community.

Of these sentiments of our's you might have been apprized before now; for having occasion to write on this very subject in the Preface to the English translation of Baron Swedenborg's *Brief Exposition of the Doctrine of the New Church,* published more than two years ago, I therein a few words stated the wisdom and propriety of there being an established religion in every nation;

nation; though I did not take upon me to point out what that religion ought to be in each country. If you will give me leave, I will here transcribe what I then afferted, and ftill acknowledge, as my fincere opinion, and moft mature judgment.

"*Every government in every country is influenced by the religion prevalent therein.* This is a truth, which, the more it is confidered, will, I believe, the more fully be acknowledged. Agreeable hereto, all wife governments have feen the neceffity of having an eftablifhed church, which fhould be fo united to the civil ftate, as to conftitute it's very life or foul; for the relation fubfifting between the church and ftate, in every country, exactly refembles that which fubfifts between the foul and body in man. The operations of both are likewife fimilar. Thus the laws and cuftoms of civil life are to the religious principles of a nation, juft what the actions of the body are to the fecret purpofes of the foul. Hence it is, that penetrating ftatefmen dread the fmalleft alteration in the ecclefiaftical laws, as dangerous to the prefent fyftem of politics; becaufe they know, that if the main fpring of action receives a new inclination, all the wheels of government muft neceffarily fubmit to a different motion. On this

this ground it was, that a noble Lord (Lord North, now the Earl of Guildford,) in the British senate, on a late occasion, with great propriety asserted, "That the church and state were so intimately connected, that they have ever gone, and still go, hand in hand, and must both stand or fall together." *Preface to Brief Exposition*, page xlvii.

In addition to the above, I would here observe, that every society of men, whether large or small, considered as to the uses which they mutually perform to each other, and viewed interiorly, is actually in a human form; so much so, that all the individuals therein, taken collectively, are viewed by an intellectual mind as forming only one man.*

The

---

* Mr. Paine, in his *Rights of Man*, part 2, p. 34, says, "A nation is *not* a body, the figure of which is to be re-"presented by the *human body;* but is like a body contained "within a *circle*, having a common center, in which every "radius meets; and that center is formed by representa-"tion." Such is the principle, upon which a great part of this author's reasoning is founded. But it is fallacious, because contrary to the true order of things both in the spiritual and the natural world: for to suppose, that the circumference of a circle produces the center, is the same thing as to suppose, that the outer gives birth to the inner,

that

The case is precisely the same with a whole nation, which is a large society of men uniting together in one common interest, and thus constituting one body, of which the king (where monarchical government prevails) is the head; the executive power, or magistrates, the arms; merchants, manufacturers, and productors, constitute the trunk of the body; women the loyns; and labourers the legs and feet. Such is the view of a whole nation, when considered as to the general uses of life: and as it is *use* which forms the individual into the human likeness, so is it *use* also which reduces a whole nation into the complete form of a single man. The same may be said of all the nations of the earth: as to the uses they perform, they are all viewed by the Lord as one man.

Now, that the trunk and feet produce the head, that the body produces the soul, or that the effect, which is posterior, produces the cause, which is prior. Nay, upon the same principles the visible world must be considered as having derived it's existence from a general fortuitous conflux of particles or atoms from the wide expanse of infinitely-extended space, till at last they arranged themselves into the present orderly system, and produced the sun as their center. Thus the assumption of one false principle, founded on fallacious appearances, and confirmed by reasonings of ingenuity, leads to the perversion and utter extinction of truth, by ascribing the creation of the universe to nature, and not to God.

Now, as it is highly proper, that every individual man should be possessed of a deliberate and settled judgment in matters of religion, which may serve as the secret spring from whence all the actions of his life ought to be derived; so should the grand man of the nation have a settled, established religion, from which, as from an internal dictate of justice, which may be called the national conscience, all his acts of legislation and jurisprudence ought to flow. The nation that is without an established religion, is like a man destitute of any fixed principle; what he does to-day, he may undo to-morrow; and every action discovers ignorance, caprice, and folly. But while I say thus much, do not so far misunderstand me, as to suppose, that I prefer the present established religion to the religion of the New Church. By no means. Yet, I conceive it to be a duty incumbent on every member of the community to contribute, as a citizen, towards the support of that religion, which the government, legally constituted, has thought proper to approve and adopt; for on any other principle, I do not see how the general interests and peace of the nation can be secured, which nevertheless every individual is bound to support, in return for the

protection

protection afforded him by the laws. No society can exist, unless it's members are kept in due obedience to those in office; and so long as the government will allow to the people the free and peaceable enjoyment of their own religious opinions, it is all that can or ought to be expected. As members of the New Church, we no doubt could wish that our religion were the established religion of the land, because we believe it to be more pure and universal than any other. But we are far from forcing our opinions on any man, as knowing that nothing short of a deliberate, rational conviction of the truth can be of any service. We therefore rest contented with the present dispensation of divine providence, and, thankful for the many blessings we already enjoy, pray for a more general reception of divine truth in the world at large, that men may freely and of their own accord embrace the new and true christian religion, as described in the Apocalypse under the character of the holy city New Jerusalem.

Such are the politics of the New Church, which I believe none of her members are ashamed to avow. Liberty of conscience is all we demand; and as for the honours and emoluments of civil or ecclesiastical offices, we leave them to those who can conscientiously comply

comply with the conditions on which they are bestowed. The Church of England may have enemies among certain Dissenters; but I hope it will never find one among the members of the New Jerusalem; for being men of peace, we wage war with neither Jew nor Gentile; the walls of our city are a sufficient bulwark against all that may assault us; and we are not so *over-anxious* about the success of our doctrines, as to use compulsive measures for their propagation, were it even in our power so to do, because we know that no other reception of them than such as is grounded in *freedom* and *rationality* can be either genuine or permanent; and besides, our confidence in the truth is so great, that we doubt not but it will effectually, though gradually, clear it's own way, against all opposition, purely by dint of it's own native authority. *Magna est veritas, et prævalebit.*

* * * * *

II. *Of the Human Form of God.*

Page 3 and 63, you say you agree with us " in the important belief of one God, and of *one* " *person* in the Godhead." A *person*, you know, is a *man*, the word never conveying any other idea

idea than that of a human substance and form. But in p. 50, you expressly deny that God has any such form, though you have no objection to his being in a *globular* form ; for by attributing to him the shape of *infinite space*, you in fact acknowledge that his form is that of a perfect *sphere* or *globe*. The phantasy of such a notion as this, scarcely requires a serious thought ; it is it's own reproach, and a disgrace to human understanding. To suppose, that He, whose wisdom produced all the various forms of animated beauty, and, as the very perfection of all beauty and sublimity united, the human form, should yet himself be in the shape of inanimate matter, like this globe of earth, or the vast space in which it revolves, is an idea so absurd, so irrational, so degrading to a being of infinite wisdom, that I am astonished how any one can for a moment give it a place in his mind. But I perceive, the reason of your falling into this gross error is, because you form all your ideas of the divine omnipresence from and according to time and space, which, however, bear no proper relation to what is spiritual or divine, as I hope presently to demonstrate.

With what propriety you say of yourself, that you agree with us in ascribing *personality* to God, while at the fame time you deny him the *form of a perfon*, is not eafy to be conceived. The form and fubftance of a brute is never called a *perfon* by any judicious writer that I know of; ftill lefs proper would it be to call inanimate matter a *perfon*, let it's form be what it may: the term, therefore, is folely applicable to a *human form*, and by no means to a being of an infinitely extended fhape, as you fuppofe God to be. "The greateft puzzle of all," you fay, "is, to afcribe to him the form of a man:" yet by pronouncing the Divine Being to be a *perfon*, and by informing the world that you *agree with us* in fuch a belief, you have, at leaft in this particular, virtually acknowledged that he is a *Man*, and thereby admitted a fentiment plainly contradictory to the reft of your notions.

But that this fentiment forms no part of your real creed, (having, as I apprehend, crept into your *Letters* by mere accident, without defign or reflection,) is pretty evident from the great pains you have taken to abolifh the idea of God's exifting in a human form. For "this opinion," you fay, p. 50, "befides being "highly degrading to the Divine Being, has no "countenance from the fcriptures, or from "reafon." But herein you lie under a grofs miftake;

mistake; for both the scriptures and sound reason testify that God is a Man. Whenever mention is made of Jehovah in the Old Testament, or of the Lord God in the New Testament, he is uniformly represented and spoken of as having the form of a man or an angel, which is one and the same thing. The following proofs will relieve me from the censure of dealing in mere assertions.

1. In the very first chapter of Genesis, it is expressly said, that God created man *in his own image;* the simplest and plainest inference from which is, that God himself must be in a human form. How else can it be said, that man is an *image* and *likeness* of God? Were a statuary to form the image of a man, and when he had finished it to say, that he had made a statue *in his own image and likeness;* would not every person who saw the work, and doubted not the accuracy of the performance, naturally conclude concerning the person of the artist, that it was exactly such, as to form and appearance, as his image represented? Why then should we dispute the Word of God himself, when he solemnly and expressly declares that he created man in his own image and likeness? If the form of God be, as you say, no other than that of

infinite

infinite space, why was not man created in such a form, that is, (as before observed,) in the form of a perfect sphere or globe? for I cannot conceive that any other finite form is at all representative of infinite extension on all sides. But man was not created in such a form; therefore God, of whom he is an image and likeness, is not infinitely extended, but in the complete form of a Man.

2. In Gen. iv. 4, Cain said to Jehovah, "Behold, thou hast driven me out this day "from the face of the earth; and from *thy face* "shall I be hid." And, verse 16, "Cain went "out from the *presence of Jehovah*." Here Jehovah is addressed and considered in all respects as if he was in a human form.

3. When men began to build the city and tower of Babel, "Jehovah *came down* to *see* "the city and the tower, which the children "of men builded," Gen. xi. 5. Here again Jehovah is spoken of, not as a being infinitely extended, but as a Man *coming down* from heaven, with *eyes* to see the building. In many other places he is represented as *speaking, seeing, hearing, walking, standing, thinking, writing, eating, swearing, repenting, coming down, going up,* &c. &c.

&c. all which expressions evidently imply a form, and several of them denote acts that exclusively indicate the human form. See Gen. xvii. 1, 9 to 22. chap. xviii. 1, 8, 13, 21, 33. Exod. xxiv. 12. chap. xxxii. 14.

4. As you seem to ridicule the idea of God being in a human form before the incarnation, as well as since, and wonder whether he had arms and legs, and whether he ever made use of them in removing from place to place, I shall refer you, for an answer to your curious inquiries, to those prophets who have seen God, and were sent by him. " Moses and Aaron, " Nadab and Abihu, and seventy of the elders " of Israel, saw the God of Israel: and there " was under *his feet* as it were a paved work of " sapphire-stone, and as it were the body of " heaven in his clearness. And upon the nobles " of the children of Israel he laid not *his hand*: " also they saw God, and did eat and drink," Exod. xxiv. 9, 10, 11. Jehovah himself said to Moses, who desired to see his glory, " Be-" hold, there is a place *by me*, and thou shalt " stand upon a rock. And it shall come to " pass, while my glory *passeth by*, that I will " put thee in a clift of the rock, and will cover " thee with *my hand* while *I pass by*. And I
" will

"will take away *my hand*, and thou shalt see *my* "*back-parts*; but *my face* shall not be seen," Exod. xxxiii. 21, 22, 23. "God *came* from "Teman," says Habakkuk, "and the Holy "One from mount Paran. He *stood*, and mea- "sured the earth. Thou didst *march* through "the land in indignation; thou *wentest forth* "for the salvation of thy people; thou didst "*walk* through the sea with thine horses," Hab. iii. 3 to 15. The prophet Nahum says, "The clouds are the dust of *his feet*," chap. i, 3. And "the Lord *stood* upon a wall made by a "plumb-line, with a plumb-line in *his hand*," Amos vii. 7. Lastly, the prophet Ezekiel, in his amazingly sublime vision of the four living creatures and the wheels, describes the great Jehovah in respect to the Word as having the form and likeness of a Man. "This was their "appearance," says he, "they had the *likeness* "*of a Man*. And above the firmament that "was over their heads, was the likeness of a "throne, as the appearance of a sapphire-stone, "and upon the likeness of the throne was the "likeness as the appearance of a *Man* above "upon it. And I saw as the colour of amber, "as the appearance of fire round about within "it: from the appearance of *his loyns* even "upward, and from the appearance of *his loyns*
"even

"even downward, I faw as it were the ap-
"pearance of fire, and it had brightnefs round
"about. This was the appearance of the like-
"nefs of the glory of *Jehovah*. And when I
"faw it, I fell upon my face, and I heard a
"*voice of one that fpake.*" Ezek. i. 4, 26, 27, 28.

In all thefe paffages Jehovah, even before the incarnation, is fpoken of as a Man. A face, hands, feet, loyns, and back-parts, are afcribed to him. He came, marched, went forth, walked, ftood, paffed by, and fpake. Nay, he is even exprefsly declared to have the *likenefs and appearance of a Man* upon a throne. Then blame not the members of the New Church for afcribing to Jehovah a Divine Human Form; for while they give credit to the holy fcriptures, they cannot help believing that God is a Man. I do not here enter into the fpiritual fenfe of the above paffages, becaufe I believe you are not difpofed to ac-company me into regions which are fo far elevated above time and fpace. I muft, there-fore, in a great meafure confine myfelf to the material fyftem, and fpeak to you in your own language, that is, according to the mere literal fenfe of fcripture; though I dare fay, that in the above and fimilar paffages which do not

agree

agree with your idea of an *infinitely extended Being*, you have recourse to figure and metaphor. The holy scriptures, however, are not written, in any part whatever, by mere *tropes, figures,* or *metaphors,* but every-where by *correspondences;* the difference between which and bare figurative expression I must reserve for explanation in another place.

" To give to God the form of man," you say, p. 50, " is to assign him all the functions " of man, and a mode of life similar to that of " man. The form of any particular animal, " beast, fowl, or fish, is adapted to it's own " occasions, and to nothing else. If the form " be changed, as from a catterpillar to a but- " terfly, the whole mode of life is changed in " proportion. In fact, therefore, to give to the " Divine Being the form of a man, is to make " him a man, and nothing more. In like man- " ner should the form of a horse be given to a " man, it would be nothing less than changing " the man into a horse."

When we assign to God the form of a Man, you should recollect that we consider him as a *Divine* and *Infinite Man,* whose functions and mode of life must also be infinite and divine.

We are the farthest in the world from afcribing to him mere human properties, or any thing that borders on mutability and imperfection. We fay he is and muft be a *fubftance*, becaufe all other fubftances are derived from him; and as we are affured that no fubftance can exift without a *form*, therefore we are under the neceffity of afcribing to God fome form or other. But we know of none equal in dignity and majefty to the *human form*; and our conceptions of divinity are fuch, as to lead us to felect, out of the infinite variety of forms with which the univerfe abounds, that which alone appears the fitteft for an intelligent Being to refide in, namely the *Human*, as being the very *perfection of form*, and that to which all other forms bear fome reference or analogy. Hence we take up the fentiments of the wifeft among the ancients, and fay with them, that *Man is a mortal God*, and *God an Immortal Man*.

This idea of God being in the form of a Man, is univerfal, having it's refidence in the *interiors* of every rational creature, in confequence of an univerfal influx from Him who is the *Only Man*. Even you yourfelf, Sir, although by external reafonings and perfuafions you may endeavour to ftifle the conviction, cannot

not possibly divest yourself of it. It appears, when you are least aware of it, in your writings, discourses, and conversation. You attribute to him will, understanding, eyes, ears, a mouth, hands, &c. &c. for these are all implied in your acknowledging that he is *merciful* and *wise*, that he *sees* and *hears*, *speaks* and *acts*, &c. &c. In short, you speak of him in all respects as a Man, assigning him functions of life that in many cases are only predicable of the human form; and although you ridicule the notion of his being either *male* or *female*, yet your constant language characterizes him as a *male*. " *He* is invisible," you say, p. 61, " but " *he* is the maker and constant preserver of all " things. This great Being has commissioned " various men, and especially Jesus Christ, to " communicate *his* will to mankind, and *he* " always sanctioned their missions by the power " of working miracles," &c. Again, " God, " *who* is invisible and omnipresent, *sees* and " *hears* us wherever we are, and *his* power " extends to all persons, and all things," p. 63. Many other passages might be quoted, wherein you equally admit, by implication, that God is a Man. If you say you are *obliged* to use such expressions on account of the imperfection of human language; I answer, It is no such thing, but an effect *spontaneously, unpremeditatedly,* and *naturally* flowing from an interior perception, common to all men, of the true human form of God. Nor is our language so imperfect, but it will readily admit of the variation of your terms from the *masculine* to the *neuter* gender. Thus, if you really think, that God is neither male nor female, nor in any other shape than that of infinite space, you are at perfect liberty to speak of him in the following manner: 'God, *which* is invisible, sees and hears us 'wherever we are, and *it's* power extends to 'all persons and things. Although *it* is in- 'visible, yet *it* is the maker and constant pre- 'server of all things. *It* has commissioned va- 'rious men to communicate *it's* will to man- 'kind, and *it* always sanctioned their missions 'by the power of working miracles,' &c. But I apprehend you would not venture to speak in such terms of any being possessed of common rationality; much less of him who is the sole fountain and source of all wisdom. And yet, to be consistent with yourself as a philosopher and grammarian, acknowledging God under no form but that of infinite extension, which is undoubtedly *neuter*, you are certainly bound to adopt this new style of writing for the future.

If,

If, as you say, our giving to God the form of a man, be to make him a man, and nothing more; it follows by parity of reason, that your giving him the form of infinite space, is to make him infinite space, and nothing more; for, according to your own doctrine, whatever the form be, such is the true denomination of the substance or being, of which it is the form. In consequence of our acknowledging God as existing in a human form, we, in strict conformity to our principles, declare him actually to be a *Divine Man*. So you, in your turn, to shew your consistency, ought without reserve plainly to avow your belief, that God, being in the form of infinite space, is in fact nothing else but *infinite space;* or, if you reason agreeably to your declaration in p. 50, you must naturally conclude, that as God cannot possibly have any form, so he cannot have any existence at all. Such are the consequences necessarily attendant on the false premises which you have chosen as the basis of your religion; a scheme so visionary, and destitute of all rationality, that I wonder you are not ashamed of lending your name to it's support.

The light of reason is of itself sufficient to overthrow your whole system: but if we come to examine your assertions by the Word of God, we shall find them no less opposed to the plain language of divine inspiration, than to the dictates of sound reason. You say, "should the form "of a horse be given to a man, it would be "nothing less than changing the man into a "horse." Now in Apoc. ix. 7, it is said, that "the *shapes* of the *locusts* were like unto horses "prepared unto battle." Here I would ask you, whether the locusts, in consequence of being in the form of horses, were real horses; or whether they remained locusts still ? Again, the devil is represented as being in the form of a *dragon* or *serpent*, Apoc. xii. 3, 9. Is he therefore no more than a dragon or serpent? And is the whole mode of his life thereby so changed, that he cannot perform any other functions, than such as are proper to a reptile of the earth? So again, the seven churches were seen by John in the form of seven *golden candlesticks*, Apoc. i. 12. Is the church therefore nothing more than a candlestick? Jesus Christ, whom you allow to be a man, is spoken of as appearing in the form of a *Lamb* standing upon mount Sion, Apoc. xiv. 1. Do you, on that account, consider him as having been actually transformed into a lamb? Again, the Spirit of God descended from heaven like a

dove,

dove, and rested on Jesus, John i. 32. Will you therefore insist upon it, that the Spirit of God is no more than a dove? Lastly, you yourself have acknowledged, p. 30, that " the " one true God, besides whom there is no other, " is the *Word*." Now the Word has made it's appearance among men literally in the form of a book: from your own principles therefore it necessarily follows, that the one true God, who is the Word, is nothing else but a book. I should be very sorry to draw any unfair conclusions from the premises you lay down; but really, Sir, according to the best of my understanding I cannot help judging, that both your theological and philosophical systems are radically defective; and therefore, as I am myself in pursuit of truth, I hope I may be permitted, without offence, to inform my neighbours where I think it is *not* to be found. The traveller, who avoids the paths of error, cannot fail to take the right road.

Before I quit this subject, I find myself disposed to answer with seriousness a question, which you apparently put by way of ridicule. Your words are as follow: " Was the divine " form *male* or *female*? Since the two sexes " correspond to each other, he ought to be
" both,

" both, or neither." To which you add, " Indeed, gentlemen, it is impossible to con- " sider your opinions on serious subjects with " perfect seriousness." Now, Sir, if for a moment you will put away the smile that sits upon your countenance, I will endeavour to give you all the satisfaction in my power, by stating, in a few words, my reasons for considering the great Creator of the universe to be a *Male Man*, and not a female. But as every question relative to the Divine Being ought to be treated with all the reverence due to his holy name, I hope no expression that may drop from my pen, will give any just occasion of offence to the reader.

The distinguishing characteristic of a male is *activity;* while that of a female is *re-activity*. Thus God, as an *active* Creator, is properly *male;* and the whole creation, as a *re-active* subject, is properly *female*. In a more particular point of view, the Lord is the *Bridegroom*, and the church his *Bride;* or, to be still more explicit, primary love, which is a love that produces wisdom, is *masculine*, while secondary love, which is the love of that wisdom when produced, is *feminine*. The Lord, as to his proper person, is divine love or divine

divine good, not however to the exclusion of wisdom or truth, but rather to it's propagation; for divine truth is not so much *in* the Lord, as *proceeding from* the Lord, just as light is not *in* the body of the sun, but *proceeds from* the sun. Now as divine good, or primary love, constitutes the person of the Lord, while divine truth, together with it's secondary love, is only a proceeding from the Lord, it follows, that the *male* principle essentially resides *in him*, and that the *female* principle commences *out of him*. Thus the human soul, although it came *from God*, and is also conjoined *to God*, yet being *out of God*, and consequently *female* in respect to God, is *not a part of God*. Hence I infer, that God, as Creator, Redeemer, and Regenerator, is truly and properly a *Divine Male Man*; and that the whole angelic heaven, as created, redeemed, and regenerated, is truly and properly a *Grand Female Man*; or in other words, that the Lord God Jesus Christ is an *Husband*, who hath taken to himself, in celestial marriage, the church universal for his *Wife*.

To enter more fully into the discussion of this grand subject, perhaps may not be prudent in the present instance, as I know not how my readers may be affected with what has been already advanced. For my own part, such an

H h   investiga-

investigation would be highly agreeable, and I think equally serviceable in assisting us to form just conceptions of the person and attributes of the Creator, and the necessary distinction between him and his creatures. But as I have neither time nor ability to do justice to the subject, I must leave all deficiencies to be supplied in the mind of the true spiritual philosopher. I may however just remark, that that must be a gross system of materialism indeed, which excludes from the Divine Being all form or personality whatever, and reduces to a state of mere *neutrality* that God, from whom both the *male* and *female* principles of humanity, with all their innumerable felicities, are continually derived.

To say, that love, wisdom, and life, have no relation to form, as you do p. 51, appears to me the same as if you had asserted, that sight has no relation to the eye, nor hearing to the ear; yet in both cases the faculty is inseparably united with it's organ. But the sentiments you now express seem in direct opposition to the hypothesis laid down in your *Disquisitions on Matter and Spirit*. You there assert, vol. i. p. 48, " that the powers of sensation and thought are " the *necessary result* of a particular *organization*" of the brain; that is, of a particular *form*. But here you ask, " What relation have wif- " dom, love, and life, to *form?*" and then add, " It refembles Addifon's apparition, which was " in the fhape of *the found of a drum*." Really, Sir, I cannot but think you have been ridiculing our fyftem, at the expence of your own. If neither thought nor fenfation can exift in man, without being connected with form, which is a doctrine you have taken great pains to eftablifh; how comes it to pafs, that you fhould have fo far forgotten your own principles, as to declare, that wifdom, love, and life, when predicated of the Divine Being, cannot poffibly have any relation to form? Perhaps you will fay, it is true of man, but not of God. I afk, How do you know this? Sound philofophers, I have ever underftood, reafon from and according to what they actually know. But here you draw conclufions plainly repugnant to your premifes, and form a judgment in defiance of evidence.

In the aforefaid volume of your *Difquifitions on Matter and Spirit*, throughout, particularly in p. 177, 182, 185, your avowed fentiments are, that God is fubject to extenfion, that he has properties in common with matter, that he bears relation to fpace, and laftly, that he is himfelf himself absolutely *material*. Now all matter is form; it follows therefore from your own principles, that God, if he be material, must also have a form; for as an individual atom cannot exist without it's particular form, so neither can the universal bulk of matter, of which the individual atom is a part, exist without it's form. And God, you say, is extended through all matter, insomuch that he is in all respects material, having nothing of immateriality about him; wherefore it again follows, according to your hypothesis, that God is in the exact form of the universal bulk of matter. If you suppose matter to be infinitely extended, then you also allow God to be infinitely extended along with it. But if your scheme admits of a limitation to the extension of matter, then God himself must be limited to that form, be it what it may; for such is the necessary consequence of ascribing to God a material existence, or allowing him no properties but such as are inseparably connected with matter.

As to the shape of the sound of a drum, to which you pleasantly enough resemble the form of wisdom, love, and life; give me leave to observe, that by such a comparison you only

expose

expose your own principles, and furnish me with an additional occasion of pointing out their absurdity. The sound of a drum, you know, is propagated in all directions from the center of percussion. Consequently it's shape can be no other than that of a circle, the nearest resemblance of infinite space, among all the forms with which we are acquainted. Now you have already acknowledged, that God, if he has any form at all, must be in the form of infinite space; therefore I have a right to turn the tables upon you, and say, that the God, whom Dr. Priestley worships, exactly " resembles Addison's apparition, which " was *in the shape of the sound of a drum.*"

But waving these considerations, let me seriously hope, that you will re-examine your peculiar tenets, and on pure conviction be led to adopt a more rational system of religion; a system that can present to your view a God arrayed in all the glory of a Divine Human Form, and as such visible, accessible, and in some sort comprehensible by his finite creatures; a system that represents God as the mild and gracious *Father* of the human race, rejoicing in their joy, and sympathizing with them in their sorrows, from those *bowels* of

infinite

infinite mercy and compassion, which are alone predicable of a *Divine Humanity*, and *Human Divinity*. You will then perceive the true import of those words in John's gospel, " In the beginning was the Word, and the Word was with God, and God was the Word. And the Word was made *Flesh*, and dwelt among us, (and we beheld his glory, the glory as of the only-begotten of the Father,) full of grace and truth," John i. 1, 14.

* * * * *

III. *Of the Union of Divinity and Humanity in the Person of Jesus Christ, and at the same Time of the Divine Omnipotence.*

It may naturally be expected, that the person, who denies the possibility of the Divine Being assuming to himself a human form, will object likewise to the means whereby such an event was accomplished. Accordingly in p. 34, you take occasion to remark, " that of what kind soever was the union that was to be formed between the divine essence and the human body, and whatever purpose it was intended to answer, it is extraordinary that he who is omnipotent, and who made all things by a word speaking, should not have

" effected

"effected this union but in a course of time;
"and Mr. Swedenborg gives us no assistance
"whatever in forming any idea of the manner
"in which trials or temptations promoted this
"union, or why one degree of union (if there
"be such degrees) might not have answered the
"purpose as well as another. But, admitting
"all this, why different modes of speaking
"should be adopted by our Saviour in the
"different stages of this union, is particularly
"incomprehensible, since, in all the cases, both
"the person speaking, and the person spoken
"to, must have been the very same, the divine
"mind."

I have already explained, in a preceding part of this *Defence of the New Church*, p. 112 to 118, and 125 to 136, how the person speaking, and the person spoken to, may with propriety be said to be one and the same. It is therefore unnecessary to repeat what was there advanced, or even to add any thing further on the same subject; for if the principle on which I reasoned be just, it will of itself be sufficient to clear up all the apparent difficulties respecting the different modes of speaking, which our Lord adopted during the different stages of his union with the Father;

but

but if, on the contrary, the truth of my obfervations be not admitted, any further reafoning on the fame principle would be needlefs and fuperfluous.

You feem to think it an extraordinary thing, that fuch union, if it ever took place, was not effected inftantaneoufly, but gradually. But herein you only difcover how crude and undigefted your ideas of the divine omnipotence are; imagining no doubt, that God, becaufe he is omnipotent, can do whatever is propofed, even though the propofition fhould imply a breach of divine order. This, indeed, is the common belief of the prefent day, from whence have arifen fo many phantafies refpecting the power of God, as, that he created the univerfe out of nothing merely " by a word fpeaking;" and that this creation was effected in an inftant; that God, by virtue of his omnipotence, is able to fave all the human race, nay even to turn devils into angels, and hell into heaven; that man cannot live after death, until the foul is re-united with the body, and again endued with it's external fenfes; and that the material body, although devoured by worms and fifh, and in a variety of forms entering into the conftitution of other bodies, will by a

fovereign

sovereign act of divine omnipotence be again raised and collected together, at the supposed time of the general judgment, when the visible heavens and the whole habitable earth are to pass away and perish. These and many other groundless notions about the divine omnipotence are in daily circulation both among the learned and the simple; few being able to see, that the power of God is bounded by the laws of his own order, which cannot be transgressed even by omnipotence itself; because this would imply, that God, who is essential order, could go out of himself, and thereby act contrary to himself, which is a manifest absurdity.

Of all such as entertain an idea of God's absolute, unlimited power, and who suppose that the universe was created by the mere utterance of a word, I would ask, 1. Why was the omnipotent hand of God employed six* days in arranging the work of creation, when " a word speaking" could as completely and as instantaneously have brought it to it's present order,

---

* The creation spoken of in the first chapter of Genesis, does not at all allude to the creation of the visible universe, but solely to the regeneration of man, as may be seen abundantly proved by Emanuel Swedenborg in his *Arcana Cœlestia*.

order, as originally called it into being? 2. Why did not God, on the creation of man, immediately place him in heaven, without laying him under the necessity of first passing through this present state of probation? particularly as it is his desire, that all men should be saved, and be happy for ever? 3. If he needs must place him in this natural world, why has he ordained, that he shall pass so many years in a state of helpless infancy, before he can possibly have any true knowledge of him as his Creator and adorable Benefactor? 4. Why has not God, by his omnipotence, established one true religion over the whole earth? And why has he permitted so many heresies to distract the christian world in particular? 5. Why did he not send the Messiah into the world immediately after the fall, in order to recover man from the lost state into which he had plunged himself, without waiting for the lapse of so many ages; when from the beginning he foresaw that wickedness would increase on the earth, and that all the endeavours of his prophets, forerunners of the Messiah, would be ineffectual to reclaim the world? 6. Why does not God miraculously and irresistibly compel every rational being to acknowledge him alone as the sovereign of the universe, and

by

by a sudden interposition of divine authority at once put an end to the present controversy, and remove every possible doubt from every human mind with respect to the true and proper divinity of Jesus Christ? These, and a great variety of other questions of a similar nature, will be found extremely difficult to be answered by any person who imagines, that the divine omnipotence has no bounds or limits, but that it can be equally exerted in the performance of what is contrary to order, as of what is agreeable to order. All these things, however, are easily accounted for, when we know the laws of divine order, within and according to which every act of omnipotence must necessarily be confined and determined. The reason why the angels of heaven so far excel the spirits of hell in respect to power, is because the former act agreeable to order, while the latter are in opposition to it; and in proportion to their love of, and agreement with order, such invariably is their power. Were they to depart from order, their power would depart from them at the same time. Just so, God, being infinite and essential order, is in consequence thereof possessed of infinite and essential power. Were he in any measure to depart from his own order, he would in the same

same proportion immediately lose his omnipotence. But as to depart from order would be the same thing as to depart from himself, it is evident, that the divine omnipotence can perform nothing but what is consistent with the laws of order, and that every supposition to the contrary is both irrational and absurd.

With respect to the union of the divine essence with the human, which you object against not only in point of fact, but also as to the manner of it's completion, in that it is stated to have been gradual, and not instantaneous, the following passages from the Word will be sufficient to establish the truth of the proposition. " The child (Jesus) *grew* and *waxed* " *strong in spirit*, filled with wisdom; and the " grace of God was upon him. And Jesus " *increased* in wisdom and stature, and in favour " with God and man." Luke ii. 40, 52. Jesus said, " Father, glorify thy name. Then came " there a voice from heaven, saying, *I have both* " *glorified it*, and *will glorify it again*," John xii. 28. " When Judas was gone out, Jesus said, " *Now is the Son of man glorified*, and *God is* " *glorified in him*. If God be glorified in him, " God shall also glorify him in himself, and shall " *straightway glorify him*." John xiii. 31, 32.

Hence

Hence it is plain, that the union of the Humanity and the Divinity, which by the evangelists is called *glorification*, was not effected all at once, but by degrees; and that it became more and more perfect by means of temptations or sufferings which the Lord underwent during his continuance upon earth, until by the passion of the cross it was perfectly completed. Wherefore the Lord, after his resurrection, saith, " Ought not Christ to have *suffered* these things, " and to enter into *his glory* ?" Luke xxiv. 26.

But you object, p. 35, " It happens unfor-
" tunately for your hypothesis, that when Christ
" spake of the Father as being *one with himself*,
" it was at a period prior to his last sufferings,
" by which you say this union was completed."
To which I answer, His last suffering was indeed the last act of glorification in this world; but as the union of Humanity and Divinity was gradually effected, in every stage of his sufferings the Lord was *so far* one with the Father, as that union was promoted, and *no farther*. This is the sense in which we uniformly understand the Lord's words prior to his last sufferings : but after his resurrection he says, " *All power* is given unto me in heaven " and in earth," Matt. xxviii. 18 ; plainly implying,

plying, that a full union had taken place between his divine and human nature. It may not, however, be amiss here to remark, that as the gospels were written a considerable time after the Lord's full glorification and ascension, consequently at a time when he was perfectly one with the Father, the terms of inspiration are occasionally such as to have some respect to that circumstance, as well as to the gradual process of the glorification under an historical point of view; and it is not unusual for the precision of the literal sense to give way to the spiritual sense, which is within or above it. Two or three remarkable instances of this kind may be seen in the note below.*

I am

---

* 1. It is said, Exod. xii. 40, that "the sojourning of the "children of Israel, who dwelt in Egypt, was four hun- "dred and thirty years." But according to the scripture chronology they were in Egypt no more than 215 years, which is only half of the time stated in the above passage; for Moses sprung from Amram, Amram from Kohath, and Kohath from Levi, and Kohath went with his father Levi into Egypt, Gen. xlvi. 11. Now the age of Kohath was 133 years, Exod. vi. 18; the age of Amram 137 years, verse 20; and the age of Moses, when he stood before Pharaoh, 80 years, Exod. vii. 7. All these years added together make only 350, which are considerably short of 430; and therefore it is impossible the children of Israel could have been 430 years in Egypt. No mention is made

how

I am fenfible, that while you deny the fact of the Lord's glorification, or union with the Divinity, it will be to little purpofe to explain the mode of it's accomplifhment. However, as

how old Kohath was when Amram was born, nor how old Amram was when Mofes was born; but in all probability they were advanced in years. If we fuppofe them to have been about the age of 67, and for both their ages deduct 135 from 350, it will leave 215, the real number of years the Ifraelites fojourned in Egypt, according to the chronology of the fcriptures. This variation from the hiftorical truth of the fact, is on account of the internal fenfe, which requires the number 430 as it's proper correfpondent expreffion, and not 215, although this latter would have been more ftrictly conformable to the literal tranfaction. But as in the fpiritual world there is neither time nor fpace, and the Word of God is written as well for the ufe of angels and fpirits, as of men; therefore the literal fenfe, which is *in* time and fpace, occafionally gives way to the fpiritual fenfe, which is *above* time and fpace, juft as a fervant or an inferior gives way to his mafter or fuperior.

2. Another inftance, wherein the literal fenfe of the Word diverges from the ftrictnefs of hiftorical fact, by way of fubmiffion to it's fpiritual fenfe, is the following in Matt. xxvii. 9, 10. " Then was fulfilled that which was " fpoken by *Jeremy* the prophet, faying, And they took the " thirty pieces of filver, the price of him that was valued, " whom they of the children of Ifrael did value; and gave " them for the potter's field, as the Lord appointed me." Now this paffage is not to be found in *Jeremiah*, but in
Zechariah,

as you have thought proper to state your objections to the manner, as well as to the thing itself, I must beg leave to add a few more observations on this very important subject.

All

Zechariah, chap. xi. 12, 13; yet so far is this circumstance from invalidating the authority of Matthew's gospel, that, when properly understood, it rather furnishes a proof of the evangelist's divine inspiration, as I have already shewn in the *Magazine of Knowledge*, &c. vol. i. p. 451; the substance of which explanation I shall here transcribe. It is to be observed, that all the prophets represent the Word, or doctrine drawn from the Word, or the state of the church as to it's reception of the Word. Consequently every particular prophet represents some specific doctrine taught by the Word, and deducible therefrom. Thus the prophet Jeremiah represents that doctrine of the Word, which treats of the rejection of the Lord by the Jews, and the vastation of the church; and this not only in the particular prophecy which bears his name, but in *every other book of the Word* where that is the subject treated of. Hence it is, that Matthew, being under the burden of divine inspiration, when he would quote that part of the Word, which points out the low estimation in which the children of Israel valued the Lord, (signified by the thirty pieces of silver given for the potter's field,) brings forward a passage to that puport from *Zechariah*, and says, " Then " was fulfilled that which was spoken by *Jeremy* the pro- " phet ;" for *that doctrine is the prophet Jeremy* wherever it occurs throughout the Word, whether it be, according to the letter, in Isaiah, or in Jeremiah, or in Ezekiel, or in Daniel, or in Zechariah, or in any other of the prophets.

In

All temptation arises from a disagreement between the internal and external man, and is permitted for the purpose of promoting their union. But this union cannot be effected, unless the satisfactions or delights of the external man, which are in opposition to the delights of the internal man, be resisted, overcome, and removed. Now as it is impossible for those delights to be resisted, except during the moments of their excitation; therefore, by the Divine Providence of the Lord, which operates for the sake of salvation, they are permitted occasionally to affect every man, who has entered upon a state of regeneration. He who is influenced by the love of what is good and true, will not at such times suffer himself to be seduced

In like manner *Moses* means all the historical part of the Word, and *Elias* all the prophetical part.

3. Of the many other instances of a similar nature to be found in the scriptures, I shall only adduce a third. In Gen. xiv. 14, 16, Lot is called the brother of Abram, although in reality he was Abram's brother's son, as may be seen in verse 12 of the same chapter. This likewise was for the sake of the internal sense, which required that Lot should first be considered as the nephew of Abram, and afterwards as his brother. Had it been expressed otherwise, the series of the internal sense would have been interrupted, which is yet more necessary to be observed than that of the literal sense.

K k

seduced by the delights of the senses; but throwing them as it were behind his back, he breaks the force of habitual evil, and by degrees elevates his mind to pleasures of a more rational and spiritual nature, into the full enjoyment of which he at length enters. This comparison may help to give a faint idea how and in what manner the Lord's Humanity and Divinity were united by means of repeated temptations, trials, or conflicts with the powers of hell: for as the regeneration of man is an image of the Lord's glorification, or union with the Divinity, so the orderly accomplishment of the one marks out the gradual process of the other.

It is an undoubted truth, that the Lord could not be tempted as to his divinity; for it is impossible that the powers of hell should assault what is divine. For which reason, and that he might put himself into a capacity of fighting against them as it were *upon their own ground*, he was pleased to assume the human nature by actual birth from a virgin; which human nature, so received from a woman, was such that it might be tempted, suffer hunger and thirst, and lastly die. To this Humanity adhered the evils not only of Mary his mother, but of the whole human race; in consequence

of

of which his temptations were, more terrible and grievous than those of any other man; for singly and by his own power he fought against, and overcame all hell. This is expressed by Isaiah in the following terms: " Surely he hath "*borne our griefs*, and *carried our sorrows*: he " was wounded *for our transgressions*, he was " bruised *for our iniquities*: the chastisement of " *our peace* was upon him, and with his stripes " we are healed. Jehovah hath laid on him " *the iniquity of us all*: for the *transgression of my* " *people* was he stricken." Isaiah liii. 4, 5, 6, 8. Without an adherence of evil it would have been impossible for the Lord to be tempted at all; for evil is that by which temptation comes, and which at such times is excited by the approach of infernal spirits. With the Lord however, let it be well remarked, *there was no actual or proper evil*, as there is with all men, but *only hereditary evil* from the mother; and even this hereditary evil, which is barely an inclination or incitement to evil, the Lord also afterwards completely exterminated from his Humanity, insomuch that he is now no longer in any wise the son of Mary, there not being in him the smallest particle of dust, or any thing else derived from her. So that, as from the beginning he was never the son of Joseph, Matt. i. 25.

Luke ii. 49, in like manner after the crucifixion he was not the son of Mary, according to his own words in John xix. 26, 27.

There is therefore a great distinction to be made between the Humanity derived from Mary, and the Humanity derived from Jehovah. The former Humanity had an adherence of hereditary evil, and was capable of being tempted and of suffering death: but the latter, which is properly the Divine Humanity, was, like the pure Divinity itself, ever incapable of both. The Humanity from Mary was *infirm*, like that of any other man: but the Humanity from Jehovah was *omnipotent*, being the very *arm of Jehovah*, Isaiah liii. 1. The Humanity from Mary was *put off:* but the Humanity from Jehovah was *put on.* The Humanity from Mary was a *receptacle of life:* but the Humanity from Jehovah was, like the Divinity, *life itself,* John v. 26. chap. vi. 48. chap. xi. 25. chap. xiv. 6. The Humanity from Mary was forty days in the wilderness *tempted of the devil,* who *carried him about, placed him* on the pinnacle of the temple, and *took him* to an exceeding high mountain: but the Humanity from Jehovah, when Jesus *took himself* into an high mountain, and was there transfigured before Peter, James, and John, did shine as the sun in it's brightness. Such was the appearance of his face; and as to his raiment, it was white as the light, Matt. xvii. 1, 2. The same Humanity from Jehovah, so far from being tempted or assaulted by devils, *put them* to instant consternation and flight; " and they cried out, saying, *What have we to* " *do with thee*, Jesus, thou *Son of God?* Art " thou come hither to torment us before the " time?" Matt. viii. 29. Luke iv. 41. chap. viii. 28. Again, the Humanity from Mary was *material*, and as such, subject to the laws of material visibility, tangibility, gravity, and locality; witness his apprehension, crucifixion, and burial. But the Humanity from Jehovah is *not material*, but *substantial*, and as such, incapable of being seen by a material eye, or touched by a material hand; neither is he subject to any laws of gravity or locality, but is *omnipresent* with his Humanity as well as his Divinity.

In proof of these assertions, I need only bring the following passages from the New Testament. That the Humanity of Jesus, after his resurrection, was *not material*, is plain from John xx. 19, where it is said, that Jesus

came

came and stood in the midst of his disciples, *when the doors were shut*. That his Humanity is nevertheless *substantial*, is declared in these words: Jesus said, "Behold *my hands* and *my* "*feet*, that it is I myself: *handle me*, and see; " for a spirit hath not *flesh and bones*, as ye see " *me have*," Luke xxiv. 39. He also took a piece of a broiled fish, and of an honey-comb, and *did eat* before them, verse 42, 43, of the same chapter.

That the Divine Humanity of the Lord is *incapable of being seen* by a material eye, is proved from this circumstance, that his apostles, even before his crucifixion, could not see it, except when they were in the spirit; as at the time of the transfiguration before Peter, James, and John, they could not see his glorified body until their spiritual eyes were opened; for it is said, "As he prayed, the fashion of " his countenance was altered, and his raiment " was white and glistering. But Peter, and " they that were with him, were *heavy with* "*sleep*: and *when they were awake*, they saw " *his glory*, and the two men that stood with " him," Luke ix. 29, 32. Their being heavy with sleep, and afterwards waking, denotes their change from a natural state to a spiritual one;

one; for the life of the body, with all it's external sensations, compared to the life of the spirit, is like a state of sleep compared to a state of wakefulness. But that the Divine Humanity is incapable of being seen by a material eye, is further evident from the circumstance of the Lord's being invisible to all after his resurrection, except to those whose spiritual eyes were first opened for the express purpose of beholding him: wherefore it is written, that "*their eyes were opened*, and they "knew him; and he *vanished out of their sight*," Luke xxiv. 31. The case was the same with the women who visited his sepulchre after his resurrection, and saw two angels, whom it was impossible to see with the material eye, but with the eyes of their spirit only; for it is a true maxim, That *like only can see it's like.*

That the Divine Humanity cannot be *touched* by a material hand, is a consequence of it's not being material, but substantial, as already proved. A material hand can touch nothing but what may equally as well be touched or obstructed by material doors and walls. But Jesus entered among his disciples when the doors were shut: therefore as his glorified body had no relation to the materiality of a door,

door, fo neither can it have any relation to the materiality of an hand. Whence it follows, that the Divine Humanity is not tangible by material hands. It may poffibly be objected, 'Did not Jefus himfelf fay to his 'difciples, "*Handle me*, and fee;" and to 'Thomas in particular, "Reach hither thy "*finger*, and behold my hands; and reach " hither thy *hand*, and *thruft it into my fide?*" I anfwer, He did fo; but not till the difciples and Thomas were in the fpirit; and a fpiritual eye, and a fpiritual hand, can fee and touch a fpiritual or fubftantial body, but a material eye and hand cannot.

That the Divine Humanity is *not fubject to the laws of gravity*, is evident both from his refurrection out of the grave, and from his afcenfion into heaven. Concerning his afcenfion it is thus written: " And it came to " pafs, while he bleffed them, he was parted " from them, and *carried up into heaven*," Luke xxiv. 51. Now no material body ever did or can afcend to heaven; but the divine body that came down from heaven, that alone hath returned back to heaven. The circumftance of Enoch and Elijah being tranflated to heaven, is not to be underftood literally, but fpiritually;

for

for our Lord says, "*No man* hath ascended "up to heaven, *but he that came down from* "*heaven*, even the *Son of Man* who is in heaven," John iii. 13.

Lastly, That the Divine Humanity is *omnipresent*, may not only be gathered from the passage in John last quoted, where it is said, that the Son of Man, even while on earth, was still in heaven, but also from the following words, which Jesus uttered immediately before his ascension: " Lo, *I am with you always* even "unto the consummation of the age," Matt. xxviii. 20. It also appears from the promise which the Lord made to his disciples, that on his leaving them he would send the comforter to abide with them for ever; which comforter or spirit of truth, he at the same time gave them to understand, was no other than himself: " I will not leave you comfortless; *I will come* "*to you*," John xiv. 18. From which it is plain, that although the Lord hath ascended up into heaven, yet he is still upon earth; consequently that his Divine Humanity is omnipresent.

Such is the doctrine of the New Church concerning the Divine Humanity, and it's distinction

tinction from the infirm humanity derived from Mary; the former being the object of our worship, and not the latter. All therefore that you have said in p. 63, about the union of an infirm human body to the divine nature, and the necessity of it's impeding, instead of facilitating the divine operations, as it does not apply to our doctrines, when rightly understood, falls to the ground of it's own accord, and loses itself among those numerous other objections, which are frequently started by persons who have not made themselves masters of the subject.

To be well acquainted with the doctrines of the New Church, particularly in respect to the glorification of the Lord's Humanity, it is necessary to study Baron Swedenborg's *Arcana Cœlestia* with great attention; for therein not only the fact itself is clearly demonstrated, but the reasons are also stated why such a process was inseparable from the work of redemption. I shall here only quote the following passages respecting the infirm humanity which the Lord derived from Mary. "The Lord," says he, *Arc. Cœl.* n. 1414, "was as another man in every respect but as he was conceived of Jehovah; nevertheless he was born

born of a woman, a virgin, and confequently by his nativity contracted infirmities from the virgin mother, fuch as are common to other men; which infirmities were corporeal. There are two hereditary principles connate in man, one derived from the father, the other from the mother; the hereditary principle of the Lord derived from the Father was divine, but that from the mother was an infirm humanity. This infirm part or principle, which man deriveth hereditarily from the mother, is fomewhat corporeal, which is difperfed during regeneration; but what man deriveth from the father, remaineth to eternity." And again, explaining Gen. xiii. 7, where it is faid, that the Canaanite and Perizite were then in the land, by whom are underftood evils and falfes in the Lord's external man, he adds, n. 1573, " It may be matter of furprize to many to hear fpeak of hereditary evil from the mother being with the Lord; but whereas it is here declared fo manifeftly, and the fubject treated of in an internal fenfe is concerning the Lord, there can be no reafon at all to doubt it's being fo. For it is altogether impoffible for one man to be born of another man, but he muft thence derive evil: neverthelefs there is a difference between hereditary evil which is derived from

the father, and that which is derived from the mother: hereditary evil from the father is of a more interior nature, and remaineth to eternity, for it cannot by any means be eradicated. The Lord, however, had no such evil appertaining to him, inasmuch as he was born of the Father Jehovah, and was thus divine or Jehovah as to his internals: but hereditary evil from the mother appertaineth to the external man, and this evil was with the Lord, and is called the Canaanite in the land, the false thence derived being called the Perizite. Thus the Lord was born as another man, and had infirmities as another man. That he derived hereditary evil from the mother, appears evidently from the circumstance of his enduring temptations; for it is impossible that any one should be tempted who hath no evil, evil being that in man which tempteth, and by which he is tempted. That the Lord was tempted, and that he endured a thousand times more grievous temptations than any man can possibly endure, and that he endured them singly, and by his own proper power overcame evil, or the devil and all hell, is also manifest; concerning these temptations it is thus written in Luke, " Jesus was led in the spirit into the " wildernefs, being forty days tempted of the
" devil,

"devil, so that he did not eat in those days;
"but when the devil had finished all the temp-
"tation, he desisted from him for a time;
"thence Jesus returned in the power of the
"spirit into Galilee," iv. 1, 2, 13, 14: and in
Mark, "The spirit driving Jesus, caused him
"to go forth into the wilderness, and he was
"in the wilderness forty days, being tempted,
"and was with the wild beasts," i. 12, 13;
where by wild beasts is signified hell; not to
mention further, that he was tempted even
unto death, so that his sweat was drops of
blood: "And being in an agony, he prayed more
"earnestly, and his sweat was as drops of
"blood falling to the ground," Luke xxii. 44.
It is not possible for any angel to be tempted
by the devil, because whilst he is in the Lord,
the evil spirits cannot approach him even
distantly, being instantly seized with horror
and fright; much less could hell approach
to the Lord, if he had been born divine, that
is, without an adherence of evil from the
mother. That the Lord also bore the iniquities
and evils of mankind, is a form of speaking
commonly used in the pulpit; but to derive
iniquities and evils upon himself, was impossible, except in an hereditary way from his
mother. The divine nature or principle is not

susceptible of evil; wherefore that he might overcome evil by his own proper strength, which no man ever could, or can do, and might thus alone become righteousness, he was willing to be born as another man; otherwise there would have been no need that he should be born; for he might have assumed the human essence without nativity, as he also did assume it occasionally, when he appeared to the most ancient church, and likewise to the prophets. But he came into the world for this reason, that he might also put on evil, in order to fight against and overcome it, and might thus join together in himself the divine essence and the human essence. The Lord however had no actual or proper evil, as he himself declareth in John, " Which of you convinceth " me of sin?" viii. 46."

Before I close this subject, I will just add a short remark on the forty days which passed between our Lord's resurrection and ascension into heaven. After quoting an explanation of that circumstance from the *Magazine of Knowledge*, vol. i. p. 277, wherein, among other things, the reason is stated to be, because the number *forty* corresponds to temptations, you say, p. 36, " What authority this writer had
" for

"for this ingenious speculation, does not ap-
"pear. But a much more obvious use of
"Jesus continuing on earth these forty days,
"and one that is plainly indicated in the scrip-
"tures, was, that time might be given for a
"sufficient number of successive appearances to
"the disciples, in order to give them the most
"complete satisfaction concerning the resur-
"rection of their master." The *ingenious speculation*, as you are pleased to call it, having
flowed from my pen, it may not be improper
to inform you from what authority I derived
it. After stating that the spiritual reason why
the Lord's ascension was protracted till forty
days after his resurrection, was because the
number forty corresponds to temptations, and
signifies complete deliverance therefrom, and
victory over all enemies, thus a plenary state of
glorification; I asserted, that the Lord ascended
above all the heavens into the sun of the
spiritual world, in the midst whereof he eter-
nally resides, as Jehovah God, in glorious
human form. As you do not agree with me
in admitting the testimony of Baron Swedenborg on this matter, I shall produce such
other authority as I hope you have no objection
to acknowledge. David says, "God is *gone*
"*up* with a shout, Jehovah with the sound of
"a trum-

"a trumpet," Pſalm xlvii. 5. "Thou haſt *aſcended on high*, thou haſt led captivity captive," Pſalm lxviii. 18. And Paul, alluding to the laſt cited paſſage, ſays, "He that deſcended is the ſame alſo that *aſcended up far above all heavens*, that he might fill all things," Eph. iv. 10. And further, he calls our Lord Jeſus Chriſt "the bleſſed and only Potentate, the King of kings, and Lord of lords; who only hath immortality, dwelling *in the light which no man can approach unto*," 1 Tim. vi. 15, 16. This inacceſſible light, in which Jeſus dwells, can ſurely be no other than the ſun of the ſpiritual world. But to make it more evident ſtill, John in the Apocalypſe expreſsly ſays, "I ſaw *an angel ſtanding in the ſun*," Apoc. xix. 17. Now it is not poſſible for any angel to ſtand in the ſun of the ſpiritual world; for that ſun is ſpiritual fire, the intenſity of which is ſo great, that were any finite creature to approximate too near it, he would inſtantly be conſumed, in like manner as would a man, were he to approach the ſun of the natural world, which is material fire. Wherefore it follows, that the angel, whom John ſaw ſtanding in the ſun of the ſpiritual world, could be no other than Jehovah God himſelf, who in Pſalm lxxxiv. 11, is even called a *Sun*.

Again,

Again, "O Jehovah our Lord, how excellent is
"thy name in all the earth! who haft set thy
"glory *above the heavens*," Psalm viii. 1. "Be
"thou exalted, O God, *above the heavens;* thy
"glory above all the earth," Psalm lvii. 5, 11.
"Jehovah is high above all nations, his glory
"*above the heavens.* Who is like unto Jehovah
"our God, who dwelleth *on high?* Who *hum-*
"*bleth himself* to behold the things that are *in*
"*heaven*," Psalm cxiii. 4, 5, 6. From all these
passages it appears, that the Lord's most immediate and personal residence is far above all
the heavens, and consequently in the sun of the
spiritual world, which is the proximate sphere
of his divine emanation.

With respect to the number *forty* signifying a
plenary state of temptations from beginning to
end, this is plain from all those passages of the
Word where that number occurs; as where
it is said, that the flood continued *forty* days
upon the earth; that Moses abode *forty* days
upon mount Sinai; that the children of Israel
sojourned *forty* years in the wilderness; and
that the Lord was tempted by the devil *forty*
days in the wilderness. But you say, a much
more obvious use of Jesus continuing on earth
forty days after his resurrection, was, that time
might

might be given for a sufficient number of successive appearances to the disciples, in order to convince them he was risen. Now it appears from the gospels, that the Lord was seen only a few times by his disciples: therefore it is evident, that the protraction of his ascension for forty days, could not be merely for the reason which you assign; for three or four days only would have been sufficient for the purpose you mention, without waiting forty. His last appearance to his disciples, as recorded in Luke and John, is by the latter declared to be " the " *third* time that Jesus shewed himself to his " disciples, after that he was risen from the " dead," John xxi. 14. There must therefore have been some other secret and particular reason why the Lord did not ascend till forty days after his resurrection; and I know of none more likely to be the true one, than that already offered, as coinciding so perfectly with other parts of the sacred scripture, where the number *forty* is used.

* * * * *

IV. *Of the Holy Scripture, and the Science of Correspondences.*

One of the objections, which you bring against the members of the New Jerusalem is, is, that they believe the holy scriptures contain a spiritual sense, different from, though concealed under, the sense of the letter. But it is your opinion, that there is no such sense; for you say, p. 17, " As to any spiritual sense " of the scriptures, *it cannot be attended to*, till " there be some evidence of the reality of such " a sense of them." And again, p. 57, " The " sacred writers are far from saying that they " had any other meaning than that which ap- " pears *on the face of their writings,* and which " is to be found in the *customary sense of their* " *words;* * and if other senses be once admitted, " there is no end of diversity of opinion. Dif- " ferent

---

* This passage reminds me of a little anecdote, which I will here subjoin. Some time ago, a person was relating to me, that a letter was sent to a distant friend by his Majesty's sloop the *Bull-Dog*. A child about seven years of age was present, and, as I afterwards found, was struck with astonishment at the discourse; for immediately on the person's retiring, the child with great simplicity said to me, " What, papa, can a *bull-dog* carry a letter for any one?" I told him, that the *Bull-Dog* we had been speaking about, was not a *dog*, but a *ship*, so called to distinguish it from other ships.—It then occurred to me, how common it was for mankind, as it were by general consent, to adopt such kind of language, and to convey in their discourse ideas very different from the first or *customary sense of their words*.

"ferent perfons interpret even the literal fenfe
"differently. What then will be the cafe, if,
"befides this literal fenfe, there be another
"concealed one, with refpect to which every
"perfon will, of courfe, think himfelf at li-
"berty to form his own conjectures?" From
this and other paffages of your *Letters* it is
very plainly to be feen, that you have not fufficiently informed yourfelf of what Baron Swedenborg advances with refpect to the fpiritual
fenfe of the Word. You feem to think it is a
mere *arbitrary* meaning put upon words, without any *certain rule* to determine their fignification. In this, however, you are greatly miftaken; and therefore all you have faid about
the uncertainty of the fpiritual fenfe, is no
better than breath fpent in the air. Perhaps
you have yet to be informed, that the *fcience
of correfpondences* is now difcovered, which is
the only true key that can unlock the cabinet
of the literal fenfe of fcripture, within which
are contained the jewels of it's fpiritual and
celeftial fenfe. The great diverfity of opinions
refpecting the letter, of which you are fufficiently apprized, is in a great meafure owing
to the want of fuch a key; for the more we
are acquainted with the fcience of correfpondences, fo much the more fhall we be agreed

in.

in judgment, and in the true understanding of the scriptures. Indeed so regular and certain is that science, that were any given number of persons, properly acquainted with it, required to give their opinion of any part of scripture, they would all uniformly agree in the same explanation, if not in words, yet in substance; which is a circumstance not even pretended to by those who reject the spiritual sense, but at the same time a striking proof of the reality of correspondences, and that the Word of God is written according to that science.

It is a well-known fact, that the sacred writings abound with parables. The prophets make frequent use of them; and of our Saviour it is said, that "without a parable spake he not," Mark iv. 34. Now the sense of a parable is not that which appears on the face of it, nor is it to be understood according to the customary sense of the words; but it conveys, in many cases, a very different meaning. Paul likewise informs us, that the history of Abraham and his two sons, Ishmael and Isaac, is an allegory, Gal. iv. 24: and in the same chapter he explains what is meant by it; shewing, that it was representative of the two dispensations of the law and the gospel.

That

That the Word of God, in many instances, cannot possibly be understood according to the sense of the letter, may appear evident from the following passages.

1. In the prophecy of Israel it is said of Dan, "Dan shall be a *serpent* on the way, a *darting-serpent* on the path, biting the heels of the *horse*, and his rider shall fall backwards," Gen. xlix. 17, 18. It is impossible for any one to understand the meaning of this prophecy without some knowledge of the science of correspondences, which teaches what is meant by a serpent, and what by a horse and his rider.

2. The prophet Habakkuk says to God, "Thou didst ride upon *thine horses*, thy *chariots* of salvation: thou didst walk through the sea with *thy horses*," Hab. iii. 8, 15. Here again the science of correspondences only can inform us what is meant by the horses of God, and by his riding upon them through the sea. The mere literal sense gives us no satisfaction at all.

3. "In that day, saith Jehovah, I will smite every *horse* with astonishment, and his rider with madness; and I will open mine eyes

" upon the house of Judah, and will smite
" every *horse of the people* with blindness,"
Zech. xii. 4. Without a spiritual sense, what
can be meant by smiting every horse with
astonishment, and the horse of the people with
blindness?

4. When Elisha saw Elijah carried up by a
whirlwind into heaven, he cried out to him,
" My father, my father, the *chariot* of Israel,
" and the *horsemen* thereof," 2 Kings ii. 12.
Joash the king also said to Elisha, " O my
" father, my father, the *chariot* of Israel, and
" the *horsemen* thereof," 2 Kings xiii. 14. Here
both Elijah and Elisha are called the chariot of
Israel, and the horsemen thereof, which, if
taken " according to the customary sense of the
words," would be ridiculous and absurd.

5. " And I saw an angel standing in the sun;
" and he cried with a loud voice, saying to all
" the *fowls* that fly in the midst of heaven,
" Come and gather yourselves together to the
" *supper of the great God;* that ye may eat the
" flesh of kings, and the flesh of captains, and
" the flesh of mighty men, and the flesh of
" horses, and of them that sit on them, and the
" flesh of all men, both free and bond, both
" small

"small and great," Apoc. xix. 17, 18. This is another passage that cannot by any means be taken in the literal sense; and therefore it must be plain to every unprejudiced mind, notwithstanding your assertion to the contrary, that the sacred writers had some other meaning than that which appears on the face of their writings.

6. " Thou shalt suck the milk of the gen-
" tiles, and shalt suck the *breast of kings*, and
" thou shalt know that I Jehovah am thy Sa-
" viour, and thy Redeemer, the mighty One
" of Jacob," Isaiah lx. 16. Here mention is made of sucking the breast of kings; which in the literal sense must appear strange and unaccountable, but in the spiritual sense is beautiful beyond description.

7. " My well-beloved hath a vineyard *in a*
" *horn the son of oil*," Isaiah v. 1. This is the proper translation of the original Hebrew, though in our common bibles it is rendered, " My beloved hath a vineyard *in a very fruitful*
" *hill*." But taking the passage as it really is, what can be made of a vineyard in a horn the son of oil, if we confine ourselves to the mere literal sense of the expressions?

8. " The

8. "The city (New Jerusalem) lieth four-square, and the length is as large as the breadth: and he measured the city with the reed, *twelve thousand furlongs:* the length, and the breadth, and the height of it are equal," Apoc. xxi. 16. If this description be understood literally, the city must be no less than *fifteen hundred miles* in square dimensions. But on what spot of ground can such a city as this descend? Not on this island, for it is not large enough to contain the half of it's base. And although the height of the city is represented as fifteen hundred miles, yet it's wall is only an hundred and forty-four cubits, (216 feet,) which is likewise said to be according to the measure of a man, or an angel. Such are the difficulties attendant on the mere literal construction of the scriptures, which, however, do not in the least incumber their spiritual sense.

A great variety of other passages might be produced from the sacred writings, of which we can form no just idea, without having recourse to a different signification of the words from that which they usually bear. But the above are sufficient to prove the fact: and it only requires a proper knowledge of the science of correspondences, to be possessed of a rational,

rational, satisfactory, and determinate manner of explaining them. For example, wherever mention is made of a *horse*, it invariably signifies the *understanding;* and a *chariot* means *doctrine.* Hence God is said to ride on a horse, and in a chariot, when he communicates to man an understanding to understand the doctrine of his Word: and hence to smite every horse with astonishment, and every horse of the people with blindness, denotes that there is no longer in the church the understanding of truth. The reason why Elijah and Elisha were called the chariot of Israel, and the horsemen thereof, is because each represented the Lord as to the Word; and by chariot is signified doctrine drawn from the Word, and by horsemen intelligence. To this I shall take the liberty of adding a further remark of Baron Swedenborg, in explanation of the same subject.

" That such was the signification of chariot and horse, was perfectly well known in the ancient churches, for those churches were representative churches, and with the people thereof the science of correspondences and representations was the chief of all sciences. From those churches the signification of horse, as expressive of the understanding, was derived to the wise men round about, even to Greece. Hence it was, when they would describe the sun, in which they placed the God of their wisdom and intelligence, that they attributed to it a chariot and four horses of fire: and when they would describe the God of the sea, since by the sea were signified sciences derived from the understanding, that they also attributed horses to him. And when they would describe the rise of the sciences from understanding, that they also feigned a winged horse, which with it's hoof broke open a fountain, at which were nine virgins called the sciences; for from the ancient churches they received this knowledge, that by horse is signified the understanding, by wings spiritual truth, by hoof what is scientific from the understanding, and by fountain doctrine from which sciences are derived. Nor is any thing else signified by the Trojan horse, than artifice or cunning exercised by their understanding in destroying the walls. Indeed, in our day, when the understanding is described after the manner received from those ancients, it is usual to figure it by a flying horse or Pegasus; so likewise doctrine is described by a fountain, and the sciences by virgins; but scarce any one knows,

that

that by horse in the mystic sense is signified the understanding; still less that those significatives were derived from the ancient representative churches to the gentiles." *Treatise on the White Horse*, n. 4.

You further object against the same great author, p. 57, that "he finds Christ in every "passage of the scriptures, even those in which "before him they who made the most of the "doctrine of types, never suspected any such "reference." This is certainly one of the truest charges you have brought against him, and forms a striking contrast between his doctrine of christianity and your's. Let us examine it again. Baron Swedenborg is *so much* a christian, as to make Christ all in all, seeing nothing but him and his kingdom in every passage of the scriptures: But Dr. Priestley has *so little* of Christ in his doctrines, that he is scarcely to be found in them; or if he be there, there is no room for him, but in the character of a *mere man*. Baron Swedenborg acknowledges the divinity and sanctity of the Word, because in the supreme sense it treats solely of the Lord Jesus Christ: But Dr. Priestley admits of it's sanctity upon no such principle; for in the first place, (as might

might naturally be expected from his denying the divinity of the Lord's perfon, and afferting that he was no more than a mere man, becaufe he had the appearance of one,) he denies that the fcriptures have any other meaning than that " which is to be found in the " cuftomary fenfe of the words;" and in the fecond place, he fuppofes, that Jefus Chrift was typified and fpoken of in no other light than as a mere man, like the reft of his brethren the prophets. That the fcriptures, however, in *every part* treat of the Lord, agreeable to the affertion of Baron Swedenborg, is plain from the following paffages in the evangelift: Jefus faid unto his difciples, "O fools, and " flow of heart to believe all that the prophets " have fpoken! And beginning at Mofes, and " all the prophets, he expounded unto them " *in all the fcriptures* the things *concerning him-* " *felf.* And he faid unto them, Thefe are " the words which I fpake unto you, while " I was yet with you, that all things muft be " fulfilled which were written in the *law of* " *Mofes*, and in *the prophets*, and in *the pfalms*, " *concerning me*," Luke xxiv. 25, 27, 44. In the Apocalypfe alfo it is written, " *The tefti-* " *mony of Jefus is the fpirit of prophecy*," Apoc. xix. 10. To object, therefore, againft this

part

part of the doctrines of the New Church, is in fact to object against the scriptures themselves, as well as against their divine Author, from whom they are derived, and of whom they constantly treat.

It is asserted by the New Church, not only that the Word treats of the Lord, but that the Lord himself is the Word: on which you remark, p. 58, "that it is a manifest absurdity "to make a real person, whether God or man, "to be the same thing with *a writing* con- "cerning him." However strange this may appear at the first mention of it, like many other things equally difficult of comprehension, it will, when rightly understood, be found to be a great truth. It is said in John i. 1, "In the "beginning was the Word, and the Word was "with God, and *God was the Word.*" Here the very thing which you object to, is plainly, asserted of God. God is a *real person*, as you have acknowledged, p. 63; yet he is declared to be the same as the Word, which is *a writing* concerning him; and what is singular enough, even you yourself have subscribed to the same sentiment in p. 30, although in the present case, p. 58, you reject it as a manifest absurdity.

To

To obtain a clear comprehension of this subject, it will be necessary to attend to the following considerations. Every man is a man by virtue of his two constituent principles of life, which are the will and understanding. These two principles in union, or what amounts to the same thing, the good and the truth of which he is receptive, form the very substance of his spiritual body, and are what distinguish him from all others. So that it may with propriety be said, that every man is his own particular love, and his own particular wisdom: and wherever these are manifested, whether in his works or words, in his life or writings, they are of the same essence with himself, and in this respect are really the man himself existing as it were out of himself; every thing that is predicable of the one, being (generally speaking) equally so of the other. It is upon this principle, and this alone, that the laws of justice in every nation take cognizance of a man's conduct in life, and punish or reward his *person* according to the quality of his *words* and *actions;* for there is in all justice, as such, an intuitive discernment, that whatever proceeds from a man is of the same essence with the man himself, and that his person, principles, and practice, are inseparably united. For the same reason

reason also it is said in the scripture, that after death men will be judged according to their words and works. "I say unto you, that every idle *word* that men shall speak, they shall give account thereof in the day of judgment," Matt. xii. 36. "Blessed are the dead which die in the Lord, from henceforth; their *works* do follow them," Apoc. xiv. 13. "They were judged every man according to their *works,*" Apoc. xx. 13. Now if it be true of every man, that he is his own particular good and truth, the human form being the continent thereof, and that whatever proceeds from him is of the same essence with himself; how plain is it to see, that the Lord must, in a supereminent degree, be his own essential good and essential truth, or essential love and essential wisdom; and that when these are said to proceed from him, being of the same essence with himself, they are in this respect the same thing as himself. Agreeable hereto, the evangelist John declares, that the Word, which proceeded forth from God, is nevertheless still God. And when it is said, that the Word was made flesh, it is the same thing as if it had been declared, that God was made flesh. From all which the following conclusion may be fairly drawn, That as the Word, when made flesh, still continued to be the Word; so flesh, after the Word became such, was and is the same with divine truth; consequently that God and his Word are inseparably one.

* * *

I observed, in a former part of this *Defence*, p. 225, that the holy scriptures are not written, in any part whatever, by mere tropes, figures, or metaphors, but every-where by correspondences; the difference between which and bare figurative expression, I also promised to point out. This I shall now attempt to do in the best manner I am able.

Correspondence in general may be defined, the relation subsisting between the essence of a thing and it's form, or between the cause and it's effect: thus the whole natural world corresponds to the spiritual world; the body of a man, with all it's parts, corresponds to his soul; and the literal sense of the Word corresponds to it's spiritual sense. So that wherever there is a correspondence, there is necessarily implied such an *union* between two things, as only takes place when the one is derived from the other, in the same manner as an effect is derived from it's efficient cause, or as speech is derived from thought, and the gestures of the body from the affections of the mind; in all which cases the exterior forms can no more be separated from the interior essences, without losing their existence, than the body of a man can be separated from his soul without death. Such is the nature and power of *correspondences*. Let us now see whether the same can be said of mere *figure* and *metaphor*.

A mere figure or metaphor is the resemblance, in some certain way, which one thing bears to another, not according to the true nature and fitness of things, so much as by the arbitrary choice of a speaker or writer, who is desirous of illustrating his subject, and rendering it familiar to the comprehension. Consequently there is no necessary union between the subject and the figure, nor is the one an effect of the other, or in any wise dependent on it for it's existence and subsistence, as is the case in all correspondences. An example will illustrate the truth of my observation. Virgil, in his Æneid, lib. 2, likens the destruction of Troy, with her lofty spires, to the fall of an aged oak on being hewn down by the woodman's hatchet. This is a simile, or figure, but not a correspondence; for there is no necessary connection between the city of Troy and a mountain oak, nor between her

lofty

lofty spires and the wide-extending branches of a tree. The one is not *within* the other, as it's life and soul; nor can the relationship subsisting between them be considered like that of cause and effect, essence and form, prior and posterior, soul and body, which nevertheless, as before observed, is the case with all true correspondences.

The difference between a mere figure and a correspondence may again appear from the following consideration. A mere figure or simile is the resemblance which one *natural* object or circumstance is supposed to bear to another *natural* object or circumstance; whereas a correspondence is the actual relation subsisting between a *natural* object and a *spiritual* subject, or a *natural* form and a *spiritual* essence; that is, between *outer* and *inner*, *lower* and *higher*, *nature* and *spirit*; and not between *nature* and *nature*, or *spirit* and *spirit*. This distinction should be well attended to. The language of correspondences is the language of God himself, being that in which he always speaks, both in his Word, and in his works: but figure and metaphor, together with the language of fable, are the mere inventions of man, which took

their

their rife when the divine fcience of correfpondences began to be loft in the world.

This being a fubject of confiderable importance, I fhall take the liberty of adding a few further remarks, which, though not immediately connected with it, may yet ferve to illuftrate the doctrine of the New Church with refpect to the language in which the literal fenfe of the Word is written.

Numbers, as well as names, in the holy Word, are fignificative and correfpondent: therefore it is faid, Apoc. xiii. 18, " Here is " wifdom : let him that hath underftanding " count the number of the beaft: for it is the " number of a man; and his number is fix " hundred three-fcore and fix." Many commentators have puzzled both themfelves and their readers in attempting to unfold the fignification of the number 666: but I believe they are all agreed in applying it to the Romifh church exclufively. Herein, however, they are much miftaken; for the whole chapter, in the fpiritual fenfe, treats of the Reformed churches only. Indeed I muft fay, the more I reflect on the learned, the laboured, and the ingenious explanations given by the moft celebrated

brated writers on the subject, who have confined their ideas to natural, historical, and external things, the more I am convinced, that *not one of them all*, however eminent or distinguished his name, has had even a faint glimpse of it's real and genuine meaning. I speak this without any derogation from the talents or acquirements of any writer; for I wish to pay a proper respect to every man of learning, who has in any measure laboured for the improvement and information of the world. But it appears to me impossible, that the most acute natural understanding could ever, by virtue of it's own powers, penetrate into the interior recesses of the holy Word, which can only be brought to light by means of a revelation from the same Spirit which dictated it. It further appears, that the book of revelation, called the Apocalypse, was in divine providence sealed from the eyes of all the world until the present day; and that it is a series of prophecies particularly designed for the use of the New Church, the true meaning of which cannot be understood without the science of correspondences; which science is revived in the writings of Baron Swedenborg, and has it's foundation in the Word of God, as well as in the works of creation.

I re-

I remember to have read, some years ago, many curious explanations of the number 666, all having reference to the titles of the pope, in Hebrew, Greek, or Latin, or in some other way alluding to the church of Rome. The words *Lateinos, Romiith, Vicarius Generalis Dei in terris, Vicarius Filii Dei*, with various others, were by dint of numeral powers, and such like calculations, all made to produce the exact complement 666. At that time I thought some attention was due to those ingenious speculations; but on further inquiry I soon found, that not only the names above mentioned would make up the required number, but perhaps an hundred and fifty other names, that could no more be supposed to have any connection with the contents of the Apocalypse, than the *man in the moon*. I then saw, that *all such explications* could not be the effect of that wisdom spoken of in the 13th chapter, and to which we are invited; but that there must be some other hidden meaning, with which the learned were unacquainted. It did not satisfy me, that *Lateinos, Romiith, Vicarius Filii Dei*, or even *Ludovicus*, made up the complement 666, when other words were to be found, that did the same, such as *Joseph Smith, Tomkins, Benjamin Bennet*, and what is singular enough,

the

the *Rev. Jof. Priefley;* for by the magical power of numerals I can bring them all to fing the fame fong, *fix hundred and fixty fix.* It was indeed a *curious* circumftance; but I thought *that* not fufficient for one who is in fearch of genuine truth; neither did I then, nor do I now think, that a mere *rebus* or *conundrum* is worthy a place in thofe oracles of divine truth, whofe Author is no lefs than the great Jehovah, the God of heaven and earth.

The Apocalypfe, like every other book of divine infpiration, is couched in *natural* terms, to reprefent and point out *fpiritual* things; and there is as great a diftinction between the *type* and *antitype*, as between what is *natural* and *fpiritual*. Now the *antitype* and *type* ought never to be underftood as exifting in one and the fame *gradus*, but in two diftinct, *difcrete* modes of being. Underftand me right: I mean, that a prophecy couched in *natural* terms, ought not be expected to have it's fulfilment in a *natural* manner, but in a manner *difcretely diftinct* from it, that is, in a *fpiritual* manner. Thus, when in fcripture it is faid, that *feven* or *ten kings* fhall arife; that a *beaft had feven heads and ten horns,* &c. &c. we are not to underftand, that in the accomplifhment of this prophecy there shall literally arise *seven* or *ten kings*, or that there shall be any *real beast with seven heads and ten horns*, for this would be confounding the *antitype* with the *type* in the same *gradus*, or same *mode of existence;* but we are to understand, that the prophecy will be accomplished when *what is signified by seven or ten kings*, and when *what is signified by seven heads and ten horns*, shall take place in the church; and this is placing the *antitype* in a *degree* or *mode of existence above* the *type*. All the prophecies in the Apocalypse are of this sort; and therefore it appears to me contrary to the true sense of scripture, to suppose that a fulfilment of that prophecy in the 13th chapter can be discovered in any man's name that happens to make up the number 666; for this would be taking both the type and antitype in one and the same *gradus*, as before observed, when nevertheless I believe there is not a single prophecy either in the Old or New Testament, but what it's accomplishment ought to be understood as principally belonging to the internal sense; though I will admit, that many of them have also been literally fulfilled.

As the true meaning of the number 666 may be seen at large in Baron Swedenborg's
Apocalypse

Apocalypse Revealed, I shall here only observe, that the whole chapter, in which it is contained, gives a description of the faith of the Protestant or Reformed churches, particularly in respect to it's separation from charity or good works, and that the number of the beast denotes the quality of that faith, as being a complex of the most enormous falses. It is called the *number of a man*, because number signifies quality, and man signifies wisdom and intelligence, but in the opposite sense, as in the present case, self-derived wisdom; for it is said of those who separate faith from charity. I have already observed, that a whole church, or community of men, appears before the Lord as *one man*: it is for this reason that the *quality of a church* is, in the letter of scripture, said to be the *number of a man*. See a further explanation of this subject in the *Magazine of Knowledge*, &c. vol. i, p. 210.

I shall conclude my remarks on the holy scriptures and the science of correspondences with the following quotation from the work entitled *True Christian Religion*, n. 200 to 207. " It is asserted in the church, that the Word is holy, inasmuch as Jehovah the Lord spake it; but because it's holiness doth not appear in it's

literal

literal sense, therefore they who once begin to doubt about it's holiness on that account, in the future course of their reading confirm their doubts by many passages they meet with, suggesting these scrupulous questions, 'Can this be holy? Can this be divine? Now to prevent the influence of such doubts on men's minds, lest they should become general, and in consequence thereof the Word of God should be rejected as a common trivial writing, and thereby the Lord's conjunction with man should be cut off, it hath pleased the Lord, at this time, to reveal it's spiritual sense, for the purpose of discovering to mankind in what part of it it's divine sanctity lieth concealed. But to illustrate this, let us apply to examples. In the Word we find frequent mention made sometimes of Egypt, sometimes of Ashur, sometimes of Edom, of Moab, of the children of Ammon, of the Philistines, of Tyre and Sidon, and of Gog: they now, who do not know that by those names the things of heaven and of the church are signified, may easily be led into an erroneous notion, that the Word treateth much of people and nations, and but little of heaven and the church, consequently much about earthly things, and but little about heavenly things; whereas, were such persons acquainted

quainted with what is signified by those people and nations, or by their names, this might be the means to lead them out of error into truth. In like manner, when it is observed, that in the Word frequent mention is made of gardens, groves, woods, and also of the trees that grow therein, as the olive, the vine, the cedar, the poplar, and the oak; and also of lambs, sheep, goats, calves, oxen; and likewise of mountains, hills, valleys, fountains, rivers, waters, and the like; he who knoweth nothing of the spiritual sense of the Word, must of necessity be led to suppose, that nothing further is meant by these things than what is expressed in the letter; for he little thinketh, that by a garden, a grove, and a wood, are meant wisdom, intelligence, science; that by the olive, the vine, the cedar, the poplar, and the oak, are meant the good and truth of the church, under the different characters of celestial, spiritual, rational, natural, and sensual; that by a lamb, a sheep, a goat, a calf, and an ox, are meant innocence, charity, and natural affection; that by mountains, hills, and valleys, are meant the higher, the lower, and the lowest things relating to the church; also, that by Egypt is signified what is scientific, by Ashur what is rational, by Edom what is natural, by Moab the adulteration of good, by the children

dren of Ammon the adulteration of truth, by the Philiftines faith without charity, by Tyre and Sidon the knowledges of goodnefs and truth, by Gog external worfhip without internal; in general, by Jacob in the Word is underftood the church-natural, by Ifrael the church-fpiritual, and by Judah the church-celeftial. When the mind is opened to this knowledge, it may then be able to conceive that the Word treateth folely of celeftial things, and that the earthly things mentioned in it are only the fubjects wherein thofe celeftials are contained. But let us take another inftance from the Word, for the illuftration of this truth. We read in Ifaiah, " In that day fhall
" there be a highway out of Egypt to Affyria,
" and the Affyrian fhall come into Egypt, and
" the Egyptian into Affyria, and the Egyptians
" fhall ferve with the Affyrians. In that day
" fhall Ifrael be the third with Egypt, and
" with Affyria, even a bleffing in the midft
" of the land; whom Jehovah of Hofts fhall
" blefs, faying, Bleffed be Egypt my people,
" and Affyria the work of my hands, and Ifrael
" mine inheritance," chap. xix. 23, 24, 25. By thefe words, in their fpiritual fenfe, is fignified, that at the time of the Lord's coming, the fcientific, the rational, and the fpiritual fhould make

make one, and that then the scientific should serve the rational, and both the spiritual; for, as was said above, by Egypt is signified the scientific, by Ashur or Assyria the rational, and by Israel the spiritual; by the repetition of the words, *in that day*, is meant the first and second coming of the Lord.

"What is meant by correspondence, hath to this day remained unknown, notwithstanding it was a subject most familiar to the men of the most ancient times, who esteemed it the science of sciences, and cultivated it so universally, that all their books and tracts were written by correspondences. The book of Job, which was a book of the ancient church, is full of correspondences. The hieroglyphics of the Egyptians, and the fabulous stories of antiquity, were founded on the same science; all the ancient churches were churches representative of spiritual things; their ceremonies, and even their statutes, which were rules for the institution of their worship, consisted of mere correspondences; in like manner, every thing in the Israelitish church, their burnt-offerings, sacrifices, meat-offerings, and drink-offerings, with all the particulars belonging to each, were correspondences; so also was the tabernacle,

with

with all things contained in it; and likewife their feftivals, as the feaft of the unleavened bread, the feaft of tabernacles, the feaft of the firft-fruits; alfo, the priefthood of Aaron and the Levites, and the garments of their holinefs. Now, forafmuch as divine things fix their exiftence in outward nature in correfpondences, therefore the Word was written by mere correfpondences; and for the fame reafon, the Lord, in confequence of fpeaking from the Divinity, fpake by correfpondences; for whatever proceedeth from the Divinity, when it comes into outward nature, manifefts itfelf in fuch outward things as correfpond with what is divine, which outward things become then the repofitories of divine things, otherwife called celeftial and fpiritual, that lie contained within them in a hidden and myfterious manner.

" The fcience of correfpondences was not only known, but alfo cultivated in many kingdoms of Afia, particularly in the land of Canaan, Egypt, Affyria, Chaldea, Syria, Arabia, in Tyre, Sidon, and Nineveh, and from thence it was conveyed into Greece, where it was changed into fable, as may appear from the works of the moft ancient writers in that country.

" To

"To shew that the science of correspondences was long preserved amongst the Asiatic nations, but chiefly amongst those who were called diviners and wise men, and by some magi, I shall adduce a remarkable instance from 1 Sam. chap. v. and vi. We are there informed, that the ark, containing the two tables, whereon were written the ten commandments, was taken by the Philistines, and placed in the house of Dagon, in Ashdod, and that Dagon fell to the ground before it, and afterwards, that his head and both the palms of his hands were separated from his body, and lay on the threshold, and that the people of Ashdod and Ekron, to the number of several thousands, were smitten with emerods, and that the land was devoured with mice; and that the Philistines, on this occasion, called together their priests and diviners, and that to put a stop to the destruction which threatened them, they came to this determination, viz. that they would make five golden emerods, and five golden mice, and a new cart, and would set the ark on this cart, and have it drawn by two milch-kine, which lowed in the way before the cart, and thus would send back the ark unto the children of Israel, by whom the kine and the cart were offered up in sacrifice, and the God of Israel was appeafed. That all thefe devices of the Philiftine diviners were correfpondences, is evident from their fignification, which is this; the Philiftines themfelves fignified thofe who are influenced by faith feparate from charity; Dagon reprefented their religious worfhip; **the emerods, wherewith they were fmitten,** fignified the natural loves, which, if feparated from fpiritual love, are unclean; and **mice** fignified the devaftation of the church, by falfifications of truth; a new cart fignified natural doctrine of the church; for chariot, in the Word, fignifieth doctrine derived from fpiritual truths; the milch-kine fignified good **natural affections;** the golden emerods fignified the natural loves purified and made good; the golden mice fignified the devaftation of the church removed by means of goodnefs; for gold, in the Word, fignifieth goodnefs; the lowing of the kine in the way fignified the difficult converfion of the concupifcences of evil in the natural man into good affections; the offering up of the kine and the cart as a burnt-offering, fignified that thus the God of Ifrael was rendered propitious. All thefe things then, which the Philiftines did by the advice of their diviners, were correfpondences;

from

from which it appears, that that science was long preserved amongst the gentiles.

"Forasmuch as the representative rites of the church, which were correspondences, in process of time, began to be corrupted by idolatrous and likewise magical applications of them; therefore, the science of correspondences was, by the Divine Providence of the Lord, successively darkened, and, amongst the Israelitish and Jewish people, entirely obliterated. Indeed, the divine worship of that people consisted of mere correspondences, and consequently was representative of heavenly things, but still they had no knowledge of a single thing represented; for they were altogether natural men, and therefore had neither inclination nor ability to gain any understanding of spiritual and celestial subjects; for the same reason they were necessarily ignorant of correspondences, these being representations of things spiritual and celestial in things natural.

"The reason why the idolatries of the gentiles of old took their rise from the science of correspondences, was, because all things that appear on the face of the earth have correspondence, consequently, not only trees and vegetables,

vegetables, but also beasts, birds, and fishes of every kind, and all other animals. The ancients, who were versed in the science of correspondences, made themselves images, which corresponded with things celestial; and were greatly delighted therewith, by reason of their signification, and that they could discern in them what related to heaven and the church; and therefore they placed those images both in their temples, and also in their houses, not with any intention to worship them, but to serve as a means of recollecting the celestial things signified by them. Hence, in Egypt and in other places they made images of calves, oxen, serpents, and also of children, old men, and virgins; because calves and oxen signified the affections and powers of the natural man; serpents, the prudence and likewise cunning of the sensual man; children, innocence and charity; old men, wisdom; and virgins, the affections of truth, &c. Succeeding ages, when the science of correspondences was obliterated, began to adore as holy, and at length to worship as deities, the images and pictures set up by their forefathers, because they found them in and about their temples. For the same reason, the ancients performed their worship in gardens and in groves, according to the

different

different kinds of trees growing therein; and also on mountains and hills; for gardens and groves signified wisdom and intelligence, and every particular tree something that had relation thereto, as the olive the good of love; the vine, truth derived from that good; the cedar, good and truth rational; a mountain, the highest heaven; a hill, the heaven beneath. That the science of correspondences remained amongst many eastern nations, even till the coming of the Lord, may appear also from the wise men of the east, who visited the Lord at his nativity; wherefore a star went before them, and they brought with them gifts, gold, frankincense, and myrrh, Matt. ii. 1, 2, 9, 10, 11; for the star which went before them signified knowledge from heaven; gold signified celestial good; frankincense, spiritual good; and myrrh, natural good, which are the three constituents of all worship. But still the science of correspondences was annihilated amongst the Israelitish and Jewish people, although all parts of their worship, and all the statutes and judgments given them by Moses, and all things contained in the Word, were correspondences; the reason was, because they were idolaters at heart, and consequently of such a nature and genius, that they were not willing to allow that any part of their worship had a celestial and spiritual signification, for they believed that all the parts thereof were holy of themselves; wherefore had the celestial and spiritual significations been revealed to them, they would not only have rejected, but also have prophaned them; for this reason, heaven was so shut up against them, that they scarce knew whether there was such a thing as eternal life; and that such was the case with them, appears evident from the circumstance, that they did not acknowledge the Lord, although the whole scripture throughout prophesied concerning him, and foretold his coming; they rejected him solely on that account, because he instructed them about an heavenly kingdom, and not about an earthly one; for they wanted a Messiah, who should exalt them above all nations in the world, and not a Messiah, who should provide only for their eternal salvation.

"The reason why the science of correspondences, which is the true key to the spiritual sense of the Word, was not discovered to later ages, was, because the christians of the primitive church were men of such great simplicity, that it was to no purpose to discover it to them; for had it been discovered, they would have found no use in it, nor would they have understood it. After those first ages of christianity, there arose thick clouds of darkness, which overspread the whole christian world, first in consequence of many heretical opinions propagated in the church, and soon after in consequence of the decrees and determinations of the Council of Nice, concerning the existence of three divine persons from eternity, and concerning the person of Christ, as the Son of Mary, and not as the Son of Jehovah God; hence sprung the present faith of justification, in which three Gods are approached and worshipped, according to their respective orders, and on which depend all and every thing belonging to the present church, as the members of the body depend on the head; and because men applied every part of the Word to confirm this erroneous faith, therefore the spiritual sense could not be discovered; for had it been discovered, they would have applied it also to a confirmation of the same faith, and thereby would have prophaned the very holy Word, and thus would have shut up heaven entirely against themselves, and have removed the Lord from the church.

"The

"The reason why the science of correspondences, which is the key to the spiritual sense of the Word, is revealed at this day, is, because the divine truths of the church are now coming to light, and of these the spiritual sense of the Word consisteth'; and whilst these are in man, the literal sense of the Word cannot be perverted; for the literal sense is capable of being turned any way, but if it be turned to favour the false, then it's internal sanctity is destroyed, and the external along with it, whereas, if it be turned to favour the truth, then the sanctity is preserved. That the spiritual sense of the Word should be opened now, at this time, is signified by John seeing heaven open, and the white horse; and also by his seeing and hearing the angel, who stood in the sun, calling all people together to a great supper, Apoc. xix. 11 to 18. But that it would not be acknowledged for some time, is signified by the beasts and the kings of the earth, who were about to make war with him that sat on the white horse, Apoc. xix. 19; and also by the dragon, which persecuted the woman, that brought forth the man-child, into the wilderness, and cast out of his mouth water as a flood after her, that he might cause her to be carried away of the flood, Apoc. xii. 13 to 17."

V. Of

* * * * *

V. *Of the Second Coming of the Lord.*

It is written in Matt. xxiv. 29, 30, 31. "Immediately after the tribulation of those days, the sun shall be darkened, and the moon shall not give her light, and the stars shall fall from heaven, and the powers of the heavens shall be shaken. And then shall appear the sign of the Son of Man in heaven: and then shall all the tribes of the earth mourn, and they shall see the sign of the Son of Man coming in the clouds of heaven, with power and great glory. And he shall send his angels with a great sound of a trumpet, and they shall gather together his elect from the four winds, from one end of heaven to the other." From this and similar passages in the Word, understood merely according to the literal sense, has arisen the generally prevailing notion, that the Lord will appear personally in the clouds of heaven, at which time all who have ever lived since the creation of the world, are to be raised up out of their graves, and their souls again clothed with their bodies; and when thus assembled in one place, that they who have lived

lived well, will be judged to eternal life or heaven, and they who have done evil, to eternal death or hell. Into this opinion, I obferve, that you, Sir, in common with the reft of your neighbours, have fallen; not knowing, that by the clouds of heaven, in which the Lord is to make his appearance, is meant the literal fenfe of the Word, and by glory it's fpiritual fenfe; confequently, that the Lord, when the church is at an end, will reveal to mankind the fpiritual fenfe of the Word, and thus manifeft divine truth fuch as it is in it's purity, which is the true fign of the laft judgment taking place.

It is one of the charges you bring againft the members of the New Jerufalem, that they do not believe on this fubject in like manner with yourfelf; and that they take the bare affertions of Baron Swedenborg in the room of rational proof. The firft part of the charge is true enough; but as to the latter, you are miftaken; for although we fet a very high value on his folemn declarations, yet we do not receive them *merely as fuch*, independent of proper evidence, but as fatisfactory illuftrations of the true fcripture doctrine of the

Lord's

Lord's second advent, the last judgment, and the resurrection.

With respect to the Lord's *second advent*, the doctrine of the New Church is this; that the Lord cannot come *in person* into the material world, because since his ascention into heaven he is in his glorified humanity, and in this humanity, although it is omnipresent, he cannot be seen by any man unless his spiritual eyes be first opened, as was the case with all who saw him after his resurrection; for as a material eye can see nothing but matter, so the Lord's glorified body being substantial, and not material, can only be seen by a spiritual eye. Indeed it is a clear case to me, that, were the Lord to make his *personal* appearance among men in the unclouded splendor of his Divine Humanity, it would be attended with more certain destruction to the whole race of mankind, than if this ball of earth, together with all it's inhabitants, were cast into the sun. But although the Lord cannot, consistently with divine order, come personally into the world, yet he can in his Word, which being the divine truth proceeding from himself, is in this respect the same thing as himself. " In " the beginning was the Word, and the Word " was

"was with God, and *God was the Word*," John i. 1.

To this you object, p. 39, "When the dis-ciples were viewing Jesus ascending to heaven, the angels who stood by said to them, Acts i. 11, "Ye men of Galilee, why look ye up to heaven? This same Jesus, who is taken up from you into heaven, shall so come in like manner as ye have seen him go into heaven." "What" (you ask) "can be more evident from this, than that as the ascent of Jesus was personal and visible, his return will be the same, personal and visible, not figurative or emblematical only, meaning not himself, but his doctrines?" In answer to this, I have to observe, that the whole passage from which you have drawn the objection, is the record of a transaction that occurred, *not in the natural, but in the spiritual world;* for, as has been already proved, the Lord never was, nor could be, seen after his resurrection, by the material eyes of any man. He was then in the lower parts of the spiritual world; consequently his personal ascent must have been from *thence* into heaven, and not from the material world, which he had left forty days before, viz. at the time of his resurrection. Besides, there are

clouds

clouds in the spiritual world, equally as well as in the natural world; and the clouds of the former are more properly called the *clouds of heaven*, than the latter, which in fact are nothing but the *clouds of the earth*. It is evident, therefore, that what the angels said of Jesus returning from heaven in like manner as he went up into heaven, ought to be understood as alluding to his appearance in the spiritual world, at the time of his second coming, and not to any personal appearance in the natural world. To men on earth who are enlightened so as to discern the spiritual sense of the scriptures, the Lord appears as divine truth: but to those inhabitants of the spiritual world, who in heart acknowledge him as the only God of heaven and earth, he not only manifests himself in the character of divine truth, but also occasionally presents himself in person, descending in the same glorious manner, as the men of Galilee saw him ascend. And thus the event, which the angels foretold, hath actually taken place.

That the above passage in the Acts of the Apostles cannot with propriety be understood in any other sense than that already explained, may further appear from this consideration, that

that the Lord's afcenfion was vifible only to his followers, whofe eyes were opened, and not to the bulk of mankind. Now if he is to come again *in like manner*, as is exprefsly declared, it follows, that his fecond advent will be witneffed and acknowledged, not by the bulk of mankind in general, but (as before, fo now again) by his followers only, whofe fpiritual eyes or underftandings are opened to difcern him in his Word. And all fuch, in confequence of clearly comprehending the meaning of John, when he fays, that God was the Word, will fee that the Lord's advent in his Word, confifting of a revelation of it's internal contents, is neither a mere figure nor an emblem, but a divine reality.

It was before obferved, that by the clouds of heaven, in which the Lord is faid to come, is meant the Word in it's literal fenfe. This is proved from the following paffages. " God " rode upon a cherub, and did fly; yea, he " did fly upon the wings of the wind. His " pavilion round about him were dark waters, " and *thick clouds* of the fkies. At the bright- " nefs that was before him, his *thick clouds* " paffed," Pfalm xviii. 10 to 13. " Afcribe " ye ftrength unto God; his excellency is over
" Ifrael,

"Israel, and his strength is in the *clouds*," Psalm lxviii. 34. "And Jehovah will create upon every dwelling-place of mount Zion, and upon her assemblies, a *cloud* and smoke by day, and the shining of a flaming fire by night; for upon all the glory shall be a covering," Isaiah iv. 5. "Behold, Jehovah rideth upon a *swift cloud*," Isaiah xix. 1. "He bindeth up the waters in his *thick clouds*, and the *cloud* is not rent under them. He holdeth back the face of his throne, and spreadeth his *cloud* upon it," Job xxvi. 8, 9. In all these passages clouds denote the literal sense of the Word; and riding upon a cloud signifies instruction in divine truth. The same was represented by the thick cloud in which Jehovah descended upon mount Sinai, when the law was delivered to Moses, that being the *first-fruits* of the Word. From all which circumstances it is evident, that the Lord's second coming in the clouds of heaven, which is for the purpose of bringing into his church the *full harvest* of the Word, can have no other meaning than his more immediate presence in the literal sense of the Word, in consequence of the revelation which is now taking place of it's spiritual sense.

* * * * *

VI. *Of the Last Judgment.*

Baron Swedenborg afferts, that the laft judgment was accomplifhed in the fpiritual world, in the year 1757. On this you take occafion to raife three objections, the firft of which is, p. 38, that "to all appearance no difference "whatever then took place in the power of "man to contend with vice or prejudice." The fecond occurs in p. 39, where you charge the members of the New Church with holding, "that no future judgment is to be looked for." And the third is, p. 42, that "according to "Mr. Swedenborg the laft judgment took place "in the fpiritual world only, and of courfe "none could be judged befides thofe who had "been dead:" whereas it is your opinion, that "thofe who fhall be found alive at the coming "of Chrift, and who will not die at all, are to "be judged, as well as thofe who have been "dead;" confequently that the whole procefs of the laft judgment is to be as literal and formal as any trial in Weftminfter Hall.

As to the firft objection, that has been already anfwered in the preceding part of this

Defence, p. 51 to 55, where it is shewn, that a most extraordinary change has manifestly taken place, since the year 1757, throughout every nation in christendom, particularly in regard to the liberty of thinking about religious and civil concerns. The restoration of this spiritual liberty to mankind was announced by Baron Swedenborg in his *Treatise on the Last Judgment* so long ago as the year 1758; which was at a time when the general operation of that liberty could not be perceived in the natural world; for as yet the spiritual judgment had not descended as an efficient cause into natural effects: wherefore it required some length of time to manifest, in the outward actions of men, the change which had passed in their interiors, that is, in the spiritual world. But the event has since proved the truth of his assertion; and I doubt not but every year's experience will in future tend more and more to confirm it.

Exclusive of these reasons for believing that the judgment, spoken of in the scriptures, is already accomplished, there are others of considerable weight, amounting to little less than a kind of demonstrative proof. When mention is made of the last judgment in the Word of God, it is generally represented as an event
which

which is to be succeeded by an extraordinary degree of illumination, and knowledge of divine things, vouchsafed to the human mind, by means of a new revelation. Thus the coming of the Son of Man is compared to *lightning shining out of the east*, Matt. xxiv. 27. After the judgment of the great whore, John says, "I saw "*heaven opened*, and behold a *white horse*: and "he that sat upon him was called *The Word of* "*God*," Apoc. xix. 11, 13; evidently alluding to the understanding of the spiritual sense of the scriptures, which was to take place after the judgment. The same is further described in chap. xxi. by the new heaven and new earth, and the holy city New Jerusalem coming down from God out of heaven; which event, as it is now taking place, is a proof that the last judgment, according to the scriptures, has been already performed, the one coming to pass as the certain consequence of the other.

The truth of our doctrine concerning the actual accomplishment of the last judgment, is further confirmed by the following consideration. Our Lord says, "The time cometh, "when I shall *no more speak unto you in proverbs*, "but *I shall shew you plainly of the Father*," John xvi. 25. The speaking no more in proverbs,

verbs, can mean nothing elfe but revealing in plain terms the fpiritual fenfe of his Word. This is effected in the writings of Emanuel Swedenborg; which is a corroborating proof, that the prefent day is the time to which our Lord alluded, as the æra of his fecond advent. But above all, his promife, that in that day he would fhew us plainly of the Father, is to me a moft certain and indubitable proof, that the laft judgment is actually accomplifhed; for prior to this, men were no more difpofed to hear that Jefus himfelf was the Father, than they were in the days of his flefh; therefore he faid, " I " have yet many things to fay unto you, but " *ye cannot bear them now*," John xvi. 12. Now no church, or fet of men, that have heretofore exifted fince the firft inftitution of chriftianity, have ever yet pretended to any *plainer knowledge of the Father*, than was enjoyed by the apoftles, and immediate difciples of the Lord; and yet it was predicted, that a day would come, when fuch knowledge would be communicated to the church. The prophet Ifaiah indeed long ago declared, that the *Child* which was to be *born*, the *Son* which was to be given, fhould be called *God*, the *Father of eternity*, Ifaiah ix. 6. But who ever believed his report? Where is the church, that ever acknow-

acknowledged Jesus Christ to be the *Father of eternity*, as well as the *Son* that was *born in time?* Where are the builders that ever made *Him* the *chief corner-stone* of their building? directing all their worship to *Him* alone as the *Head* of the church, and not to another being whom they vainly imagined to be superior to him? Where are such churches, such christians to be found, as will bring *all* their praise, *all* their glory, and *all* their honour, and lay them down at *his* feet, in humble and prostrate adoration, acknowledging *Him alone* as the *Father* and *Saviour* of mankind? I know of none that have ever had such a *plain* and *direct knowledge* of the Father as dwelling in the person of Jesus Christ, except the members of the New Jerusalem. This circumstance is therefore to me a demonstrative proof, not only that the last judgment is accomplished, and thereby an end put to the former christian church, but also that the New Church and kingdom of Christ is begun, that he hath taken to himself his great power, and that henceforth he shall reign for ever and ever.

Your second objection, in which you charge the members of the New Church with holding, " that no future judgment is to be looked for,"

is

is not a true reprefentation of our belief in that refpect: for although we really believe, that the laft *general* judgment was accomplifhed in the year 1757, yet we alfo maintain, that every man *in particular* will be judged immediately after death, and that he will be rewarded according to the deeds done in the body, whether they have been good or evil. The laft judgment we confider to be of various fignification, general, particular, and fingular; *general*, as having refpect to the end of a church; *particular*, in reference to the death of individuals; and *fingular*, with refpect to the future flate of man as determined by every thought and affection, every word and work.

The common idea of the laft judgment being *univerfal*, and decifive of the fate of all mankind without exception, the deceafed among whom are fuppofed to be referved in fome unknown place till that great day, is not only hoftile to the true fenfe of fcripture, but alfo repugnant to found reafon. By the fcriptures we are informed, that two general judgments have taken place on the inhabitants of this earth, prior to that in the year 1757. The firft was the laft judgment of the moft ancient church, when all charity and faith perifhed, and which is defcribed in Genefis by the flood. At that time, according to the language of the Word, heaven and earth paffed away, that is, the internals and externals of the church perifhed, and a new heaven and a new earth were created, that is, a new church, which fucceeded the former, and may be called the ancient church. The laft judgment of this fecond general church, which included many particular churches, together with the reprefentative of a church eftablifhed among the pofterity of Jacob, took place at the time of the Lord's firft coming into the world. The prophet Ifaiah fpeaks of this judgment, to be accomplifhed by the Lord, in the following terms: "Who is this that cometh from Edom, "with dyed garments from Bozrah, travelling "in the greatnefs of his ftrength? I that fpeak "in righteoufnefs, mighty to fave. I have "trodden the wine-prefs alone: *I will tread* "*them in mine anger, and trample them in my* "*fury;* and *their blood* fhall be fprinkled upon "my garments, and I will ftain all my raiment. "For the *day of vengeance* is in my heart, and "the year of my redeemed is come," Ifaiah lxiii. 1, 3, 4. Hence it appears, that judgment and redemption commence at the fame time; which is further evident from the following

lowing passages: "Zion shall be *redeemed with* "*judgment*, and her converts with righteousness. "And the destruction of the transgressors and "of the sinners shall be together," Isaiah. i. 27, 28. "The Lord shall purge the blood of Je-"rusalem from the midst thereof, by the *spirit* "*of judgment*, and by the *spirit of burning*," Isaiah iv. 4. Not to mention many other places to the same effect in this and other prophets. The Lord himself also, when he was in the act of fulfilling those prophecies, and executing the judgment, says, "*Now is the* "*judgment of this world; now shall the prince of* "*this world be cast out*," John xii. 31. In another place, "Verily verily I say unto you, "the hour is coming, and *now is*, when *the* "*dead* shall hear the voice of the Son of God; "and they that hear shall live. For as the "Father hath life in himself, so hath he given "to the Son to have life in himself; and *hath* "*given him authority to execute judgment also*, "because he is the Son of Man," John v. 25, 26, 27. Again, "Be of good cheer, *I have* "*overcome the world*," John xvi. 33. From which passages it is evident, that a day of judgment is not spoken of in the scriptures, as an event the like of which has never yet in any former period taken place, or as decisive

of

of the fate of every individual of the human race; for we find, that the Lord, when on earth, actually accomplished a judgment, not upon the whole race of mankind, but only upon those who were deceased, and consequently in the spiritual world.

These considerations sufficiently obviate your third objection, and prove, that the doctrine of the New Church respecting the last judgment is perfectly consistent with the Word of God; while all those systems, which suppose the destruction of the universe as the necessary consequence of that event, can be considered in no other light, than as so many idle dreams, and dreadful chimeras, calculated to frighten mankind, and to inspire them with no one useful or rational sentiment, but on the contrary with dismal expectation and useless alarm.

The end of creation is the formation of an angelic heaven out of the human race, which, as an image of the Creator, may bear some respect to his infinity and eternity. But this respect to infinity and eternity would cease, were the habitable earth to be destroyed at the day of the last judgment; for then, by a period being put to the procreations of mankind, the

extent

extent of heaven, together with the number of it's inhabitants, would be limited: whereas, it is highly reasonable to suppose, that as the human mind, which is an heaven in it's smallest form, increases in perfection according to the plurality of it's knowledges, so the angelic heaven will likewise advance in perfection, and thus more and more resemble it's Creator, according to the perpetually increasing number of it's inhabitants. Hence the doctrines which attribute to the Divine Being an end worthy of himself in the creation of the world, by making provision for the perpetual generations and eternal successions of mankind, must be the most rational in themselves, as well as most conformable to divine revelation, when properly understood. That the habitable earth is not to be destroyed at the time of the last judgment, is plain from the Lord's words in Luke, " I tell " you, in that night there shall be two men " in one bed; the one shall be taken, and *the* " *other shall be left*. Two women shall be grind- " ing together; the one shall be taken, and *the* " *other left*. Two men shall be in the field; " the one shall be taken, and *the other left*," chap. xvii. 34, 35, 36. Here the last time of the church is called night, because there is no genuine faith remaining, in consequence of

there

there being no true charity : but that the world would not then be destroyed, is plainly declared by the circumstance of some being left while others are removed. The same doctrine may be confirmed from the following passages: " Jehovah built his sanctuary like high palaces, " like the earth which he hath established *for* " *ever*," Psalm lxxviii. 69. " Thou hast esta- " blished the earth, and it *abideth*, Psalm cxix. 90. " One generation passeth away, and another " generation cometh: but *the earth abideth for* " *ever*," Eccles. i. 4.

In addition to the above, I will here transcribe the following passage from the Treatise on the *Last Judgment*, n. 30, 32, shewing why men are judged in the spiritual world, and not in the natural. " No one is judged from the natural man, consequently not whilst he is living in the natural world, inasmuch as man is then in a natural body: but all are judged in the spiritual man, consequently when they come into the spiritual world, for man is then in a spiritual body. It is the spiritual part of man that is judged, but not the natural; for this latter is in no respect faulty or criminal, inasmuch as it does not live of itself, but is merely a servant or instrument, whereby the spiritual man acts. Hence also it is, that judgment passes on men, when they have put off their natural, and put on their spiritual body. In this body a man also appears according to his true quality with respect to love and faith; for every one in the spiritual world is an image or likeness of his own love, not only with respect to his face and body, but with respect to his speech and actions. Hence it is, that all are known and distinguished as to their real quality, and immediately separated, when it is the good pleasure of the Lord. From what has been said it also appears evident, that the judgment takes place in the spiritual world, and not in the natural world or on the earths.

"Every one after death is bound to, or in fellowship with, a certain society, and this immediately on his entering into the spiritual world. As soon as ever spirits are gathered together, and separated, they are also judged, and every one is instantly fixed in his own place, the good in heaven, and in society there with their like, and the evil in hell, and in society there with their like. Hence it is manifest, that the last judgment can only take place in the spiritual world, as well because every one there is an image of his own life, as becaufe all are affociated together who are in a fimilar life, confequently every one is in fellowfhip with his like. It is otherwife in the natural world, where the good and the bad are intermixed; there no one knows the real quality of another, nor are they feparated from each other according to the affection of their life. Befides, it is impoffible for any man with his natural body to be either in heaven or in hell; wherefore, in order that man may enter into one or the other, it is neceffary that he put off his natural body, and afterwards be judged in his fpiritual body. Hence it is, as obferved above, that the fpiritual man is judged, and not the natural."

* * * * *

VII. *Of the Refurrection.*

As the notions commonly entertained about the refurrection of the dead, are, like thofe on the laft judgment and the fecond coming of the Lord, drawn from the mere letter of fcripture, without any knowledge of it's fpiritual fenfe, it is not to be expected, that they fhould approach any nearer the truth than them. From the idea you entertain of heavenly happinefs, that it it cannot be perceived by the soul, except while united to a grofs material body, you take it for granted, that all men, on their death, are reduced to a state of torpor, inactivity, or extinction, in which condition they are to remain till the last day, when you suppose the spark of life will be re-kindled, and again animate the same body which had been consigned to the grave, notwithstanding it's having been devoured by worms, &c. In this opinion you likewise seem to be confirmed by the circumstance of the resurrection of Jesus Christ with his whole body, which, like the first-fruits under the law, you consider as a sample of the general harvest at the resurrection of all mankind, in like manner with their whole bodies. Hence, p. 37, you remark as follows: "According to the scriptures, the resurrection of Christ is a pattern of our own resurrection, and therefore he is called *the first-fruits from the dead.* What were the first-fruits under the law, but a sample of the general harvest? Whatever, therefore, Christ now is, we shall be also, when with us, as with him, corruption shall have put on incorruption, and this mortal shall have put on immortality."

If by the *first-fruits* from the dead you understand the *first body* that was raised from the dead, (which evidently appears to be the sense in which you take that expression,) your premises are false, and consequently the whole of your reasoning founded thereon must be inconclusive. According to the scriptures, Jesus was not the first that was raised from the dead; for he himself raised Lazarus, John xi. 43, 44; likewise Jairus's daughter, Mark v. 41, 42; and the widow's son, Luke vii. 14, 15. The prophet Elisha also raised the Shunamite's son, 2 Kings iv. 34, 35. And even after his death, when a dead man was let down into his sepulchre, and touched the bones of Elisha, he revived, and stood up on his feet, 2 Kings xiii. 21. All these are instances of persons rising from the dead, previous to the resurrection of our Lord; which are sufficient to prove, that the expression of Christ's being *the first-fruits from the dead*, is not to be understood according to the sense which you seem to put upon it, but rather as implying the same thing that is signified by his being called the *first-begotten of the dead*, Apoc. i. 5; the *first-born*, Psalm lxxxix. 27; and the *resurrection itself*, John xi. 25; that is, the primary and sole fountain, from whom all other beings derive their life.

I may

I may here take occasion to observe, as a striking proof of the divinity of Jesus, that his body, after the resurrection, so essentially differed from those of Lazarus, Jairus's daughter, and the Shunamite's son, who were also raised from the dead, that while these latter were again conversant with mankind, in like manner as they had been before their deceafe, that is, in grofs material bodies, which were liable to a second natural death, the Humanity of the Lord was only occasionally visible to his difciples, and no more subject to sufferings or death. That the body of Lazarus after his being raised from the grave, was not exempt from the usual infirmities of human nature, is plain from the circumstance of the chief priests confulting how they might put him to death, John xii. 10. But of Jesus, after his resurrection, no such circumstance is related, nor could such a defign by any possibility be put in execution. This, therefore, furnishes an additional argument in favour of his divinity, and proves that Christ was more than a man.

You say, " Whatever Christ now is, we shall " also be, when with us, as with him, cor- " ruption shall have put on incorruption," &c.

By

By these words you seem to insinuate, that Jesus was no more than a mere man, and that, as such, he saw corruption in common with the rest of the dead. But had you studied to invent a declaration more contrary to the true sense of the scriptures than this, I am inclined to believe you would have found some difficulty in the attempt. David, who represented the Lord, says, " My flesh shall rest in " hope: for thou wilt not leave my soul in hell, " *neither will thou suffer thine Holy One to see cor-* " *ruption,*" Psalm xvi. 9, 10. That these words were spoken of Jesus, is plain from this circumstance, that David in his own person saw corruption, whereas Jesus saw no corruption, for before corruption could take place he rose from the dead. With this agrees the testimony of Peter in Acts ii. 25, 30, 31, where he expressly says that David in that psalm spake of Christ. The same is asserted by Paul in these words, " David, after he had served his " own generation by the will of God, fell on " sleep, and was laid unto his fathers, and *saw* " *corruption:* but he whom God raised again, " *saw no corruption,*" Acts xiii. 36, 37. Herein then is to be seen a striking distinction between Jesus and other men; such a distinction as at once raises him above the whole of the human

race,

race, and characterizes him as their God, and not as a mere man, their fellow-creature. What he is, therefore, we can never be; for he is Lord and Master, but we are only servants: he is the Head of the church, but we are scarcely members: he is Creator, Redeemer, Saviour; but we are the created, redeemed, saved: he is the King; we are the subjects: he is Alpha and Omega, the First and the Last, the All in all; but we are—nothing. Such is the disparity between God and man, Jesus Christ and ourselves.

You seem, p. 40, to lay great stress on the account which Paul gives of the resurrection, in 1 Thess. iv. 15 to 17, where he says, " For this " we say unto you by the Word of the Lord, " that we who are alive and remain unto the " coming of the Lord, shall not prevent them " who are asleep. For the Lord himself shall " descend from heaven with a shout, with the " voice of the archangel, and with the trump " of God; and the dead in Christ shall rise " first. Then we who are alive and remain, " shall be caught up together with them in the " clouds, to meet the Lord in the air: and so " shall we ever be with the Lord." But all this may very easily be explained, consistently with

with the doctrines of the New Church, by considering it as spoken according to the appearances of the literal sense of the Word, which describes spiritual things by such images and expressions as are accommodated to the apprehension of men in the natural world. We have already seen, p. 305, that the Lord's second coming in the clouds of heaven is not to be understood as alluding to the atmospherical clouds over our heads, but to the literal sense of the Word, and to the appearance of clouds in the spiritual world. In this view, the above passage perfectly coincides with our sentiments; for we maintain, that the new heaven is formed before the new earth, that is, the New Church takes place in the spiritual world before it does in the natural world; which agrees with this saying, that *the dead in Christ shall rise first*. And as the church on earth will be conjoined with the church in heaven, so as together to form only one church, like internal and external, therefore it is said, that we who are alive and remain, shall be *caught up together with them in the clouds, to meet the Lord in the air;* that is, we shall be enabled, at the Lord's second coming, when the spiritual sense of his Word shall be revealed, to penetrate through the shade and obscurity of the letter,

and,

and, discerning the glory of it's inner contents, be elevated into the heat and light of heaven, by virtue of which we shall worship the Lord alone in spirit and in truth, as angels do above. In any other sense, what can be meant by being caught up in the clouds, and meeting the Lord in the air? Surely every rational and intelligent person must know, that heaven is no more in or above the clouds, than it is under them; and that the presence of the Lord is equally as well to be found upon the earth, as in any heights of the air or atmosphere!

Another passage which you quote as apparently favourable to your hypothesis, is that in 1 Cor. xv. 51, 52, 53, where the apostle Paul says, "Behold, I shew you a mystery; we "shall not all sleep, but we shall all be changed, "in a moment, in the twinkling of an eye, at "the last trump; for the trumpet shall sound, "and the dead shall be raised incorruptible, and "we shall be changed. For this corruptible "must put on incorruption, and this mortal "must put on immortality." In whatever sense these words of the apostle are to be interpreted, they ought at least to be taken in connection with the preceding verses of the same chapter. The construction which I observe you put upon them, is, that the same material body which is committed to the earth, will rise again, and be made immortal. But this is not the doctrine of Paul; for he distinguishes between the natural corruptible body which is sown, and the spiritual incorruptible body which is raised. " Thou fool," says he, " that which thou sowest, *thou sowest not that* " *body that shall be*," verse 37. " There are *ce-* " *lestial bodies*, and *bodies terrestrial*," verse 40. " There is a *natural body*, and there is a *spiritual* " *body*," verse 44. " Now this I say, brethren, " that *flesh and blood cannot inherit the kingdom of* " *God; neither doth corruption inherit incorrup-* " *tion*," verse 50. Hence, I think, we may fairly conclude, that Paul maintained the resurrection of man's spiritual body, and not of his material, earthy, and corruptible body. In agreement with this, then, must the succeeding verses, which you have quoted, be understood. He begins, " Behold, I shew you *a* " *mystery*;" plainly implying, that what he is going to add, is not to be understood literally, but spiritually; for were it to be taken according to the express tenor of the words, there would be no mystery in the case, but a simple prophetic narration. A mystery is something hidden from public view, being under the cover of

appearances;

appearances, which may either be misinterpreted or properly understood, according to the different degrees of illumination which different persons may possess. Paul, in most of his epistles, writes according to the literal sense of the Word; which indeed could not have been otherwise, inasmuch as the genuine spiritual sense was not at that time clearly revealed. Hence the appearance of calvinism, and the doctrine of justification by faith alone, so visible in various parts of his writings, is by many confirmed as the genuine sentiment of Paul; when yet it is sufficiently clear from other parts, that he in reality maintained no such doctrines. See 1 Cor. xiii. 13: "Now abideth "faith, hope, and charity: but the *greatest* of "these is *charity*." This also is the express doctrine of the New Church. But writing as he did according to the appearances of truth in the letter of scripture, it is no wonder that he should have been misunderstood by those who penetrated no further. Let us now see what is the real import of his words, agreeable to the true sense of scripture. To be changed in a moment, in the twinkling of an eye, at the last trump, means nothing else but the certainty of passing from a natural into a spiritual state, at the time of the Lord's second coming; and this

change

change may take place, according to it's measure, as well with those who are now living, as with those who are already dead. Not that a material body shall be ever converted into a spiritual body, for this is a thing impossible, as being contrary to divine order; but on the death and removal of the former, together with all the imperfections of it's nature, man will be endowed with a spiritual substantial body, in which he will live for ever, and no more see the corruption of death.

"Paul," you say, p. 41, "compares the re-
"surrection of the dead, 1 Cor. xv. 36, to the
"revival of seed that has been put into the
"ground; and we read, Rev. xx. 13, of the
"sea giving up it's dead. But according to
"you, nothing that is ever committed to the
"ground, or to the sea, will appear again, or
"any thing else in the place of it." With respect to the revival of seed that has been put into the ground, it is well known, that it is *not the same gross earthy substance* of the seed which grows up in the form of a new plant or tree, but only the spirit within it, which accumulates *fresh matter* from the juices of the soil in which it is sown. Hence Paul, in the very next verse to that which you mention, says,
"And

" And that which thou foweſt, *thou foweſt not that body which ſhall be*, but bare grain, it may chance of wheat, or of ſome other grain." This is a true emblem of man's reſurrection; the material body, which is laid in the grave, forms no part of that ſpiritual and ſubſtantial body, with which man riſes; but the ſpirit, which is within the material body, quits it after death, and then man lives as a man in all reſpects as before, only in a more perfect ſtate, in conſequence of being diſencumbered of the groſs body of clay. You therefore do juſtice to the members of the New Church, when you report as their belief, that " nothing that is ever committed to the ground, or to the fea, will appear again:" but you by no means do juſtice to their ſentiments, when you repreſent them as holding, that " nothing elſe is to appear in the place of it."

As to the paſſage in Apoc. xx. 13, where it is ſaid, that " the ſea gave up the dead which were in it," it has no reſpect whatever to the *ſea* in the natural world, or to the men whoſe dead bodies have been there conſigned. This indeed may appear even from the circumſtance, that no notice is taken of the bodies which have been committed to the *earth*, although the

number

number of these latter immensely exceeds that of the former, comprising in fact the general bulk of mankind. But it is still more plain from the words immediately following those above quoted, viz. "And *death and hell* de-"livered up the dead which were in them." And again, verse 14, "*Death and hell* were "cast into the *lake of fire.*" If we take these last words in their mere literal sense, we shall be under the necessity of supposing, that *hell shall be cast into hell*, which is a manifest absurdity. And if hell deliver up the dead, in order to present them before the judgment-seat, it will follow, that some men are consigned to hell, immediately on their death, not only before sentence of condemnation is passed upon them, but even before they are arraigned at the bar, and tried; which is utterly inconsistent with every principle of justice, whether human or divine. This doctrine, moreover, is particularly unfavourable to the scheme which you have adopted, respecting the state of souls after the death of the body; for you suppose, that then the life of man becomes extinct, and that he neither goes to heaven nor to hell, until the arrival of a certain grand but awful day, usually called the end of the world, and day of judgment, when souls and bodies are to be re-united,

united, and for the firſt time either raiſed to heaven, or thruſt down into hell.

That man, however, riſes again immediately after death, is evident from many paſſages in the Word, particularly the following: "Jeſus "ſaid to the thief on the croſs, Verily I ſay "unto thee, *To-day* ſhalt thou be with me in "paradiſe," Luke xxiii. 43. The ſame alſo appears from what the Lord ſaid concerning Dives and Lazarus, that Dives went to hell, and thence converſed with Abraham; and that Lazarus went to heaven; and all this while men were ſtill living in the world, conſequently before what is generally underſtood by the day of judgment; for when Dives intreated Abraham to ſend Lazarus from the dead to warn his brethren, Abraham anſwered, "If they "hear not Moſes and the prophets, neither will "they be perſuaded though one *roſe from the* "*dead*," Luke xvi. 31. It is further written, "I am the God of Abraham, and the God of "Iſaac, and the God of Jacob. *God is not the* "*God of the dead, but of the living*," Matt. xxii. 32. Hence it appears, that Abraham, Iſaac, and Jacob, notwithſtanding the death of their bodies, are ſtill alive. The angel likewiſe ſaid unto John, who fell down to worſhip him, "I "am "am *thy fellow servant*, and *of thy brethren the prophets*," Apoc. xix. 10. chap. xxii. 9: a demonstrative proof this, not only that man lives as a man after death, prior to the general judgment, but also that angels are of the human race, being no other than deceased men. So again, when Jesus was transfigured before Peter, James, and John, "there appeared unto them "*Moses and Elias* talking with him," Matt. xvii. 3. And in the Acts of the Apostles, chap. x. 30, "Cornelius said, I prayed in my house, "and behold, *a man* stood before me in bright "clothing;" which same man is called *an angel* of God, verse 3, 7, 23.

When a proposition is clearly proved, it is unnecessary to urge further arguments on the same subject. I shall therefore conclude my remarks on the resurrection, by briefly shewing who are the persons meant by the living, and who by the dead, that are to be judged at the last day; for I observe you all along take the account of the judgment according to the first and lowest sense of the words, when yet, to be truly rational in our conceptions, we ought to elevate our minds to their highest sense, and thus from the letter ascend to the spirit. All who die in a state of regeneration, are in the

language

language of scripture called *living men*; but all who depart in an unregenerate state, are termed *dead*. Both descriptions of men will be judged; the former, as having the spirit of true life within them, to life eternal; but the latter, as being destitute of that life, to death eternal: life eternal is the life of angels in heaven; but death eternal is the life of devils in hell. The Lord alone knoweth the true state of every man; therefore the Lord alone is the judge of every man; and he will give to every one according to his works, whether they have been good or bad. This is what is meant by judging the living and the dead, good and evil being the only proper distinction between life and death, as invariably set forth in the Word of God.

* * * * *

VIII. *Of Marriages in Heaven.*

It is no wonder, that men, who have been accustomed to understand the Word of God in no other sense than that of the letter, should raise objections against that part of the New Jerusalem doctrines, which asserts, that marriages take place in heaven, as well as upon earth. The plausibility of this objection appears the more ſtriking from the reply made by our Lord, Luke xx. 34, to certain of the phariſees, who interrogated him about the reſurrection; which, as might have been expected, is urged by you, Sir, as a deciſive argument againſt the truth of our doctrine. But upon cloſer examination it will be found, that not only in the preſent, but in a variety of other inſtances, the Lord ſpake in a language adapted to the ſtate of his hearers, who were ſo immerſed in worldly and corporeal ideas, as to have no other conceptions of the heavenly ſtate than ſuch as were groſs, earthly, and ſenſual. To have anſwered them in any other manner than he did, would have been to encourage them in their deluſion: wherefore it was neceſſary, firſt of all, to withdraw them from the groſſneſs of their imaginations, in order to prepare them for the reception of genuine truth. Marriage with them was no other than carnal conjunction, an union not of minds, but of bodies. With this view of marriage, they aſked Jeſus, which of the ſeven deceaſed brethren, who ſucceſſively had lived with the ſame woman, ſhould have her again to wife in the reſurrection? To which he wiſely anſwered, " The ſons of this age marry, and " are given in marriage," (even according to

your

your conceptions of marriage); "but they who "shall be accounted worthy to obtain that "world, and the resurrection of the dead, "neither marry nor are given in marriage," (in any such sense as you understand marriages,) Luke xx. 34, 35. Besides this interpretation of the words, they have a still further meaning, which may be explained as follows. Marriage, in the spiritual sense, signifies conjunction with the Lord; and this conjunction must be effected upon earth before death, or it never will in another life; for as the tree falls, so it lies. On this account it is said, that in heaven they neither marry nor are given in marriage; that is, regeneration, which is begun and entered into during the life of the body, is not *re-commenced* in heaven, like a *first act* of marriage, or spiritual conjunction with the Lord, but is carried on and perfected as the *sequel* or *confirmation* of a former covenant.

Many parts of the scriptures are to be understood in a sense diametrically opposite to the expression of the letter; as where it is said, that God is *angry*, that he *punishes, casts into hell*, and *destroys*; that he has *arbitrarily chosen* a part of the human race for salvation, and *rejected* the rest; instead of which the true sense is, that

that God is *loving* and *merciful to all*, hating *none*, punishing *none*, casting *none into hell*, destroying *none*, reprobating *none*. All these expressions are mere appearances accommodated to the infant apprehensions of man, who is apt to judge of the Lord by what passes in his own breast. In like manner when it is said, there are *no marriages* in heaven, the real truth is, that there *are marriages* there, not indeed such gross, carnal, and unchaste marriages as take place on earth, but marriages of a celestial kind, pure, chaste, holy, worthy of heaven, and where, in a supreme sense, the Lamb, the Lord God himself, is the husband of his church.

Again, it is said, that in heaven they neither marry nor are given in marriage, just as it is said, that no man is to be called father, master, or rabbi: that a rich man can scarcely be saved, it being easier for a camel to pass through the eye of a needle, than for a man who hath great riches to enter into the kingdom of heaven; but that the poor, the lame, and the blind, gain easy admission: that we are to make friends of the mammon of unrighteousness: that the right eye is to be plucked out, and the right hand cut off, if they offend: that

that we are not to refift evil, but to him that fmiteth us on the right cheek, to turn the other alfo: that if any man will fue us at the law, and take away our coat, we are to let him have our cloak alfo: that in order to become a true difciple of Jefus, a man muft hate his father, and mother, and wife, and children, and brethren, and fifters, yea and his own life alfo: that the Lord came into the world, not to fend peace among men, but a fword; and to fet at variance with each other the father and the fon, the mother and the daughter, &c. &c. In fhort, it is faid, that in heaven they neither marry, nor are given in marriage, in the fame fenfe as numerous other paffages of fcripture fpeak of heavenly and divine things, the literal expreffions of which are not in themfelves naked or genuine truths, but truths clothed with appearances, and thus accommodated to the apprehenfion of the fimple, and of children.

That neverthelefs there are marriages in heaven, as well as upon earth, confifting of the fpiritual union between male and female minds, is clearly deducible not only from the original defign of the creation of man, but alfo from the general fenfe of the fcriptures, which in many places reprefent heaven as a ftate of marriage.

riage. As there are two universal principles of life proceeding from the Creator, viz. good and truth, (although in him they are only one,) it is necessary that there be two universal receptacles in the intelligent creation to perceive and manifest that life. These two receptacles, in the general view of the human race, are male and female minds, separate indeed from each other while in their first and lowest state of being, but so formed that in their ascent towards their great original, they may be continually more and more united to each other: which union, as to the spirit, is so perfect and complete, that two minds, heretofore distinct from each other, at length constitute only one mind, or one angel. Their bodies, it is true, still continue distinct from each other; for the union of *mind* can never be fully set forth by any union of *body*, although there is a perpetual effort to accomplish even this. Our Lord says, "Have ye not read, that he who made them at the beginning, made them *male and female?* And said, For this cause shall a man leave father and mother, and cleave to his wife; and *they twain shall be one flesh.* Wherefore they are no more twain, but one flesh. *What therefore God hath joined together, let not man put asunder,*" Matt. xix. 4, 5, 6. Hence it appears,

appears, that marriage, which confifts in the union of male and female forms, both in the fpiritual and in the natural world, is agreeable to the original unchangeable intent of the Creator, who being effential good and truth in moft perfect union, defireth all the recipient forms thereof to become images and likeneffes of himfelf.

Were it neceffary, I might here take occafion to enlarge upon the fubject, and fhew how the two univerfal principles of life, above mentioned, manifeft themfelves in almoft every part of the creation, both animate and inanimate. In the *animate*, we obferve love and wifdom, good and truth, will and underftanding, affection and thought, works and words; alfo in the conftruction of the body, a cerebellum and cerebrum, heart and lungs, pulfe and refpiration; two eyes, two ears, two arms, two legs, &c. &c. all of which, although diftinguifhed into pairs, and thus expreffive of man's twofold life, yet in point of ufe make only one act, one life, reprefentative of that heavenly ftate of fpiritual union between the fexes, which is again reprefentative of the divine marriage of good and truth in the Lord, in whom fince his glorification they are no

longer

longer two, but one. In the *inanimate* creation we may also trace similar representations, as in the heat and light proceeding from the sun, which are both united in one ray; the two polar virtues of magnetism; and the two powers of electricity, called positive and negative, which are united in one substance, as in a kind of marriage between male and female. The same thing may be seen in the distinction of plants according to what is called the sexual system, which bears so great a resemblance to the male and female sex in animals, that the most celebrated botanists have not scrupled to call them male and female plants. But in this they are mistaken, as may be seen in the note below.* However, there is a distinction in

---

* The Linnéan system supposes plants, &c. to be male and female, because of a certain distinction between their parts, called the *stamen* and *pistil*, the union of both which is necessary to render the seed prolific. But this distinction in plants is no more a sufficient reason for calling them male and female parts of a plant, than a similar distinction, which may be observed in all male animals, is for supposing there are male and female parts in one and the same animal. The characteristic peculiar to male animals is the formation of seed in themselves, which is first conceived in the understanding, then formed in the will, and afterwards translated to the lower parts of the body, where it is enveloped with a material covering, and thence conveyed

in the parts of plants, analogous to the distinction of will and understanding in man, which under certain circumstances may be considered like male and female. Thus both the animate and inanimate creation, each in it's peculiar way,

veyed into the womb, and last of all brought forth into open day. By tracing this analogy in the vegetable kingdom, we may easily see what is male, and what female. All plants are male, because they produce of themselves *seeds-only*, and not new plants. The distinct parts of the plant, which some mistake for the male and female organs of generation, are nothing but analogous resemblances of the will and understanding, which are equally distinct in every male animal, and like them necessarily unite in the formation of seed. But this animal seed cannot produce new animals, until it is conveyed into the womb of a female, where, after undergoing a state of corruption, similar to that of death, it rises again in all the strength and vigour of a new and living animal. In like manner the seeds of plants, which are all male, cannot produce new plants; until they are sown in the womb of the earth, which is the common female, where they equally undergo a state of corruption similar to death, and after that rise up by vegetation into new plants. As therefore the *formation of seed* is peculiar to the male, and the *nourishment and expansion of it* peculiar to the female, it follows, that all the subjects of the vegetable kingdom are male, because they are concerned only in preparing seed for the production of plants; and that the earth alone is the common female, because it nourishes and expands the seed, and thus actually brings forth new plants.

Y y

way, points out and reprefents the union of good and truth, which is the fame thing as celeftial marriage.

That the fcriptures reprefent heaven as a ftate of marriage, is plain from thofe places where the Lord is fpoken of as a bridegroom or hufband, and the church as his bride or wife; as from the following, "The *marriage* " of the Lamb is come, and *his wife* hath made " herfelf ready. Bleffed are they who are called " unto the *marriage-fupper* of the Lamb," Apoc. xix. 7, 9. " I John faw the holy city, New " Jerufalem, coming down from God out of " heaven, prepared as a *bride* adorned for her " *hufband*. Come hither, I will fhew thee the " *bride*, the Lamb's *wife*," Apoc. xxi. 2, 9. Again, " The kingdom of heaven is like unto " a certain king, who made a *marriage* for his " fon, and fent forth his fervants to call them " that were bidden to the *wedding*," Matt. xxii. 2, 3. " Then fhall the kingdom of heaven be " likened unto ten *virgins*, who took their " lamps, and went forth to meet the *bridegroom*, " of whom five went in to the *marriage*," Matt. xxv. 1 to 10.

If heaven itself is compared to a marriage, why should it seem an improbable thing, that marriages should take place there? particularly as man continues to live as a man after death, the male being still male, and the female still female? It is indeed supposed by many of the learned, that souls are of no sex; but this is a gross mistake; for the distinction of sex originates in the soul, and it is that which causes the body to have either the male or female form. The masculine principle consists in this, that love is inmost, whose clothing is wisdom; whereas the feminine principle has the wisdom of the male for it's inmost, and the love thence derived (being a secondary love) for it's clothing. Thus the female principle is derived from the male, agreeable to what is said in Gen. ii. 23, that the woman was taken out of the man. Now as in all love there is a tendency to conjunction, and as the male and female were so created that they two may become as it were one man, or one flesh, there being a conjunctive principle in every part of their constitution, it follows, that in every stage of existence this tendency to union must be gratified, and consequently that there are marriages in heaven, where the end of creation is fully accomplished.

But you object, p. 43, "What is the end of marriage, but the propagation of the species? and since you allow this to have no place in the spiritual world, for what purpose is the difference of sexes, and what can you mean by conjugal delights in that state?" I have already shewn, that marriage is the union of two principles, viz. good and truth, which originally were one, as in the Creator, but since the creation became separate. Immediately on their re-union *procreation* takes place, because it is the nearest possible resemblance of *creation*, for God being essential good and truth in perfect union, is in consequence thereof in the perpetual act of creating, that is, of preserving; preservation being no other than instant and perpetual creation. In heaven, although the union of minds is more complete, and the conjugal delights more blessed, than on earth, yet there is no propagation of the species, for want of an ultimate material basis wherein their spiritual principles may rest, and as it were see corruption prior to the formation of an actual and distinctly organized offspring. But instead thereof, there is a propagation of goods and truths, the essence of their species, which without doubt terminate in, and are adjoined to, their proper receptive forms in

the

the natural world. Besides, the conjugal enjoyments of angels tend more and more to promote and confirm the union of male and female minds, and thereby to fulfil the divine law, that they twain shall be one flesh, Matt. xix. 5, 6. This therefore is the grand end of marriage.

It is said in Apoc. xii. 1, 2, 5, that " there " appeared a great wonder in heaven, a *woman* " clothed with the sun, and the moon under " her feet: and she being *with child*, cried, " travailing in birth, and pained to be deliv- " ered. And *she brought forth a man-child*, who " was to rule all nations with a rod of iron." This being spoken prophetically, and consequently in the language of correspondence, by the man-child which was brought forth, we are not to understand literally a man-child, but that to which a man-child corresponds, viz. the *doctrine of the church;* and by the woman the New Church, which is the New Jerusalem. She was seen to bring forth a man-child in heaven, because the doctrines of the New Church originate there, and descend from thence into the natural world, where the child was actually born when the *Doctrine of the New Jerusalem*, the *Doctrine of the Lord*, the *Doctrine of the Sacred Scripture*, and the *Doctrine of Life*, were

were published, these being particularly signified by the man-child. In the Word frequent mention is made of generations and births, all of which have reference to good and truth; for nothing else is generated and born of the Lord as a husband, and of the church as a wife. The male offspring born in spiritual marriage, is truth and good in the understanding, and thence in thought; and the female offspring is truth and good in the will, and thence in affection.

Human souls descend from the Lord through all the heavens, but receive their interior quality, as well as their exterior forms, from their immediate progenitors: and such is the intimate connection subsisting between the angelic heaven and men upon earth, that I have no doubt but the marriages and conjugal enjoyments of angels are among the interior causes of human prolification, which may be justly considered as a natural effect flowing from the spiritual world. But as this is a subject of intricate research, and not absolutely necessary to be enlarged upon in this *Defence of the New Church*, I shall content myself with the observations already made, referring the reader for further information to Baron Swedenborg's denborg's treatise entitled, *The Delights of Wisdom respecting Conjugal Love.*

* * * * *

IX. *That Love and Wisdom are Substances, and not mere Properties.*

I am aware, Sir, that hitherto it has been a received opinion among metaphysicians, that love and wisdom are not real *substances* themselves, but mere *properties* of something else, which they call substance. Hence, I believe, has arisen all that confusion and perplexity of idea so observable in the most celebrated writers, when treating of the being and attributes of God. While some represent him as an abstract being, destitute of all substance or form, which is the same as a mere nothing, others consider him as nature in it's first principles, consequently as something material extending itself through, and filling the expanse of the universe. Such or similar must necessarily be the ideas of all those, who ground their reasonings upon the fallacious supposition, that love and wisdom are mere properties, and not real substances.

If Baron Swedenborg has introduced into the world an entire new fyftem of metaphyfics, as well as of theology, he is certainly entitled to a candid hearing; and no perfon ought to decide either upon his philofophy or divinity, until he has well examined what he has written on thefe fubjects; for however true it may be, as you obferve, p. 44, that " Mr. Swedenborg " makes that to be fubftance, which all other " writers call property," it does not hence follow, that his diftinctions are lefs accurate, or his reafonings lefs true and conclufive. On the contrary, I believe, an impartial, unprejudiced mind may difcern more true philofophy, and more folid argumentation in his metaphyfical as well as theological difquifitions, than is to be met with in any writer that preceded, or that has hitherto fucceeded him.

"God," fays he, "inafmuch as he is an " effe," that is, an original, infinite, felf-fubfifting being, " is alfo a fubftance; for an effe without a fubftance is a mere imaginary entity; fubftance being a fubfifting entity. And whatfoever is a fubftance, is likewife a form; for fubftance too without form is a mere imaginary entity. Wherefore both fubftance and form may be predicated of God, but with this diftinction,

tinction, that he is a substance and form sole-existent, self-existent, and primary." These are Baron Swedenborg's own words in his work entitled *True Christian Religion*, n. 20; from which it appears, that you have not fairly represented his doctrine of the divine existence, in asserting (as you have done in p. 48, 49, 51, 54,) that he makes God to be *no substance* at all, but a *mere property*. What *he* calls a substance, namely, love and wisdom, *you* indeed call a property; but this ought to be no reason for commixing your distinctions with his, and then charging him with the absurdity which appears in the expressions, when all the while it is occasioned by your own inaccuracy in stating his sentiments.

Baron Swedenborg asserts, that God is love itself, wisdom itself, and life itself, on which you take occasion to observe as follows, p. 44: "That God is a being possessed of love, and "wisdom, and life, is intelligible language; "but that he is love, and wisdom, and life, is "not so, except in a figurative sense." A fundamental error seems to be contained in these words, because they imply, that in God is something which is not God, just as in man there is something which is not man. But if love, wisdom, and life, are not in God as a self-subsisting, independent substance, then he must derive them from some other being, in whom they are such; which would be reducing him to the predicament of a creature, by whom, as a recipient, such things are indeed possessed, but in whom nevertheless they do not essentially reside as his proper own. God, however, is not a recipient either of love, wisdom, or life, but the primary source from whom they proceed: and therefore he is expressly called *love itself*, 1 John iv. 8, 16; *wisdom itself*, or *truth itself*, Luke xi. 49. John xiv. 6; and *life itself*, John xi. 25. Now as every thing that is in God, is God, he being infinitely and essentially *one*, it follows, that these three, love, wisdom, and life, are not only in God as the essence of God, but also as his very substance and person.

That love and wisdom, with life which is their union, are real substance, is further evident from the following consideration. Whatever proceeds from any thing, must be a substance, and indeed of a nature similar to that from which it proceeds. A mere property, separate from a substance, cannot proceed; for in no respect does such an abstract property differ from a non-entity; and to say that nothing,

thing, or what is equivalent to nothing, proceeds from something, and is also received by something, what is this but language without sentiment, words without meaning? Now love and wisdom are acknowledged to proceed from God. But they cannot proceed from him as mere properties, for we have seen that on such a supposition they would amount to mere nothings. They must therefore proceed from him as a substance, which substance must be a form, and also of a nature similar to the fountain from whence it proceeds. Hence I conclude, 1. That God is the only self-subsisting, primary substance and form, from whom all other substances and forms are originally and perpetually derived. 2. That the divine love and wisdom in God, and proceeding from God, are also a real substance and form, giving life and being to all created substances and forms both in the spiritual and the natural world.

Perhaps you may ask, 'If love and wisdom 'be a *substance*, then what are it's *properties?*' To which I answer, The three following are the essential properties of divine love, viz. 1. To love others *out of itself*. 2. To desire to be *one with them*. And, 3. To desire to make others happy *from itself*. These are the properties,

perties, which inhere to, and are infeparable from, the divine love of God. The property of divine wifdom is, to forefee and promote the accomplifhment of thofe ends by the *beft poffible means*. Thefe being the *properties* of divine love and wifdom, it is plain, that divine love and wifdom themfelves muft be a *fubftance*; for all property has relation to fubftance, which is a fubject, and the divine love and divine wifdom in form are the fubject of all divine properties.

You acknowledge, p. 49, that you are incapable of forming any ideas at all of the diftinction between the divine *effe*, the divine *effence*, and the divine *exiftence*; and yet Baron Swedenborg, and his tranflator, whofe note you have quoted, make it very clear and intelligible to others. But it is rather fingular, that a perfon, who profeffes his ignorance of the very *terms* made ufe of in the new fyftem of metaphyfics publifhed by our Swedifh author, fhould yet take upon him to decide againft it. Can it be expected, that the public will look upon him as a competent judge, who has openly avowed his incapacity, by declaring in one place, that he *cannot form any ideas at all* about the matter; and in another place, that he finds himfelf included in the number of thofe who *do not under-*

ftand

stand the writings of Baron Swedenborg? It reminds me of a certain clerical gentleman, a doctor of divinity, who, after writing pretty freely against the doctrines of the New Church, candidly confessed to me, that he did not understand what Baron Swedenborg meant by the three terms *celestial*, *spiritual*, and *natural!*

I shall conclude this article with the following quotation from Baron Swedenborg's work, entitled, *Angelic Wisdom concerning Divine Love and Divine Wisdom*, n. 40 to 43, and 286; wherein he proves, that love and wisdom are both a substance and a form, and that this can be no other than the human form.

" The common idea of men concerning love and wisdom is as of something volatile and floating in subtil air or ether; or as of an exhalation from something of such a nature; and scarcely any one thinks that they are really and actually a substance and a form. They who see that they are a substance and a form, nevertheless perceive love and wisdom out of their subjects as issuing from it; and what they perceive out of their subject as issuing from it, although it be perceived as something volatile and floating, they also call a substance and form,

not

not knowing that love and wisdom are the subject itself, and that that which is perceived without it as something volatile and floating, is only an appearance of the state of the subject within itself. The causes why this hath not heretofore been seen are several; one is, that appearances are the first things from which the human mind forms it's understanding, and that it cannot shake them off but by an investigation of the cause, and if the cause lies very deep, it cannot investigate it, without keeping the understanding some time in spiritual light, in which it cannot keep it long by reason of the natural light which continually draws it down. Nevertheless the truth is, that love and wisdom are a real and actual substance and form, which constitutes the subject itself.

" But inasmuch as this is contrary to appearance, it may seem not to merit belief, unless it be demonstrated; and it cannot be demonstrated, except by such things as a man can perceive by his bodily senses; wherefore by them it shall be demonstrated. Man hath five senses, which are called feeling, taste, smell, hearing, and sight. The subject of feeling is the skin with which a man is encompassed, the substance and form itself of the skin cause it to feel

feel what is applied; the sense of feeling is not in the things which are applied, but it is in the substance and form of the skin, which is the subject; the sense is only an affection thereof from things applied. It is the same with the taste; this sense is only an affection of the substance and form of the tongue; the tongue is the subject. It is the same with the smell; that odours affect the nose, and are in the nose, and that there is an affection thereof from odoriferous substances touching it, is well known. It is the same with hearing; it appears as if the hearing was in the place where the sound begins, but the hearing is in the ear, and is an affection of it's substance and form; that the hearing is at a distance from the ear, is an appearance. It is the same with the sight; it appears, when a man sees objects at a distance, as if the sight was there, but nevertheless it is in the eye which is the subject, and is in like manner an affection thereof: the distance is only from the judgment concluding concerning space from intermediate objects, or from the diminution and consequent obscuration of the object, whose image is produced within the eye according to the angle of incidence. Hence it appears, that the sight does not go from the eye to the object, but that the image of the object enters the eye, and affect it's substance and form: for it is the same with the sight as it is with the hearing, the hearing does not go out of the ear to catch the sound, but the sound enters the ear and affects it. Hence it may appear, that the affection of a substance and form, which constitutes the sense, is not a thing separate from the subject, but only causeth a change in it, the subject remaining the subject then as before, and after. Hence it follows, that the sight, hearing, smell, taste, and feeling, are not any thing volatile flowing from those organs, but that they are the organs themselves considered in their substance and form, and that whilst they are affected the sense is produced.

" It is the same with love and wisdom, with this only difference, that the substances and forms, which are love and wisdom, do not exist before the eyes as the organs of the external senses; but still no one can deny, that those things of love and wisdom, which are called thoughts, perceptions, and affections, are substances and forms, and that they are not volatile entities flowing from nothing, or abstracted from that real and actual substance and form, which is the subject: for there are in the brain innumerable substances and forms, in which every

interior

interior sense, which hath relation to the understanding and the will, resides. That all the affections, perceptions, and thoughts there, are not exhalations from them, but that they are actually and really the subjects, which do not emit any thing from themselves, but only undergo changes according to the influences which affect them, may evidently appear from what hath been said above concerning the senses.

" Hence it may be seen that the divine love and the divine wisdom in themselves are a substance and form, for they are essence and existence itself; and if they were not such an essence and existence as they are a substance and form, they would only be an imaginary entity, which in itself is not any thing."

Such is the reasoning of Baron Swedenborg in favour of the existence of love and wisdom, not as mere properties of something else, but as being themselves an actual substance and form. That this form is truly and properly human, he proves in n. 286 of the same work, in the following manner. " No intelligent person can deny, that in God there is love and wisdom, that there is mercy and clemency, that there is good and truth itself, because they are from him;

and as he cannot deny that thefe things are in God, neither can he deny that God is a Man; for no one of them can exift abftractedly from man, for man is their fubject, and to feparate them from their fubject, is to fay that they do not exift. Think of wifdom, and place it without man, and then let me afk, Is it any thing? Can you conceive of it as of fome etherial principle, or as of fome principle of fire? You cannot, unlefs poflibly as exifting in thofe principles, and if in them, it muft then be wifdom in a form, fuch as man hath; yea, it muft be in every form of man's, not one muft be wanting in order that wifdom may be in it. In a word, the form of wifdom is man; and forafmuch as man is the form of wifdom, he is alfo the form of love, mercy, clemency, good, and truth, becaufe thefe act as one with wifdom."

* * * * *

X. *Of the Divine Influx.*

It is a leading doctrine of the New Church, that man is not life in himfelf, but merely a recipient of life, which continually flows from the fountain of all life, viz. God, who alone is life in himfelf; confequently that all love and wifdom, wisdom, all good and truth, come from the same source. Agreeably hereto we also maintain, in the words of Baron Swedenborg, that the spiritual world did exist, and does subsist, proximately from it's own spiritual sun, and the natural world in like manner from it's own natural or material sun. But to the first of these positions, you object, p. 45, that it is unphilosophical, because all our primary ideas are received from external objects through the medium of the bodily senses; and because Dr. Hartley has endeavoured to prove, that what Mr. Locke calls ideas of reflection, are nothing more than combinations of simple ideas, originally derived from impressions made by sensible objects. That this mode of reasoning is most agreeable to *appearances*, I readily grant; but it does not thence follow, that it is most *true* or *genuine*. The very circumstance of it's being an *appearance* accommodated to the *bodily senses*, is with me sufficient to excite a suspicion of it's fallacy; for I have ever found, that the appearances of nature, as first apprehended by the senses, are for the most part, if not altogether, *diametrically opposite to the truth of things*.

There are two kinds of order, the one of which is real, the other apparent; or in other words,

words, there is one order of the spiritual world, which has respect to the essence of things, and another order of the natural world, which has respect to the appearance of things as existing in time and space. This may be elucidated by the following comparison. In the building of a temple or house, the first thing in the natural world, and consequently the first thing in time, is the foundation, and the last a place to worship in, or to dwell in. But in the spiritual world, or what amounts to the same thing, *in the mind of the architect*, the order is entirely reversed, for the first and uppermost thing with him, which is the end in view, is a place to perform worship in, or to dwell in, and the last is the foundation. It is the same with the disposition of a garden, or the culture of land; the first thing, in point of time and bodily labour, is to level the ground, and to prepare the soil for the reception of trees and seeds to be planted and sown. But the first thing, in respect to the mind, or end in view, is a plentiful harvest, and the enjoyment of the fruits to be produced. Hence I infer, that as in the above-mentioned instances the first things in point of time, are in reality the last in true order, being produced by those which are first in end, although last as to time; so all our primary

ideas

ideas, occasioned by impressions from external objects, are in like manner produced from spiritual causes, which, though manifested last as to appearance, are yet first as to reality. Thus the order of divine influx, so beautifully explained and illustrated by Baron Swedenborg, is proved to be both rational and philosophical; while the contrary system of supposing love, wisdom, and life, to be derived from senseless matter, can boast nothing but the merit of *fallacious appearance.*

In conformity with the above-mentioned appearances, and because man is so formed, that his intellectual or perceptive faculty first opens upon effects, and thence, by a retrograde motion as it were, ascends to causes, the holy scriptures themselves, being accommodated to man's primary conceptions of truth, speak a similar language in their external sense; while internally they contain a meaning widely different, and treat of things, not as they appear in their outward forms, but as they are in their real essences. Thus in Gen. i. 14, it appears from the literal sense as if the sun was created on the fourth day, after the earth; when yet we know, or at least ought to know, that the sun, as being the fountain of natural heat and light,

light, and thus as it were the father and supporter of it's universe, must have been the primary work of creation in this natural world, and in the hands of divine omnipotence the instrument by which every material substance was originally produced.

It is an established rule in philosophy, that *subsistence* is a continuation of *existence*; and that whatever is the present cause of the one, must have been the original cause of the other. Whence it follows, that the earth, inasmuch as it is dependent on the sun for subsistence, by means of it's heat and light, must have derived it's existence also from the same fountain. That the earth is really dependent on the sun for subsistence, is sufficiently plain from it's general appearance in the time of winter, when not only the whole of the vegetable kingdom suffers a visible decay bordering on destruction, but many subjects likewise of the animal kingdom sink into a state of torpor and death-like sleep. If such effects are occasioned only by a *small withdrawing* of the sun's heat, what would not be the case, were the communication to be *totally cut off!* Could any thing short of utter destruction, if not annihilation, be the certain consequence? Yet, notwithstanding these considerations, fiderations, you moſt unaccountably aſſert, p. 45, that " the natural world, or the earth, does " not, in any proper ſenſe, exiſt or ſubſiſt from " the material ſun;" but that " they are two " *independent bodies!*" that is to ſay, bodies which have no neceſſary connection with each other. From what ſyſtem of philoſophy you derive theſe ſentiments, I know not. They are certainly foreign to that which is now generally adopted; and being equally foreign even to the appearances of truth, I believe you will find it difficult to ſupport them by any natural experiments. In moſt, if not all your other doctrines, you have ſomething plauſible to appeal to, like the evidence of the ſenſes; but in the preſent caſe I think it muſt be confeſſed, that even *appearances are againſt you.*

The doctrine of divine influx, as deſcending from God through heaven, firſt into the ſoul of man, and then into his body, is by Baron Swedenborg amply and ſatisfactorily explained. Indeed one great end of his writings is to ſet this point in it's true light, and thereby to convince mankind, that, notwithſtanding all appearances to the contrary, yet there is only one ſource of love, wiſdom, and life, for all in the univerſe; but that they are received differently

by

by each, according to the difference of their respective forms. As there is no necessity for enlarging on the subject in this place, I shall conclude it with the following remark.

It appears as if man derived all his ideas from external objects, as from a *cause;* but the truth is, he derives no idea whatever from them, as from a *cause;* which is plain from this consideration, that every cause is, in point of dignity, superior to it's effect; whereas external objects are inferior in dignity to the ideas which are improperly called their effect. But it is equally true, that without external objects we can have no ideas at all; whence it follows, that although external objects are not properly the *cause* of ideas, yet they are the necessary *occasion* of them, serving as mediating objects not only to embody ideas, but also to supply the mind with an *inert* power, which is as necessary to the rational faculty in it's contemplation and sensible perception of spiritual truth, as mercury is to a looking-glass in the reflection of the rays of natural light. For as in the latter case, without an *opaque* substance *behind* the *glass,* to arrest and as it were embody the light, no *natural image* can be produced; so in the former case, without an *inert* principle

under

under the *mind*, viz. in the bodily senses, in like manner to arrest and embody truth in it's descent from heaven, no *spiritual idea* could be formed or sensibly perceived by man. To suppose, that wisdom, intelligence, or science, actually flow from dead material objects, because our ideas *appear* to be excited thereby, is no less absurd than to imagine, that the bright image seen in a mirror is actually derived from the dark opake substance of the mercury, because the rays of light also *appear* to spring forth from it. The image really consists of natural light reflected from the mirror, according to the form of the object; and so also ideas, thoughts, and perceptions, actually consist of spiritual light, which is truth, in like manner reflected from external objects, according to the form of the human mind.

* * * * *

XI. *Of the Discovery of the Georgium Sidus.*

You object to the inspiration of Baron Swedenborg, that, though he visited not only the moon, and the other planets of our system, but also various planets belonging to other suns, he says nothing of that which has lately been discovered by Dr. Herschel. In answer to which, I have to observe, that although it is true he takes no notice of a seventh primary planet in our system, in his *Treatise on the Earths in the Universe, and their Inhabitants*, yet in another book entitled, *De Cultu et Amore Dei*, n. 11, where he treats of the origin of the different planets, he expressly speaks of seven primary ones in the following terms. " *Seven* * foetuses were excluded from the sun at one birth, namely, as many in number as there are huge bodies revolving in the grand circle of the world; every one of which being poised in it's sphere,

in

---

* The author's own words are as follow: Septem erant fœtus uno nixu editi, quot scilicet corpora in maximo mundi circo errantia; horum unumquodvis in suâ sphærâ libratum, secundum rationem molis cum pondere, ocius aut segnius, a natali centro recessit. Ita separati fratres, quisque velocitate acceptâ patenti spatio insurgebat, & simul ac in gyros, etiam per gradus a gyris in peripherias per ætherem explanatas, excursum faciebat. Quidam etiam orbiculos, plures vel pauciores, tanquam famulos & satellites, intra gyratas circum se sphæras receptos, secum a parentis aulâ abduxerunt: nostra vero tellus non nisi quam unam, tanquam vernam, quæ Luna dicitur, ut illa luminosam Solis effigiem in se ut in speculo exceptam, noctis cumprimis tempore, in telluris objectæ, suæ heræ, faciem, reflecteret: ita quocunque abirent, & utcunque se verterent, sub intuitu, & in præsentia sui parentis, nihilominus agebant.

in a ratio according to it's bulk and weight, revolved quicker or slower, receding from it's native center. The kindred globes thus separated, made excursions into the open space, each with the velocity proper to it's contents, and at the same time by spiral evolutions, extending by degrees, made large excursions into the etherial regions. Some drew with them from their fostering parent smaller globes, more or less in number, which accompanied them as humble attendants, being admitted to revolve within their orbits. Our earth had only one as an attendant handmaid, called the moon, which receiving the luminous image of the sun on her surface, like a mirror, might reflect it on the face of the earth, her mistress, more especially in the night time. Thus wherever they were carried, and which way soever they were turned, they were notwithstanding under the intuition and direction of their common parent."

In what manner Baron Swedenborg obtained his information, I do not pretend to say; but from the above passage (as I have elsewhere * observed in a note on the same,) it is plain, that he was apprized of the actual existence of *seven* primary planets in our solar system, though

---

* *Magazine of Knowledge*, &c. vol. i. p. 400.

though all the other philosophers of his day were acquainted with no more than *six*, viz. Mercury, Venus, the Earth, Mars, Jupiter, and Saturn. The moon is not a primary planet, but a secondary one, and is by the author expressly considered as such; so that it is impossible he could have meant to include the moon among the number of the seven; for he says, that *some of the seven* had satellites revolving round them in small orbits, and then instances the moon as a *secondary* planet appointed to attend this earth. Baron Swedenborg's treatise on the origin of the earth was published in Latin in the year 1745; and it was not till the year 1781 that Dr. Herschel discovered the seventh primary planet, called *Georgium Sidus*.

Whatever therefore may have been Baron Swedenborg's reasons for not giving a particular account of the Georgium Sidus, or it's inhabitants, in his treatise on the *Earths in the Universe*, it is plain, that the omission was not because he was unacquainted with a seventh primary planet in our system. But even supposing he had known nothing about it, such a circumstance would not at all affect the credit of his testimony in other matters; for I never understood, that it is absolutely essential, to form

the

the character of an inspired man, that he be acquainted with *every thing* that is to be known: it is sufficient, I apprehend, if in all his assertions about what he does know, he deliver himself in a rational, consistent manner, and prove his doctrines by the written Word of God.

* * * * *

XII. *Of Time and Space in the Spiritual World.*

Baron Swedenborg truly observes, that it is one of the most difficult things in the world for men, while living in the body, to withdraw their thoughts from time and space, and think of spiritual things with spiritual ideas, that is, with ideas that have no relation to time or space, but to *state*. Nay, so difficult does it appear to you, Sir, that in p. 49, you expressly declare, that you can easier admit the non-existence of God himself, than the non-existence of space or duration. Your words are, " Though " *we can*, in imagination, *suppose* the Divine " Being himself not to have existed, yet it is " *impossible* for us to exclude the ideas of space " or duration." From this I infer, that you conceive time and space, which in themselves are unsubstantial, inanimate, and destitute of intelligence,

ligence, to be more neceſſary and independent in their exiſtence, than him whom we call God; conſequently, that they ought rather to be conſidered as the Firſt Cauſe of all things, than any intelligent Being, whoſe exiſtence may in idea be diſpenſed with. Shocking as this may appear, I do not know that it is charging your principles with too much; for in one place you give us to underſtand, that God is in the ſhape of infinite ſpace, and in another you aſſert, that the moſt eſſential and neceſſary of all beings is ſpace and duration; which is no leſs than a virtual acknowledgment, that ſpace itſelf, or duration itſelf, is God: for that which is *moſt eſſential and neceſſary*, muſt be *primary*, and that which is *primary* muſt be the *cauſe* of all beings, and ſuch a cauſe is God. So true is the obſervation of Baron Swedenborg, that they who exclude from their minds all ideas of the Divine Human Form of God, muſt unavoidably fall into naturaliſm or atheiſm.

You acknowledge, p. 61, that God is the maker and conſtant preſerver of *all things*. Now ſpace and duration are either *ſomething* or *nothing*. If they are *ſomething*, then by your own confeſſion they muſt have been *created*, and are ſtill *preſerved* by God. But if they are

are *nothing*, I leave you to extricate yourself, as well as you are able, out of the dilemma into which you have fallen, by asserting that the existence of God is less necessary, than the actual being of that which after all has no real existence! This latter is an absurdity, which I think you will not attempt to defend: and therefore you must stand to the first proposition, viz. that time and space were both introduced by God into the world at the creation; in which case you must also of necessity acknowledge, that God himself is above time and space, and consequently that in his own proper existence he bears no relation to either of them. But the truth of this shall be made more evident still.

Because God is omnipresent, you think he must necessarily bear some relation to space, by which you mean, that he must be extended through all space. But this idea of God is both irrational and unphilosophical; for if he be a subject of *extension*, he must be a subject of *division* also; in which case the idea of his *indivisible unity* would perish, and being himself, like any finite substance, *made up of parts*, he could never be considered as a God of infinite perfections. The absurdities necessarily attendant

tendant upon the fuppofition of God being extended through all fpace, according to the rules and laws of fpace, are fo many and great, that I apprehend no intelligent perfon needs to have them recounted. I will, however, juft mention one as a fpecimen of the reft. Were God to be infinitely extended, or in other words, to fill what is called infinite fpace, then on every divifion of the whole fphere into two hemifpheres, by the horizon, it might be faid, that the *one half* of God is in the one hemifphere, and the *other half* in the other: confequently he would not be *completely* and *wholly* prefent in either of them diftinctly. Thus by fuppofing a prefence of divifible locality, the trueft and nobleft idea of the divine omniprefence is loft, which confifts in being *fully, wholly, completely,* and *indivifibly* prefent in all fpaces without fpace, and in all times without time. Any other kind of omniprefence is unworthy of God, and deferves not to be called divine.

But if the notion you entertain about the omniprefence of the Divine Being, as having relation to *fpace,* is found to be irrational, low, and unjuft; no lefs monftrous and abfurd muft muft be that idea, which fuppofes an omniprefence presence bearing relation to *time*. By bringing down the Infinite into space, and confining his being to the properties thereof, as if his person and habitation were necessarily subject to the laws of natural extension, like those of his finite creatures on earth, it is easy to see what is the form you give him in your own mind. But when you assert, that he must have relation to time, as being present in all duration as well as in all space, it is indeed hard to conceive what you can make of such omnipresence. According to the principles you lay down, viz. that the existence of God must have relation to time, it will follow, that as neither the *past* nor the *future* has at the present moment any actual existence, so neither has the omnipresence of God any actual relation to them; consequently that God is not omnipresent in respect to *all times*, but only in respect to that *one time*, which is now present. You cannot surely say, that the *past* time has any *present* existence; still less can you say, that the *future* has. If then they have no existence at the present moment, how can it be said, that the omnipresence of God, which is *something*, can have relation to that which is *nothing*? According to your own reasoning, it can only have relation to the fleeting *now*; for there is no other point of duration, on which you can lay your hand, and say, *It exists.* Thus by limiting the Divine Being to the revolutions of time, you in the same breath deny his *eternity*, which is totally independent of all times, it not being even made up of them, and make his existence in no respect to differ from that of a temporary creature, with whom the past and the future are never present, except by recollection or anticipation.

From what has been said, it is plain to be seen, that no true idea of the divine omnipresence can be formed, unless we banish from the mind both time and space. The whole immensity of space must dwindle into a point, and all successions of time into a single moment, before we can rationally and satisfactorily perceive the omnipresence of God in a human form, or in any tolerable measure comprehend the mode of his eternal existence; for with him all space is but a *point*, and all eternity a *present now*. Nay, even with man, who is but a finite being, there is a certain power inherent in his affections, capable of so contracting space, and shortening time, that they shall be to him as nothing. I can as readily think of the most distant star, as of the nearest object: it takes no more time to travel, in my thoughts,

thoughts, to the one, than to the other. Hence it appears, that whatever a person intensely thinks of, is as it were present with him, whether it's distance in the natural world be great or small. So also in respect to time; in all pleasing and joyous states of mind, the time seems short; but in contrary states long: evincing, that neither time nor space bears any strict relation to will and understanding, affection and thought, in man; and if so, still less can they be predicated of God, whose infinite perfections admit of no admeasurement.

That neither angels nor spirits have any thing to do with space, may easily be gathered from this circumstance, that even the human mind, which is an embodied spirit, is not a proper subject of it. When we say, such a person has a *great* soul, we do not mean that his soul occupies a *great space*, for this kind of extension is only applicable to body; but we mean, that he is possessed of certain qualities, which are as far superior to others, in point of real dignity or excellence, as some material objects exceed others in magnitude or bulk. The soul of a fat, lusty man, although it may fill a body which occupies much more space than that of another who is less, yet is not on that account a whit the greater. Neither in cafes of amputation of limbs, when the body evidently fuffers in it's dimenfions, is the foul on that account a whit the lefs, although the fpace it occupies is confiderably diminifhed; which is a plain proof, that *extenfion* in relation to fpace is not predicable of the foul, but *impletion* only. How abfurd would it be to fuppofe, that with every alteration in the bulk of the body, occafioned by diforders or otherwife, a fimilar change takes place in the dimenfions of the foul! And yet this muft be the cafe, if fpirits and angels bear any fuch relation to fpace as bodies do: and with equal propriety you may talk of meafuring the will and underftanding by the carpenter's rule or bucket.

But in p. 48, you object, that "according to
" Mr. Swedenborg angels are *real beings*, in the
" form of men, and have all of them been men,
" who when they die throw off the material bo-
" dy, and appear in what he calls their fubftan-
" tial or celeftial body. They muft, therefore,
" as it fhould feem, occupy a portion of real
" fpace as they did before, and confequently
" cannot refide except in real place. But what
" fpace, or place, is there in the affections,
" which are only properties of the mind? What
" room is there for a good angel in the affection
" of

" of love, or for a bad one in that of anger?"
Rather say, 'What room is there for a *bad*
'angel in the affection of love, or for a *good*
'one in that of anger?'

We have already seen, that affections are not mere properties, but that they are real spiritual substances. Therefore all your objections against the existence of space in the affections, as in mere properties of the mind, fall to the ground, having no application to the doctrines we maintain. Baron Swedenborg asserts, that angels and spirits dwell in the affections of men, and yet they are not without place. But this is to be understood in the following manner. They are connected with space in no other way than through the medium of man, who is actually in it. They reside in man's affections, these affections reside in his body, and this body is actually in space. Thus angels and spirits may be said to reside in space, or place, not *immediately* or *directly*, but *mediately* or *indirectly*. And *vice versa*, man himself, even while living in the body, is in like manner *indirectly* resident either in heaven or in hell; and after death, *actually* or *immediately* in the one or the other. Angels, therefore, do not actually occupy space in their own proper persons, although there is the same
appearance

appearance of space with them in the spiritual world, as there is with men in the natural world; but they occupy human affections, which affections occupy human bodies, and these bodies are in actual space. Such is the connection between the inhabitants of the spiritual and those of the natural world, neither of whom can subsist independently of the other.

In answer to your question, p. 48, whether there must not be some beings as necessary to the affections of angels, as angels are to those of men, it is to be observed, that angels differ from each other, according to the heavens they inhabit, as much as spirits differ from men. The angels of the third or highest heaven are invisible to those of the second or middle heaven; these again are invisible to the angels of the first or lowest heaven; and these latter in their turn are invisible to common spirits, whose temporary residence is in the middle world between heaven and hell. In each of these cases the superior dwells in the affections of the inferior, as spirits dwell in the affections of men; and it is in this way, that the links of creation are joined together. But there cannot be continued gradations of created beings quite up to the Creator himself, since between the highest

finite

finite creature and the infinite Creator, there always must be an infinite distance; and these gradations may as well terminate, where they actually do, viz. with the angels of the highest heaven, as any where else. Yet even in this case, the divine principle is accommodated to angelic affections by various descending gradations within itself, prior to it's actual reception by the highest angels; for the sphere of divinity above the third heaven is so ardent and intense, that no creature could subsist a moment in it. Whence it follows, that although there are no superior beings resident in the affections of the highest angels, as they are in those of men, yet, what is tantamount to the same, there is an *accommodated influx* of life within them, by virtue of which the Divine Being himself resides in them, as in his temple, and by their means in the good affections of mankind who are his footstool. And this is a sufficient answer to your next question, viz. " What was there to " reside in the affections of the first men, who " on their deaths only became the first angels?"

* * *

" The spiritual world of Mr. Swedenborg," you say, p. 54, " bears some resemblance to " the ideal world of Plato. Both, however, " are equally the work of imagination; and it
" is

"is remarkable, that, as in dreams, Mr. Swe-
"denborg had no real new ideas communicated
"to him in the different worlds that he vifited,
"but only fuch combinations of old ideas as
"commonly occur in dreams. Wherever he
"went, he found beings in the form of men,
"and the fame animals that we have here, hills
"and vallies, feas and rivers, as with us."

Whatever may be your opinion of the wifdom of Plato, and others of the ancients, I confider it far fuperior to that which paffes for wifdom among many of our modern philofophers, whofe conceptions of fpirit are either fo grofs as to make it one and the fame with matter, or fo attenuated as to refolve it into mere vapour or nothing. As to your objection, that Mr. Swedenborg had no real new ideas communicated to him, becaufe he defcribes the things of the fpiritual world by fimilar objects in the natural, this will apply equally as well to the fcriptures themfelves, as to his writings. Whenever the prophets fpeak of fpiritual things, or of the appearances in another life, they always do it in fuch terms as are proper to natural language, and under fuch forms as we have been accuftomed to behold. Nay, even when God himfelf delivers a new revelation,

revelation, he does it by expreſſions, which, if analyſed, are found to be no other than what you call combinations of old ideas. If therefore the circumſtance of Baron Swedenborg's deſcribing the things of the ſpiritual world by natural forms, be a ſufficient reaſon for rejecting his teſtimony, it is no leſs a reaſon for rejecting the ſcriptures alſo, theſe being written exactly in the ſame manner. And if your doctrine of influx be true, in ſuppoſing that all intelligence and wiſdom, or, to uſe your own words, all ideas, are derived from impreſſions made by ſenſible objects, and afterwards combined together, then revelation itſelf is but a particular arrangement of matter, and he, whom we ſuppoſe to be the fountain of wiſdom, and call God, turns out to be no other than nature at laſt.

* * *

The next thing I have to remark upon, is a paſſage in p. 56, where you ſay, " There is " certainly no ſmall confuſion in the ideas of " Mr. Swedenborg, when he makes the *heavens* " in the ſpiritual world ſynonomous to *angels*, " and the *hells* to *devils*; as if theſe *real beings* " and the *place* which they occupy were the " ſame thing."

However confused this way of speaking may appear to you, Sir, it is certainly very common with the best speakers, as well as the best writers, on almost every subject. What, for example, is more common, than for a politician to talk of wars, treaties, and commerce, with *France, Spain, Russia, America,* &c. ? thus with the *places* as synonomous to the *people* that inhabit them? And how frequently do we read of the *house* of lords, the *house* of commons, the *house* of Brunswick, the *house* of Bourbon, &c. &c. when at the same time nothing else is meant but the *persons* or *family* within or belonging to the house ? Nay, even you yourself, Sir, in the *Letters* you have addressed to the members of the New Church, make use of the *very same kind of language*, which you ridicule and condemn in Baron Swedenborg. I will produce your own words. Speaking of a young lady's ingenious imitation of plants in paper, and comparing to the loss of them the destruction of your library and laboratory, you exclaim, in p. x. of your preface, " How would the " *country* in general have been filled with *indig-* " *nation*, had any envious female neighbour " come by force, or stealth, and thrown all " her flowers into the fire, and thus destroyed " all the fruits of her ingenuity, and patient
" working

"working for years, in a single moment!" Now here, Sir, you speak of a *country*, which is a *place*, being filled with *indignation*, which is an *affection of the human mind;* and thus *persons* and *places* are made to be synonomous, by yourself, as well as by the Baron whom you oppose.

If we turn to the scriptures, we shall find a similar language used in them. In Apoc. xxi. 22, the Lord God almighty and the Lamb are called the *temple* of the New Jerusalem. In 1 Sam. iv. 7, the *ark* of God and *God himself* are spoken of as synonomous. In Jonah ii. 2, the *whale's belly* is called the *belly of hell;* thus the place *hell* and a *fish* are considered as synonomous terms. In Isaiah xxviii. 15, it is said, " We have made a covenant with *death*, " and with *hell* are we at agreement." And in Apoc. xx. 14, *death* and *hell* are said to be cast into the *lake of fire:* in both of which passages, *states* and *places* are mentioned instead of *persons*. So again, in Isaiah xxiii. 1, 4, the *ships* of Tarshish are addressed as *men*, and the *sea* itself is personified, and represented as saying in human language, " I travail not, nor bring " forth children, neither do I nourish up young " men, nor bring up virgins." Many other passages might be produced from the Word, wherein places and things evidently denote persons and states. But as I expect by this time you must see the impropriety of making that an objection to Baron Swedenborg's language, which equally militates against the Word of God, against the best speakers and writers on every subject, and even against yourself too, Sir, I shall leave you to reflect on the merits of the case, while I prepare to address you with a few concluding remarks.

* * * * *

XIII. *Of Charity.*

You charge Baron Swedenborg, and those who have embraced his writings, with want of charity, because he asserts, and they believe, that no one can be admitted into heaven, who acknowledges a trinity of Gods, or who denies the divinity of Jesus Christ. Had this been a mere arbitrary assertion, without having it's foundation in the Word of God, and in the true nature and fitness of things, there might have been some justness in your charge. But when it is considered, that one grand design of the scriptures is, not only to teach the unity

of

of God, but to point out *who and what he is*, in order that men may worship him in a manner the most likely to be effective of conjunction with him; and when the same scriptures inform us, that it is one of the essential conditions of salvation, to acknowledge and believe the divinity of Jesus Christ, there is reason to suppose, that, notwithstanding the *apparent uncharitableness* of such a condition, it must in reality be otherwise, because dictated by him who is the fountain of *love* and *mercy*. It therefore becomes a business of the most serious concern to be properly acquainted with this interesting subject; seeing that on such acknowledgment, both in doctrine and in life, depends no less than our eternal welfare, or what amounts to the same thing, our admission into heaven.

It is not my intention to adduce all the passages of scripture, that inculcate the necessity of believing in Jesus, as well as the Father, in order to ensure our future happiness. Let the following suffice. " He that *believeth on the Son*, hath everlasting life: and he that *believeth not the Son*, shall not see life," John iii. 36. Jesus said, " If ye *believe not, that I Am*, ye shall die in your sins," John viii. 24.
" Ye

"Ye believe in God, *believe also in me*. I am
"the way, and the *truth*, and the *life*," John
xiv. 1, 6. "This is life eternal, that they
"might know thee the only true God, *and Jesus*
"*Christ* whom thou hast sent," John xvii. 3.
Upon such passages as these is founded Baron
Swedenborg's assertion, that none can be admitted into heaven, but they who have faith
in Jesus Christ as the Son of God, or one with
the Father, and thus acknowledge the divinity
of his humanity. Arians and Socinians falling
short in this respect, are therefore condemned,
not by the testimony of Baron Swedenborg
alone, but by the holy scriptures themselves.
"He that *rejecteth me*, (saith the Lord,) and
"*receiveth not my words*, hath one that judgeth
"him: *the word* that I have spoken, *the same*
"shall judge him in the last day*,*" John xii.
48. Again, "Whosoever speaketh against
"the Holy Spirit, it shall not be forgiven him,
"neither in this world, nor in the world to
"come," Matt. xii. 32. To speak against the
Holy Spirit, is to say that what proceeds from
Jesus is not holy in itself, to deny the divinity
of his humanity, and to assert that he is a
mere man, or a *mere angel;* thus that "he hath
"an *unclean spirit*," Mark iii. 30; for in his
sight, who *alone is holy*, Apoc. xv. 4, both

angels

angels and men are *filthy* and *unclean*, Job. xv. 15, 16. Pfalm xiv. 3. Therefore to afcribe to Jefus any thing fhort of perfonal and proper divinity, as Arians and Socinians do, and to be *confirmed* therein both in *doctrine* and in *life*, is coming within the defcription of thofe who *exclude themfelves* from heaven, and who are therefore faid to be guilty of a fin unto death, 1 John v. 16, or in other words, of blafphemy againft the Holy Spirit, which cannot be forgiven in this world, nor in the world to come.

In addition to the evidence arifing from fcripture, we may alfo gather from the true nature and fitnefs of things, that no Arian or Socinian, *while he continues to be fuch*, can be admitted into heaven. If it be allowed, that heaven derives all it's effence from the Lord's humanity, which muft be the cafe if the inhabitants are members of his body, then it will follow, that no perfon can have a place therein, but he who acknowledges Chrift as his head; comparatively as no member of the human body can continue to be fuch, without receiving life from the head, and thus as it were acknowledging the fource from which it derives it's fupport.

No subject can gain admission to the court of an earthly prince, while he refuses to acknowledge his right and title to the crown; such a person, by the very nature and fitness of things, being self-excluded. It is just the same with respect to admission into heaven, which is the court of the King of kings: all who enter the gates of that palace, must bear true allegiance to their lawful sovereign Jesus Christ; they must be loyal subjects; they must love him with their hearts; they must confess him with their tongues; and none else can taste angelic happiness, or even breathe celestial air.

That men of every religious persuasion, by whatever name they are called, whether Arians, Socinians, Jews, Mahometans, or idolaters, may nevertheless be saved, as well as those who profess the truest religion in the world, provided they live a life of charity according to the best light they possess, and are not confirmed in the falses of their religion, is a doctrine to which I believe every member of the New Jerusalem most chearfully subscribes. And further, that they who know and profess the most genuine, heavenly, and divine truths, if they live not in agreement with them,

them, can have no place in heaven, where all is charity and mutual love; for the state of man after death depends not so much on the quality of his thoughts, opinions, and doctrines, as upon the quality of his affections and life. If these be good, no error of judgment will eventually exclude him from heaven: he may indeed be thereby retarded in his progress thither; but when by repeated instructions in the world of spirits his understanding is enlightened with the pure beams of angelic wisdom, he will then be prepared to enter into the full enjoyment of celestial happiness, and join the company of those blessed spirits, who unite in ascribing all blessing, and honour, and glory, and power, unto him that sitteth upon the throne, and unto the Lamb for ever and ever.

* * *

Having now, Sir, in the best manner my leisure hours would permit, made answer to every objection, which you have brought forward against the doctrines of the New Jerusalem; and having at the same time proved, as it's fundamental article, the supreme and exclusive divinity of Jesus Christ, it only remains to be observed, that the whole is submitted to your serious reflection and consideration.

tion. If what has been advanced in the prefent *Defence of the New Church*, be neither confiftent with fcripture nor reafon, it will and ought to fall to the ground, as a work of imagination, and a delufion of the mind. But if, on the other hand, it fhould appear to be fupported by the authority of both, then you, Sir, in common with every other feeker of truth for the fake of truth, muft feel yourfelf interefted, in no fmall degree, in the decifion of queftions, which, from their very nature, involve confequences of the utmoft importance. The difference between believing aright and believing amifs, is fomething like the difference between doing good and doing evil, though not altogether fo; for it is poffible, that he, whofe opinions are falfe, may yet be faultlefs, and confequently in a falvable ftate; whereas the man, whofe life and conduct is evil, can expect nothing elfe but to incur the penalties of his guilt. Truth, genuine, unadulterated truth, is, I hope, with each of us the object of purfuit. But while we have in view the difcovery of fo great a treafure, let us not forget to prepare our minds for the lafting enjoyment of it, by cultivating with all diligence that heavenly principle of love and charity, which is not only the end, but alfo the producing caufe of truth.

Thus,

Thus, whether we are now in the poffeffion of it, or not, we fhall moft affuredly obtain it hereafter, when in heaven we are admitted to the fellowfhip of angels, and there commence actual citizens of the New Jerufalem.

In this hope, and with my moft cordial wifhes for your eternal profperity,

   I remain,

     S I R,

    Your obedient Servant,

     ROBERT HINDMARSH.

London, Jan. 1792.

     F I N I S.

LIST OF BOOKS Sold by R. HINDMARSH.

		£.	s.	d.
1.	ARCANA CŒLESTIA, vol. 1, 3, 4, 5.	1	6	0
2.	A Brief Expofition of the Doctrine of the New Church	0	3	0
3.	True Chriftian Religion, or the Univerfal Theology of the New Church	0	15	0
4.	A Treatife on the Nature of Influx, or of the Communication between Soul and Body	0	1	6
5.	A Treatife concerning Heaven and Hell	0	6	0
6.	Of the New Jerufalem and it's Heavenly Doctrine	0	4	0
7.	The Doctrine of the New Jerufalem concerning the Lord	0	2	0
8.	The Doctrine of the New Jerufalem concerning the Sacred Scripture	0	2	0
9.	The Doctrine of Life for the New Jerufalem	0	1	0
10.	Of the Earths in the Univerfe, and their Inhabitants	0	2	6
11.	The Pfalms of David, with a Summary Expofition of the Internal Senfe	0	3	0
12.	Of the White Horfe mentioned in the Revelation, Chap. XIX. with curious Remarks on the Souls of Beafts, and the Life of Vegetables	0	1	0
13.	A Treatife concerning the Laft Judgment, and the Deftruction of Babylon, in 1757	0	2	6
14.	Continuation of the Laft Judgment	0	1	0
15.	Angelic Wifdom concerning Divine Love and Divine Wifdom	0	6	0
16.	Angelic Wifdom concerning Divine Providence	0	7	6
17.	The Liturgy of the New Church, in fmall Octavo, or large Quarto	0	1	0
18.	The Apocalypfe Revealed, 2 vols.	0	13	0
19.	Hymns for the New Church	0	3	6
20.	Jehovah's Mercy, a Poem, recommending the Writings of the Hon. E. Swedenborg, by J. Proud	0	0	3
21.	Nine Queries concerning the Trinity, &c. with their Anfwers	0	0	3
22.	Wifdom's Dictates	0	1	6
23.	The New Magazine of Knowledge, &c. in 20 Numbers at 6d. each, or complete in 2 vols.	0	10	0
24.	An Eulogium delivered on the Death of the Hon. E. Swedenborg	0	0	9
25.	A Short Account of the Hon. E. Swedenborg, and his Theological Writings	0	0	6

www.ingramcontent.com/pod-product-compliance
Lightning Source LLC
Chambersburg PA
CBHW032144010526
44111CB00035B/1195